Hans Scharoun and the Development of Small Apartment Floor Plans

Hans Scharoun and the Development of Small Apartment Floor Plans

Markus Peter and Ulrike Tillmann

The Residential High-Rises Romeo and Julia, 1954–1959

PARK BOOKS   AKADEMIE DER KÜNSTE

Table of Contents

Hans Scharoun in the Archive of the Academy of the Arts

by Eva-Maria Barkhofen

The architect Hans Scharoun, who from 1956 to 1968 was President of the Akademie der Künste Berlin (West), left the archives of the Berlin Academy of the Arts an extraordinary treasure trove of documents. This collection, gifted to the academy by Scharoun himself shortly before his death in 1972, remains the largest and most important estate in its architecture archive. It covers the period 1909 to 1972 and comprises some 25,000 plans and drawings, 14,000 photographs, and a vast quantity of written records pertaining to 331 building projects, around ninety of which were actually built. But it is not just in the architecture archive that traces of Scharoun's work are to be found. His name crops up in connection with ninety-four different holdings and archives in the academy database,[1] only forty-three of which are architectural in nature, while the remaining fifty-one belong to a range of categories, among them the historical archive. Clearly he created and kept alive an exceptionally dense network of contacts that included not just fellow architects, but also artists and policymakers.

Alone, the correspondence preserved in the various archival holdings is enough to show that Scharoun's involvement in public life extended far beyond his work as an architect and as the first postwar president of the West Berlin academy. Although by nature a rather reserved man, who liked to work in relative seclusion and who behind closed doors could start and finish the plans for a single-family dwelling literally overnight, he also loved to surround himself with others who, like him, had set themselves the goal of getting things moving and defining new cultural values. Scharoun was the one who, together with the first faculty of the academy's new department of architecture that he himself had founded, initiated its collection of works on twentieth-century architecture. And Scharoun was again the one who, on Hugo Häring's death, secured his archive for the academy, setting an example that would inspire others to follow suit, not least among them Max Taut, the Luckhardt brothers, and Werner Hebebrand, all of whom bequeathed their archives to the academy.

For Scharoun, building was a process that followed life. To his mind, even the most modest house had to be just as functional and humane as mass housing, the villas of the wealthy, and buildings for cultural purposes. His aim was always to harmonize space, form, function, material, and scale within the given environment. His engagement with the notion of "organic building" extended to numerous texts, in which he repeatedly drew attention to the complexity of the creative process. Even his earliest designs show him grappling intensively with a sculptural approach to space that was defined at once by clearly delimited functions and a fluidity of line that transcended any specific forms. His first high-rises, near Stuttgart, of the late 1950s were designed according to the same principle as his single-family dwellings. On his retirement in 1954, Scharoun visited Stuttgart to receive an honorary doctorate awarded by the university there. During his stay, the painter Manfred Pahl, whom he had first met in Berlin in the 1930s, introduced him to the housing developer, Universum Treubau-Wohnungs-GmbH, whose managing director, Andreas Hastenteufel, along with the architect Wilhelm Frank, was pondering the idea of building residential high-rises with owner-occupied apartments in Stuttgart. They were looking for an architect of renown to implement their innovative project and Scharoun readily agreed. The complex planning process for the two high-rises, Romeo and Julia, began that same year and they were completed in 1957 and 1959, respectively. While Pahl, through whose good offices the project had come about, was responsible for the outside color scheme, Scharoun was able to draw on the support of his Stuttgart staff, Stephan Heise and Jo Zimmermann.

Romeo rose to eighteen stories in height and had a compact footprint with six apartments per floor, accessed via a central corridor. Julia, with its lace-collar-like footprint, was conceived as an access-balcony building and the corpus staggered so that it rose from four to seven to eleven stories in height. Scharoun explained his design approach in an address given at the inauguration of Julia on September 12, 1959: "These buildings are not a product of the geometric principle, nor are they a product of perfection, which all too easily ends in formalism and the aesthetic. These buildings leave room for improvisation [...] Their design is not only artistically founded, therefore, but it is also deeply bound up with what it means to be *human* [...] Regard this world not as a definitive form, but rather as a beginning, as something still to be completed."[2] One critic, writing a few years later, went even further: "Here the issue is neither the high-rise nor the row house, but rather the world of people," he wrote. "Architecture must ensure that the world of the individual remains unblocked, unstandardized, unrestrictedly open. No building regulations, no housing standards, no financing rules can be of service here. Only a personally creative architect can. And just such an architect is Hans Scharoun."[3] ●●

1 https://archiv.adk.de.
2 Akademie der Künste, Berlin, manuscript of the inaugural address for Julia, September 12, 1959, Hans-Scharoun-Archiv, WV 187, Romeo und Julia, Mappe 1959.
3 Hermann Funke, "Romeo und Julia in der Stadt. Wohnen im Hochhaus und doch privat," in *Die Zeit*, No. 44, November 2, 1962.

"In my view, the necessary re-union, or rather: the novel union of living and working is a particularly pressing issue."

Scharoun, Lecture VI/7, June 23, 1952

S 1:50
BLOCK B
TYP 1
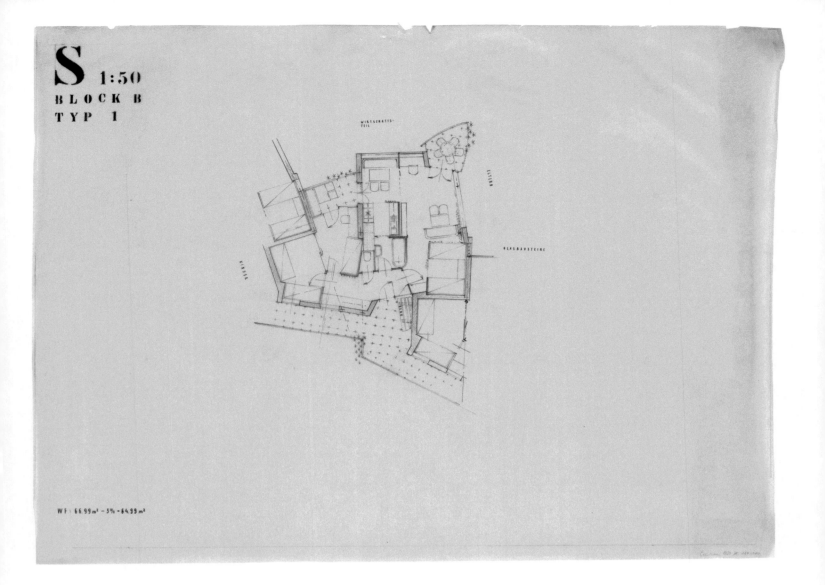

WF: 66.99 m² – 3% – 64.99 m²

The Find

Among the sketches that Hans Scharoun drew for the design of the Romeo and Julia apartment blocks is one of a residential organism whose geometry crystalizes out of overlaps, slants, and curvatures. The floor plan is striking on account of the equilibrium struck between contrary movements. The lines of the walls veer off their parallel trajectories, opening up, and multiplying their directions so that they appear to have no geometric center. Only at the lower edge of the figure, amid all the offset and broken parallel lines and the dashed regulating lines, does the underlying principle of a rhythmic movement that is at once bent inward and offset become apparent. The elegance of the planned entity is just as appealing as the meticulousness of the drawing. The matte beige sketch paper throws the precisely drawn fittings and furnishings sharply into relief. A bench fits snugly into a niche in the wall of the access balcony; some doorways are flanked by bench niches and study alcoves, and the core of the housekeeping zone with its interior kitchen and bathroom in fact consists solely of an arrangement of machines and fittings. The parents' bedroom distilled to an alcove separated by no more than a curtain, however, immediately declares itself to be in contravention of the standard specifications for subsidized housing. This room, as the best protected space in the German postwar dwelling, was subject to norms and conventions that Scharoun clearly wanted to see radically reworked.

Our analyses of this "find" from the repertoire of floor plans for the Romeo and Julia apartment blocks that were built in Stuttgart between 1954 and 1959 are part of our attempt to open a new chapter in the study of floor plans in modern German architecture. The aim of our inquiry is not to allocate these floor plans to certain categories or developmental stages in the way that floor plan manuals do, but rather to shed light on the teamwork of researchers and designers and other experts in related fields through which these residential layouts came about.

Hans Scharoun's contribution to the housing debate is strikingly idiosyncratic; yet it is also firmly embedded in the expert discourses that steered the process by which the "small apartment" was defined. His repertoire of dwelling types covers almost all the topoi of functionalist discourse, from the issue of lighting and orientation to the exploration of different access systems, and optimized "dwelling processes."[1] Yet the dwellings' distinctive mode of expression remains curiously untouched by these requirements. They are shaped, rather, by a style that is visibly anti-dogmatic, as evidenced by the creation of countless open spatial relations inside the dwelling. Thus we learn most about Scharoun's design work by studying his adoption and development of specific themes and concepts, such as the generation of circuits and polygons on the one hand and the unexpected shifts and ruptures on the other.

What interests us are the unexpected and blind collaborations which came about when designing the floor plans, whose points of reference, though not necessarily apparent, were almost always the starting point for the task in hand. Not everybody on the team knew everybody else, yet what the one chose to preclude, another brought to light. Nor were they all peers. The instruments and organisms the group of designers brought to bear on their work varied considerably, even if the questions they posed were similar. They came from different linguistic and cultural backgrounds, had trained in different disciplines, and were pursuing divergent career paths. Yet they were bound together by a concept and by the problem that they had set out to solve: by which value systems and instruments is the floor plan of the minimum dwelling defined?

The Reichsforschungsgesellschaft für Wirtschaftlichkeit im Bau- und Wohnungswesen (Berlin, 1926–1931) plays an important role in this story, and not just as an institution entrusted with tackling the housing shortage and endowed with vast resources to this end, but also because it focused the quest for a standardized, scientifically sound, rule-based approach to floor plan research on a hitherto unprecedented scale.[2] Its self-declared mission was to culminate in the "identification of functional housing types that could no longer be improved upon."[3] The director of this vast apparatus and author of *Rationeller Wohnungsbau Typ/Norm*, Wilhelm Lübbert, called on architects to turn their attention to the building of small apartments.[4] His report on the activities of the Reichsforschungsgemeinschaft enumerates the research projects undertaken by the committee:[5] "Item one, a) To set up work programs for the subcommittees: urban dwellings, minimum dwellings, residential hygiene; b) principles for the evaluation of typical principles; c) the operation and elaboration of a floor plan laboratory." Item two comprised "Investigations into the economic significance of floor plan typologies by Gustav Wolf," author of the book *Grundriss-Staffel*, excerpts from which Scharoun had copied. This handbook defines the "small apartment as the first field of interest in the study of floor plans" and claims "to attempt an orderly classification of floor plans."[6] Item three concerned the "architect's response to the demands made of the floor plan and interior design by the housewife and social hygienist." This task was delegated to Hugo Häring, who had already made a name for himself with *Die neue Küche*, a kitchen show that he and Ludwig Hilberseimer organized in 1929 with the support of the domestic science specialists Erna Meyer and Hilde Grünbaum-Sachs. The show kitchens exhibited were "ring kitchens," the

1 Scharoun, Lecture VI/8, June 30, 1952.
2 The Reichsforschungsanstalt für Wirtschaftlichkeit im Bau- und Wohnungswesen was a registered association. It was the product of a committee convened by the Reichstag in 1926, whose brief was to look into the potential for the rationalization and economically viable renewal of Germany's housing stock. In 1927, at the request of the policymaker Marie-Elisabeth Lüders, the RFG was provided with a budget to finance experimental projects. The RFG was disbanded in 1931.
3 Lübbert, *2 Jahre Bauforschung*, 1930, p. 12.
4 Lübbert, *Rationeller Wohnungsbau Typ/Norm*, 1926, p. 10.
5 Lübbert, *2 Jahre Bauforschung*, 1930, p. 30.
6 Wolf, *Die Grundriss-Staffel*, 1931, p. 9.

smaller variant of which, the "R1," needed no more than 4.5 square meters of floor space and made use of freely combinable, industrially made cabinets, which with space at a premium were closed with roller shutters instead of hinged doors.[7] Item four, "Floor plan formation and interior design of small apartments, new evaluation methods," was reserved exclusively for Alexander Klein, whose systematic "practical science" of floor plan formation counted as unsurpassed.[8] Of crucial importance was item seven, "Selection and evaluation of the best floor plans from the Reichsforschungsgesellschaft's collection of typologies," for which Lübbert himself was to be responsible.[9] Many of the methods selected for this undertaking, to say nothing of the experimental structures erected in the course of it,[10] in fact constituted new ways of steering the design process for small apartments, and in their turn applied, through the modeling and planning techniques that the designers and researchers were developing, the findings of the dwelling research being conducted at the time.

Hugo Häring, whose contribution to the Reichsforschungsgesellschaft's housing program, "Die billige, gute Wohnung" (literally, "the cheap, good apartment"),[11] took the form of some curious buildings with paraboloid roofs, was the mastermind behind "Neues Bauen" ("New Building"),[12] which within just a few years had developed and consolidated both a conceptual world and the theoretical position underpinning "organic architecture" almost in tandem. It was his intensive engagement with this theoretical stance and the original conceptual world that supplied the theoretical substrate of Hans Scharoun's world, albeit without in any way thwarting or restricting his forays into creativity. Decades later, Häring would cite Scharoun's 1951 design for an elementary school in Darmstadt as a shining example of "what, exactly, we mean when we speak of something as 'organic'"; for "the first planning act here entailed studying the essentials of this building and inquiring into what would be going on inside it and how it would serve education. It was not about studying the usual technical space requirements, but about the goals of the educational work that had yet to be set. The shape of the complex grew out of this inquiry into its essentiality."[13] His numerous essays repeatedly show Häring struggling with these "essentialities," which for him were a means of inscribing matters, things, objects, and even the "world of ideas" into a general order. These intellectual forays are certainly not easy reading and this has weighed heavily on the history of their reception. They are the products of a style of thinking, whose presumption of infallibility not even "advancing years could diminish,"[14] and are steeped in "intellectual" forces, "intellectual" plans, "intellectual" approaches, "intellectual" origins, "intellectual" ties, and "intellectual" landscapes. Häring lent the "intellectual," which he understood in the tradition of post-Kantian idealism, the status of a universal regulatory concept. In his later texts, he spoke of the "intellectual" in the same breath as the "spiritual," and by doing so resisted what he saw as the ever greater "deintellectualization" of building.[15] Scharoun, by contrast, was guided by the organic and by the "heterogeneous essentiality of spaces" that it encompassed,[16] which at the same time served him as an epistemological metaphor with which he sought to set his own architectural creations apart from both modern dogmatism and directionless formalism.

But the Ariadne's thread of organic architecture is in itself ambiguous, being at once a heuristic and an orthodoxy. It also informs Scharoun's copious—for the most part unpublished—texts, notes, and transcripts of the lectures that he gave at the Technical University of Berlin between 1947 and 1958, which as source materials attesting to the scope of his scholarly network will be drawn on here. The archived documents do not reproduce the lectures in full, but rather consist of largely impenetrable texts and fragments of texts, only some of which have been furnished with headings. These range from "Chinese Urban Planning," "The Essence of the City," and "The Transformation of the Dwelling" to "From the Dwelling to the Organization of the City" and "Style—A Form of Performance/Regional Development."[17]

What stands out in Scharoun's utterances on housing are the advances he made in the history of residential architecture, which were hitherto unknown and will be discussed further here. He produced a highly informative and systematic chart of dwelling types, both historical and modern, and presented these in drawings. His contributions to the housing debate of the 1920s also warrant attention, as do his surprising references to Alexander Klein's analytical criteria for the evaluation of small apartment floor plans and Walter Neuzil's diagrammatic method of measuring sunlight exposure and lighting. Scharoun's diversity of forms ultimately turns out to be embedded in the idea of an urban organism, which can be identified as the basis of his multiplicity of forms. But in a departure from Hans Bernhard Reichow's emphatic and inflationary use of "the organic" as a metaphor for urban planning, Scharoun endeavored to differentiate between "the organic" and the "organism-like," the division of which spelled dismemberment. While that might indeed "produce a suitable relationship between people and work after the organic model, it is scarcely conducive to, and does little to support, real-life transformations, symbioses, and disentanglements."[18] In the interaction of the individual and the community and "the development of a genuine society" that he was pondering, even the "tiniest 'organism'," he argued, was "infinitely more than the most sophisticated machine, since the organism is capable of development, in other words it is a living thing, whereas the machine and all things schematic are dead."[19] The organic is invariably put to use as a guideline that fluctuates between a model of design as a conjectural process and instructions for right thinking, which merely communicate what is already known to be right.

With just one or two exceptions, the documents on the Romeo and Julia project from the Scharoun Estate held at the Baukunstarchiv der Akademie der Künste Berlin are all unpublished drafts, through the study of which we have for the first time been able to reconstruct the planning process. The collection of plans will be supplemented by the large-scale residential models which were built as replicas in the elective course "Entwerferische Verfahren—Konstruktive Techniken" taught at the ETH Zurich in 2006. The wide-ranging interview with Scharoun's former assistants and students, namely Stefan Heise, Joachim Zimmermann, and Friedrich Mebes, was conducted in Berlin in September 2006.

This material, along with the texts, enables us to make sense of the vast hoard of Scharoun's floor plans, the drafting of which began at the Institut für Bauwesen in Berlin, founded in 1947. The first of them to be presented as part of a larger development project was the 1949 floor plan of the Wohnzelle Friedrichshain in Berlin, followed by their more extensive application in Romeo and Julia, his first major high-rise project after the war, which was built in Stuttgart-Zuffenhausen. This was the experimental field on which Scharoun, with all his many twists and turns, repeatedly pushed the boundaries of the "dwelling process."[20] By no means least of interest to us here is the messiness of Scharoun's design process, that is to say, his errors and failures, which after all prove that stumbling blocks are often just as important to development as a smooth path. Here on the fringes of architecture, the sketches that historians of architecture tend to disregard will be accorded just as much importance as the endlessly repeated planning paradigms to which contemporary architectural theory with its floor plan manuals still cleaves. ●●

7   Häring, exhibition catalog *Die neue Küche,* 1929, p. 33; Alice Simmel, "Die neue Küche," in *Die Form. Zeitschrift für gestaltende Arbeit* 4, No. 6, (1929), p. 289.
8   Klein, "Beiträge zur Wohnungsfrage als Praktische Wissenschaft," 1930.
9   The remaining items were: "Item 5: Hygiene requirements for floor plans and interior design, Professor Dr. v. Drigalski"; "Item 6: The dwelling and mental hygiene, Professor Dr. med. Gins"; and "Item 8: Standardized furniture, Adolf Rading."
10 "According to the resolutions of the board hitherto passed, the Reichsforschungsgesellschaft shall support the following experiments: 1. Prefabricated building by the City of Frankfurt a. Main: 300 000 RM. Industrial manufacture of wall panels and ceiling beams for assembly by machine on site in 900 residential units. 2. Experiments by the City of Stuttgart: a) 150 000 Reichsmarks. Observation of the Weissenhof Estate with its sixty experimental residential units built according to a range of plans and using a range of methods; b) 234 000 Reichsmarks. Erection and study of various types of house—with both timber frames and masonry walls, one or two stories high, with flat or pitched roofs, in Kochenhof (117 units). 3. Experiments by the Baugenossenschaft des Post- und Telegraphenverbandes in Munich 171 000 Reichsmarks." (Gustav Lampmann, "Reichsbauforschung," in *Zentralblatt der Bauverwaltung,* 48, No. 7, [1928], pp. 100–103, here p. 101).
11 Reichsforschungsgesellschaft für Wirtschaftlichkeit im Bau- und Wohnungswesen (ed.), *Die billige, gute Wohnung* 1930.
12 Häring, "Neues Bauen," 1947.
13 Häring, "geometrie und organik," 1951, p. 18.
14 Häring, "Gespräch über organische Baukunst," 1952, p. 10.
15 Häring, "Bemerkungen zum Normierungsbegehren," 1948, p. 312.
16 Scharoun, Lecture X/23, 9.6.1958.
17 "Assuming that almost all those students who studied under Scharoun back then understood as little as I did, and that they simply made a note of all those unknown and unexplained terms that he used, intending to look them up in dictionaries or to ask other professors to explain them, it is not hard to understand that his students had only a vague idea of what he was talking about and hence still hold widely differing views of him even today," letter from the architect Merete Mattern to Professor emeritus Anatol Ginelli, spring 2006, forwarded from the latter to Markus Peter and Ulrike Tillmann, ETH Zurich, October 10, 2006.
18 Scharoun, Lecture V/17A, October 25, 1951.
19 Scharoun, Lecture II/8, May 8, 1950.
20 In his critique of the current status of the research, Norbert Huse insisted that Scharoun had not just designed "anything," but rather "dwellings and hence a form of cohabitation in the family, in the dwelling, and ultimately in the city," letter from Norbert Huse to Markus Peter and Ulrike Tillmann, ETH Zurich, November 5, 2007.

I Drawings

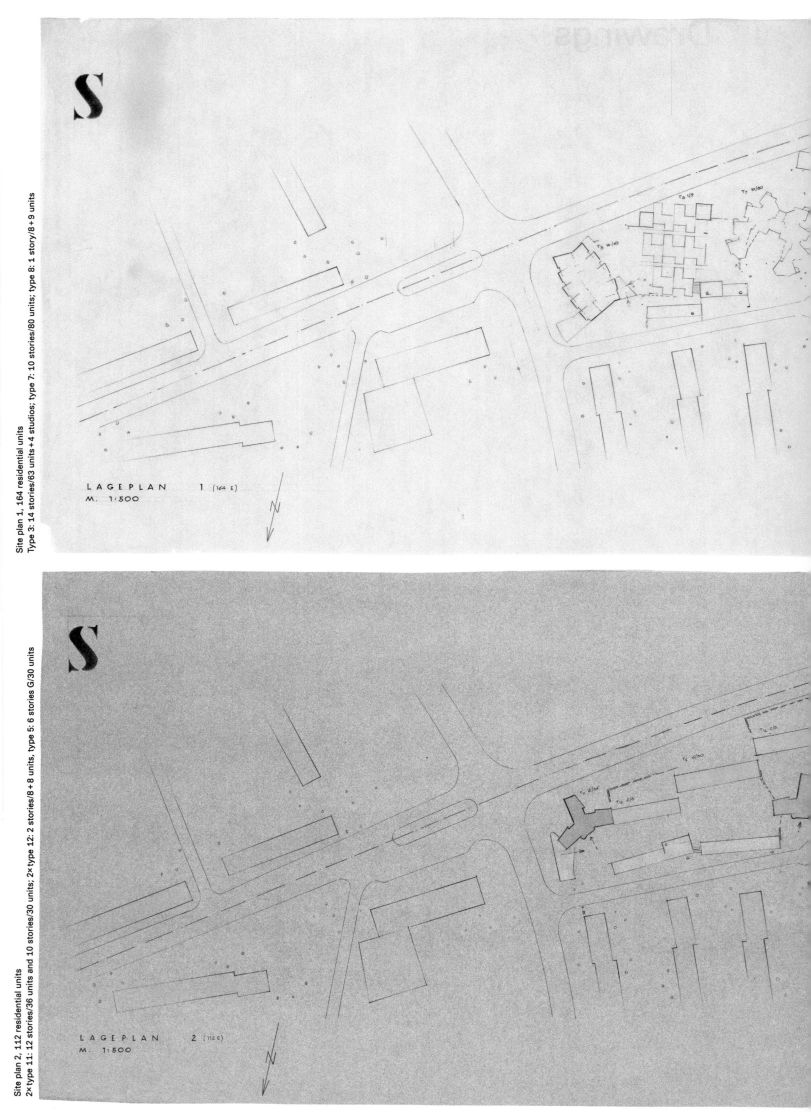

Site plan 1, 164 residential units
Type 3: 14 stories/63 units + 4 studios; type 7: 10 stories/80 units; type 8: 1 story/8 + 9 units

LAGEPLAN   1 (164 E)
M. 1:500

Site plan 2, 112 residential units
2× type 11: 12 stories/36 units and 10 stories/30 units; 2× type 12: 2 stories/8 + 8 units, type 5: 6 stories G/30 units

LAGEPLAN   2 (112 E)
M. 1:500

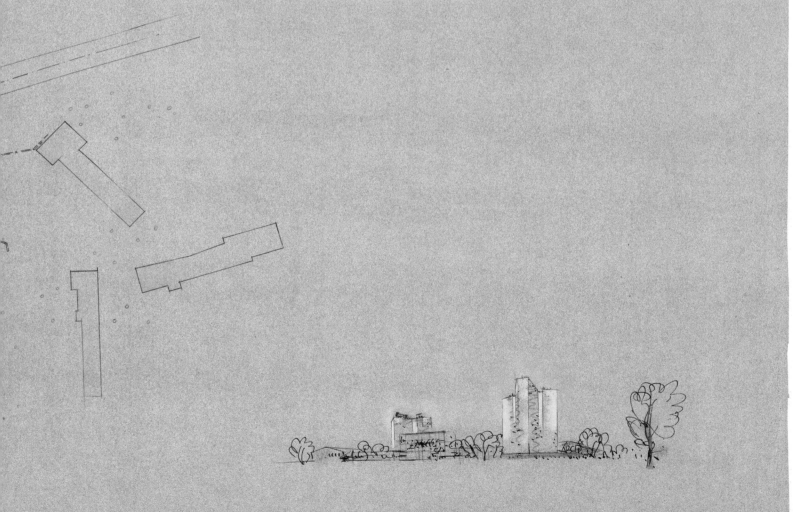

19

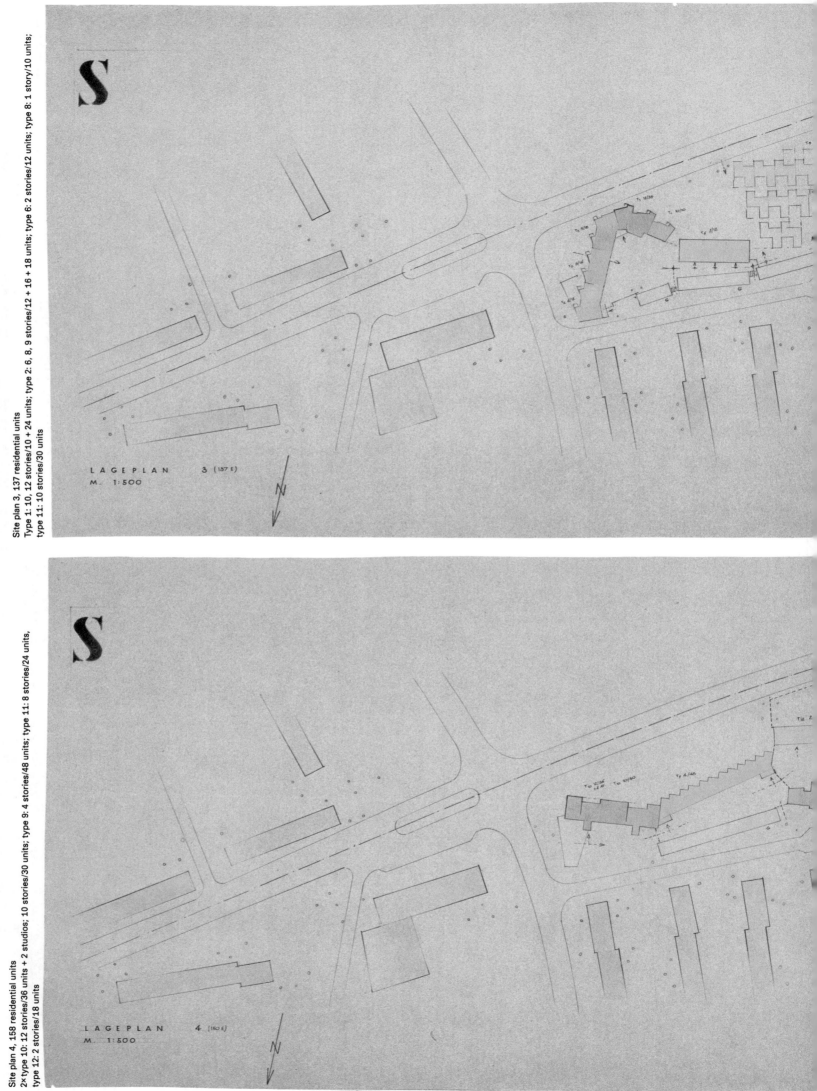

Site plan 3, 137 residential units
Type 1: 10, 12 stories/10 + 24 units; type 2: 6, 8, 9 stories/12 + 16 + 18 units; type 6: 2 stories/12 units; type 8: 1 story/10 units;
type 11: 10 stories/30 units

LAGEPLAN 3 (137 E)
M. 1:500

Site plan 4, 158 residential units
2×type 10: 12 stories/36 units + 2 studios; 10 stories/30 units; type 9: 4 stories/48 units; type 11: 8 stories/24 units,
type 12: 2 stories/18 units

LAGEPLAN 4 (158 E)
M. 1:500

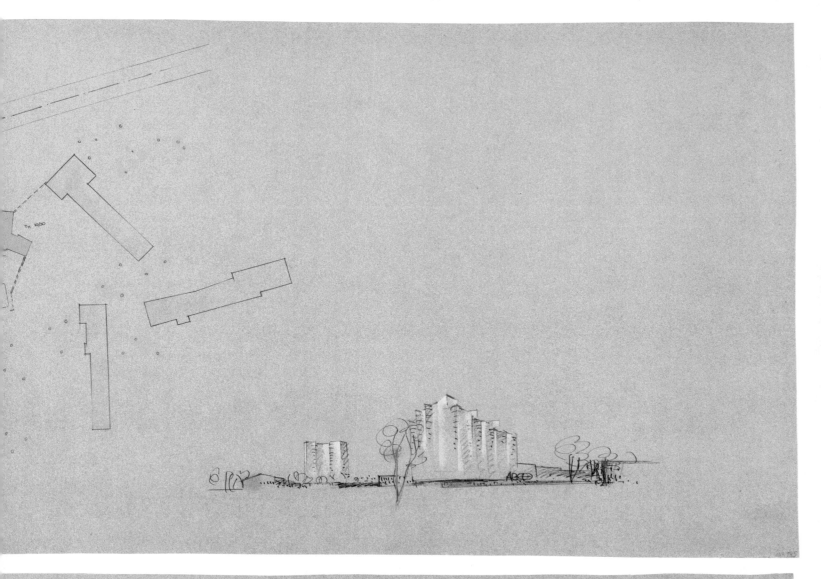

21

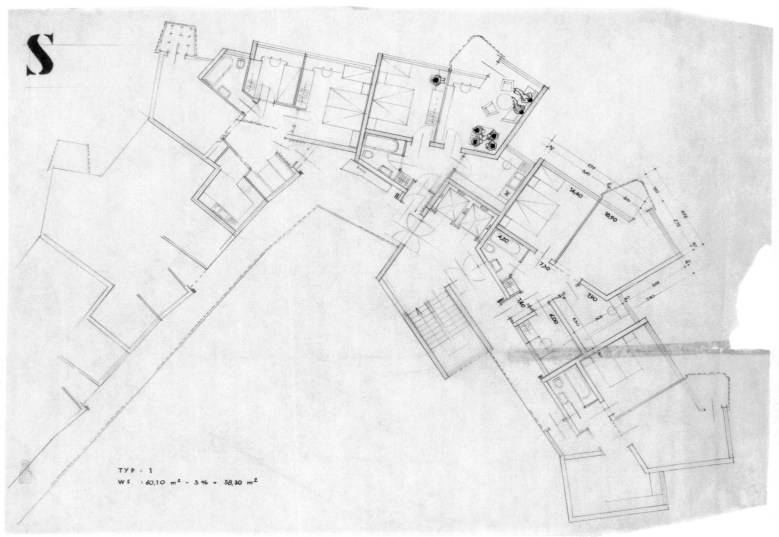

Type 1, 58.30 m²

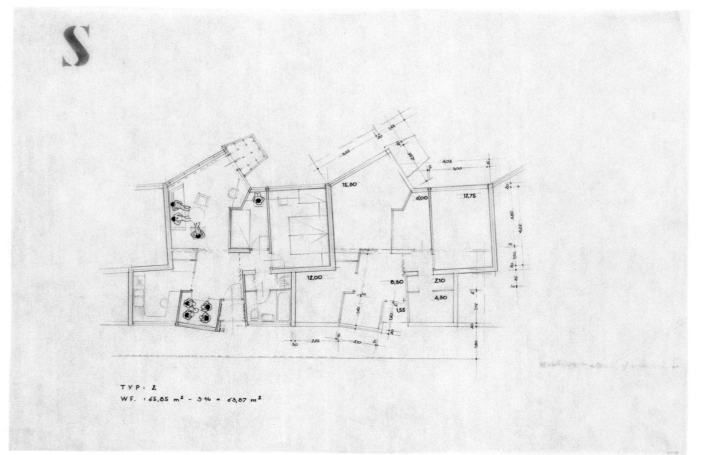

Type 2, 63.87 m²

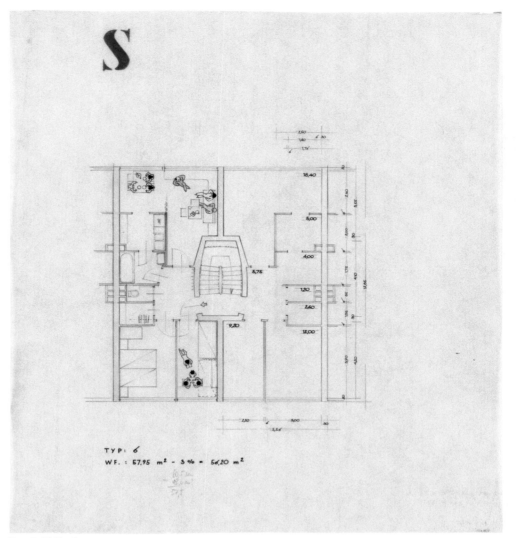

Type 6, 56.20 m²

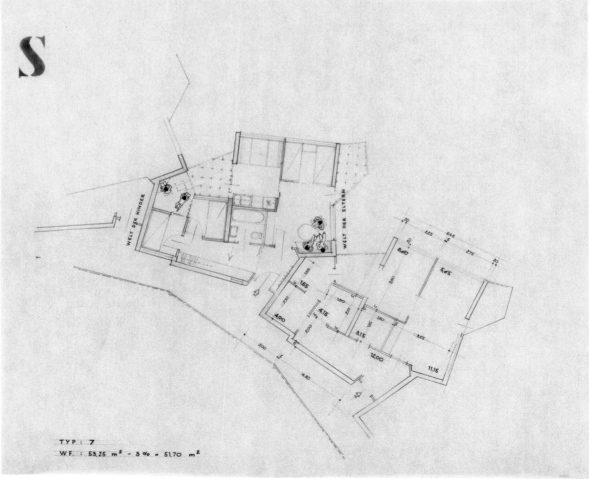

Type 7, 51.70 m²

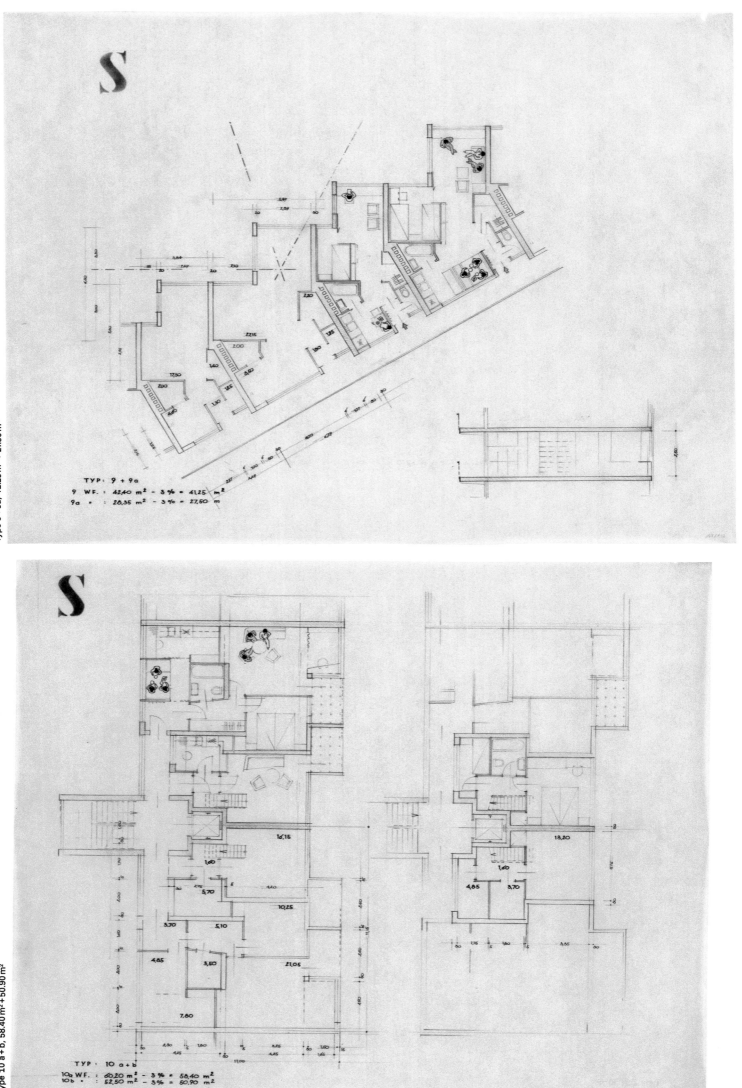

Type 9 + 9a, 41.25 m² + 27.50 m²

TYP: 9 + 9a

9 WF. : 42,40 m² − 3 % = 41,25 m²

9a " : 28,35 m² − 3 % = 27,50 m

Type 10 a + b, 58.40 m² + 50.90 m²

TYP : 10 a + b

10a WF. : 60,20 m² − 3 % = 58,40 m²

10b " : 52,50 m² − 3 % = 50,90 m²

I   Drawings   Design Phase, 1954   24

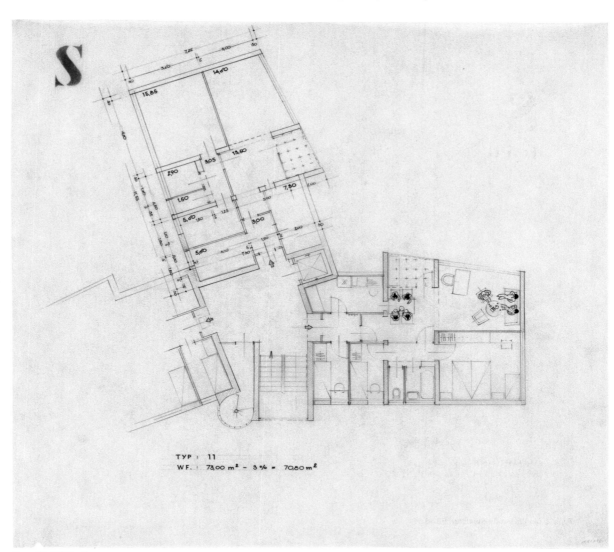

Type 11, 70.80 m²

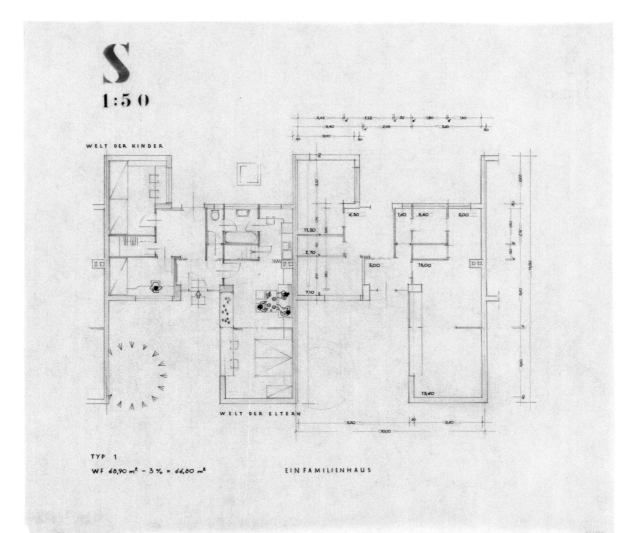

Type 1, single-family dwelling, 66.80 m²

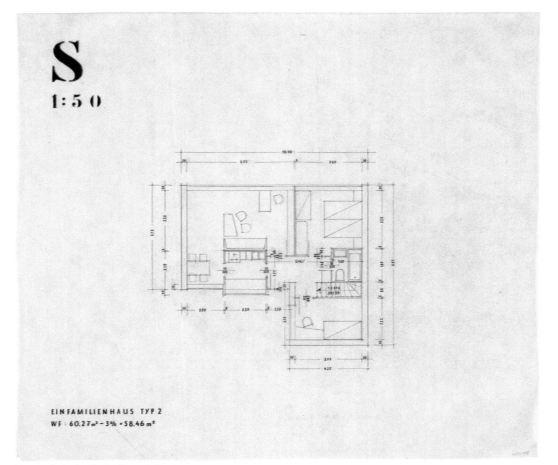

EINFAMILIENHAUS TYP 2
WF : 60.27 m² – 3% = 58.46 m²

Type 2, single-family dwelling, 58.46 m²

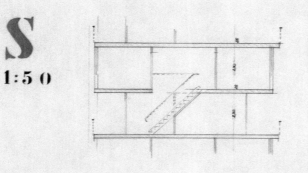

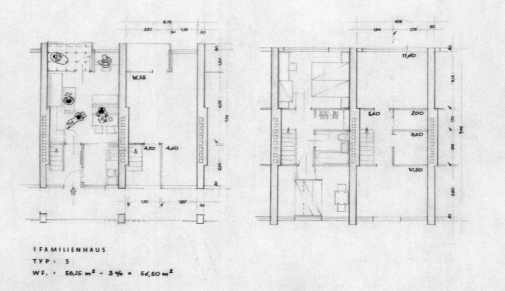

1 FAMILIENHAUS
TYP : 3
WF. : 58,25 m² – 3% = 56,50 m²

Type 3, single-family dwelling, 56.50 m²

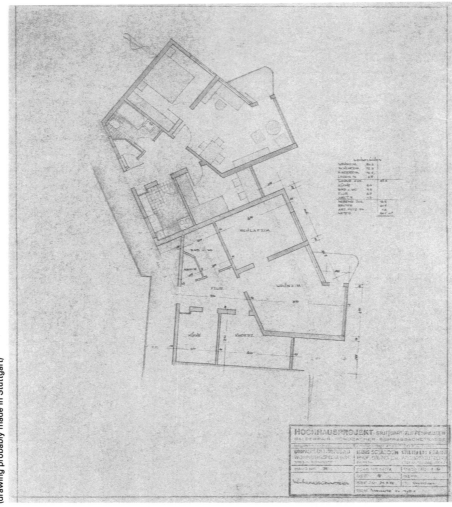

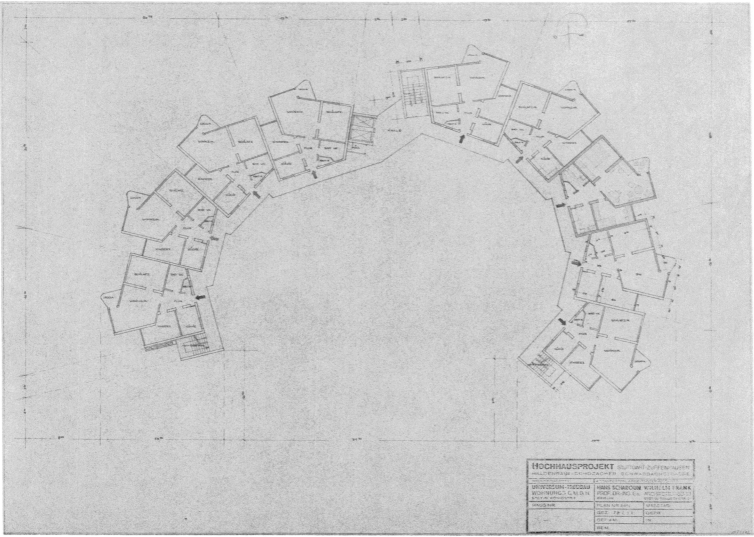

Normal floor variant with type 1, Block B, September 24, 1954

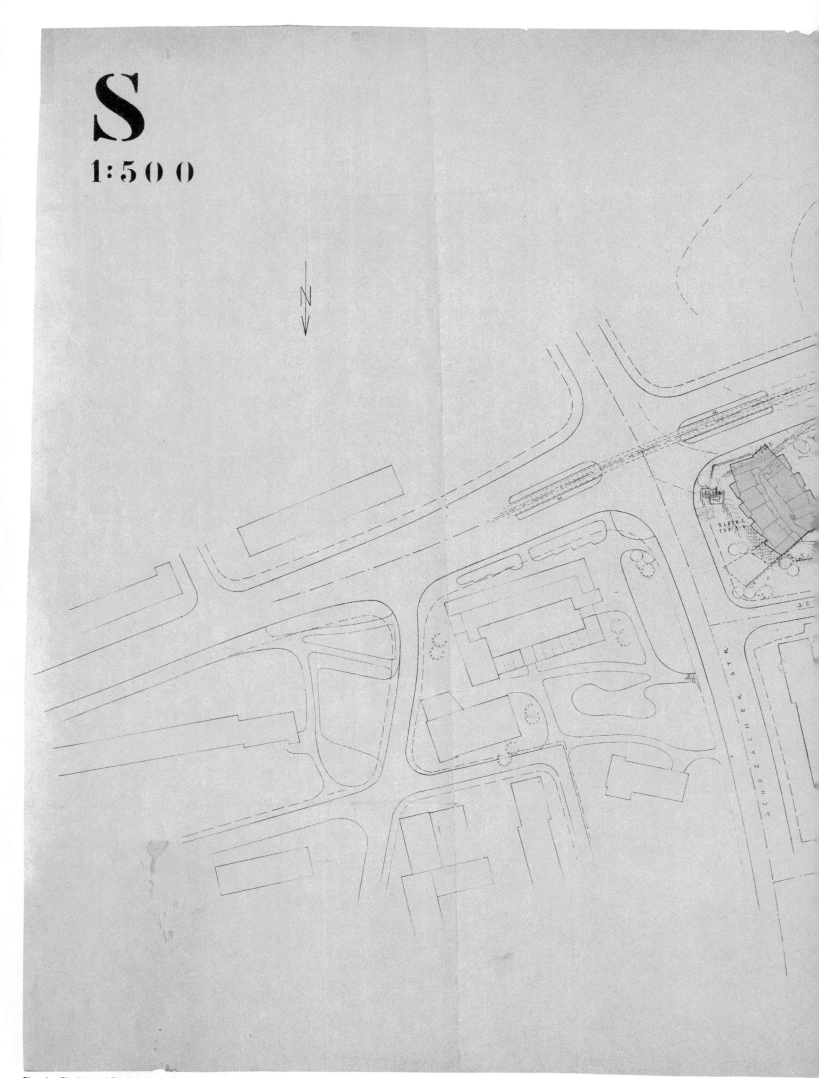

S

1:500

Site plan Block 1 and Block 2, single-family dwelling types 1, 2, 3

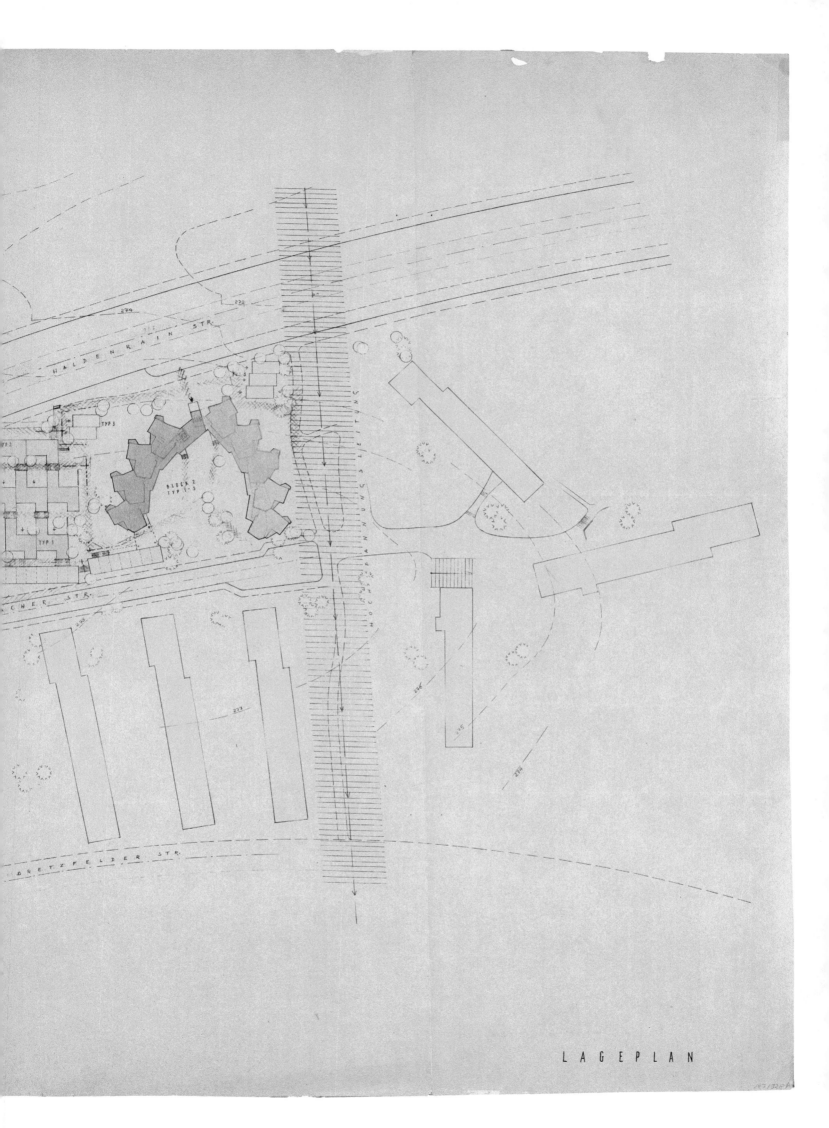

LAGEPLAN

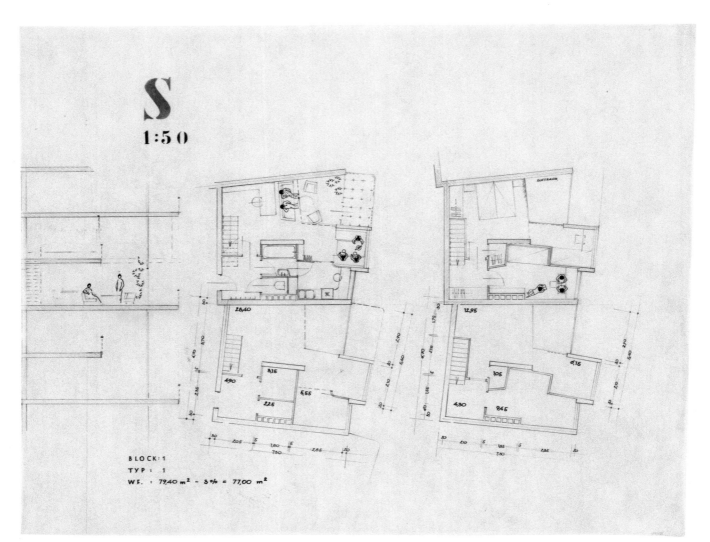

Block 1, type 1, 77 m²

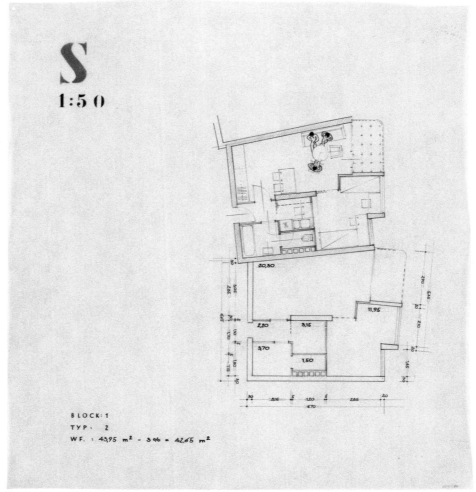

Block 1, type 2, 42.65 m²

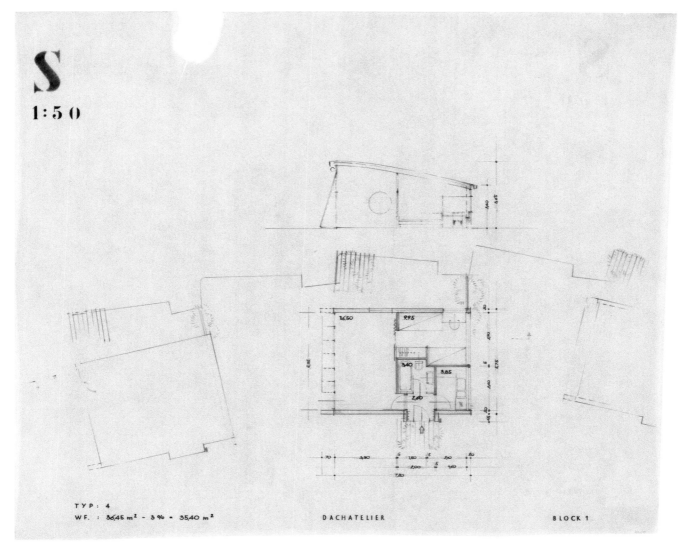

Block 1, type 4, rooftop studio, 35.40 m²

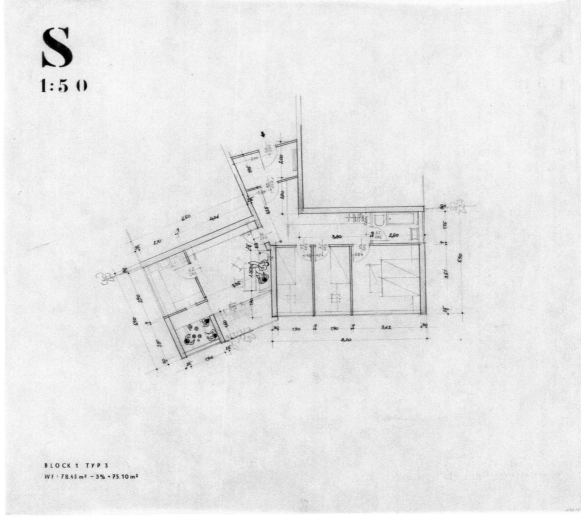

Block 1, type 3, 75.10 m²

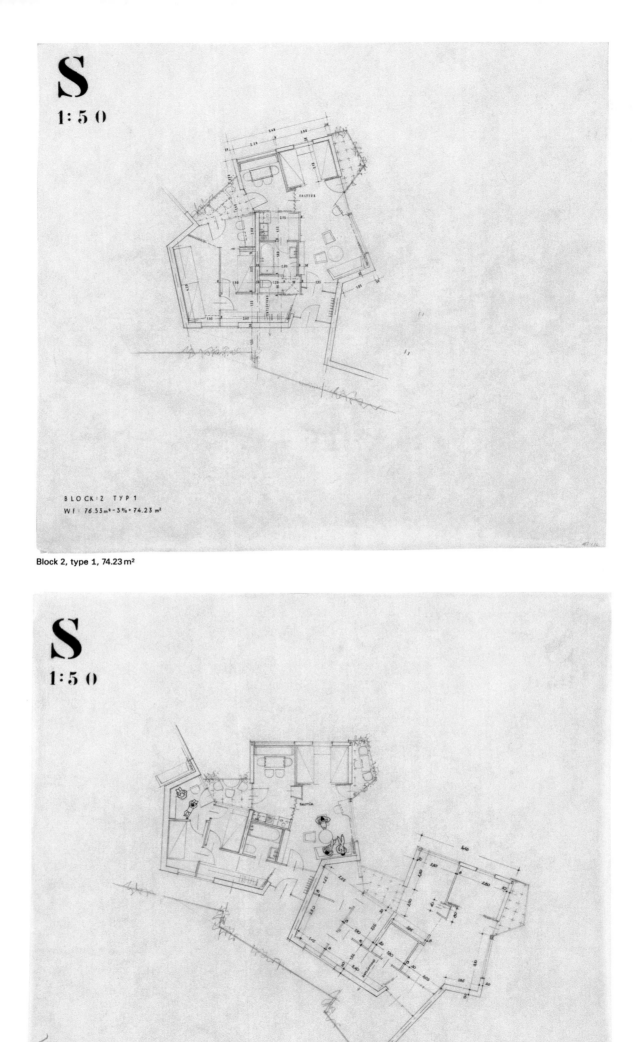

Block 2, type 1, 74.23 m²

Block 2, type 2, 61.62 m²

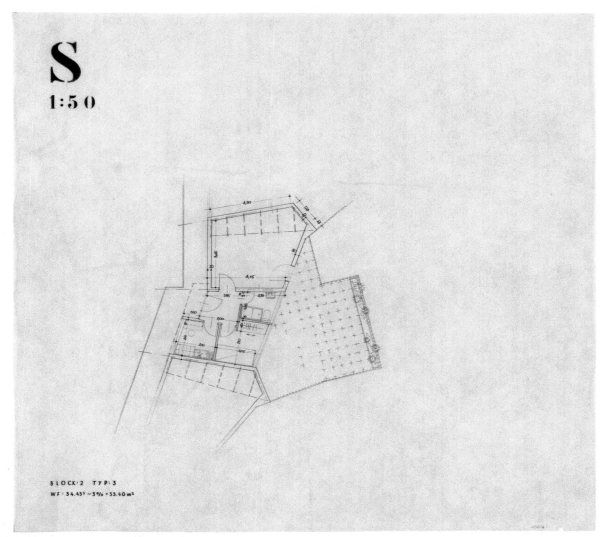

S
1:50

BLOCK:2 TYP:3
WF: 34.43⁵ –3⁰/₀ = 33.40 m²

Block 2, type 3, rooftop studio, 33.40 m²

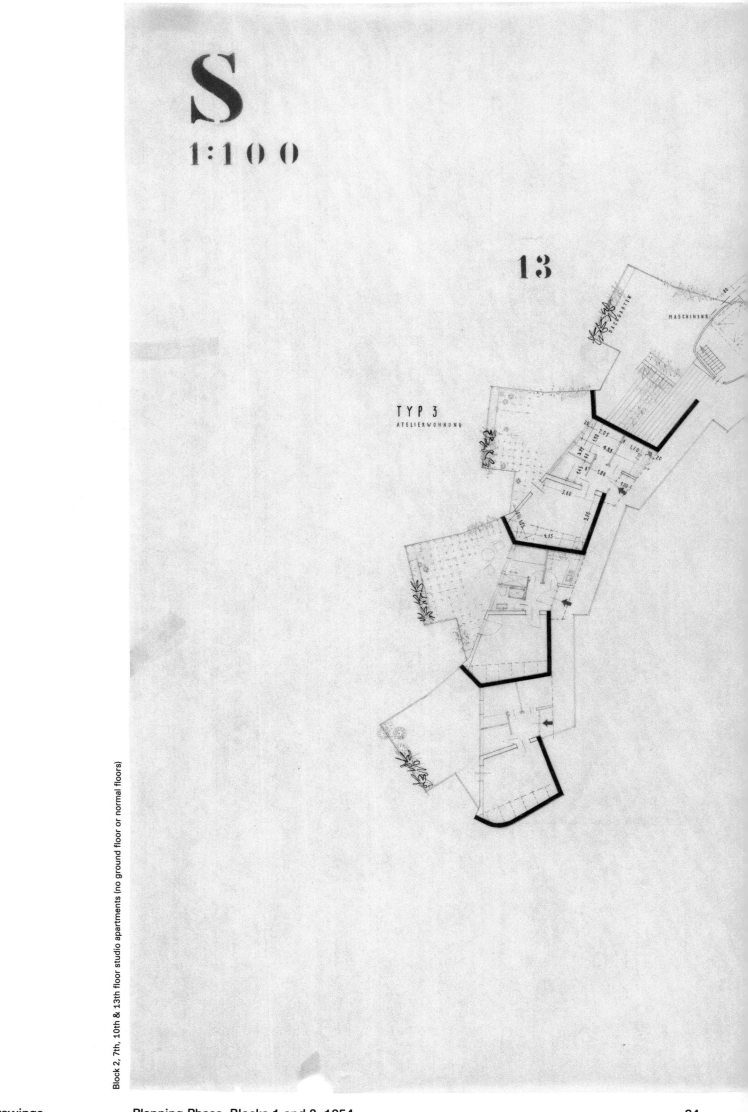

S
1:100

13

TYP 3
ATELIERWOHNUNG

Block 2, 7th, 10th & 13th floor studio apartments (no ground floor or normal floors)

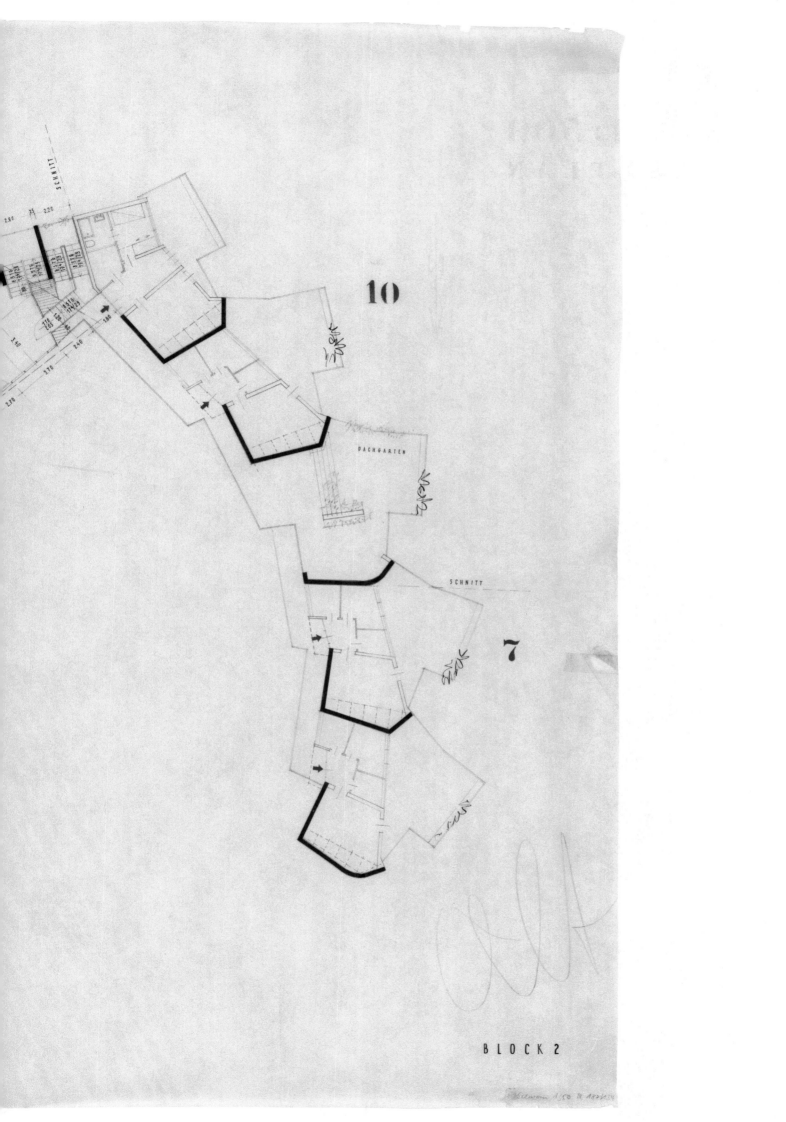

10

DACHGARTEN

SCHNITT

7

BLOCK 2

35

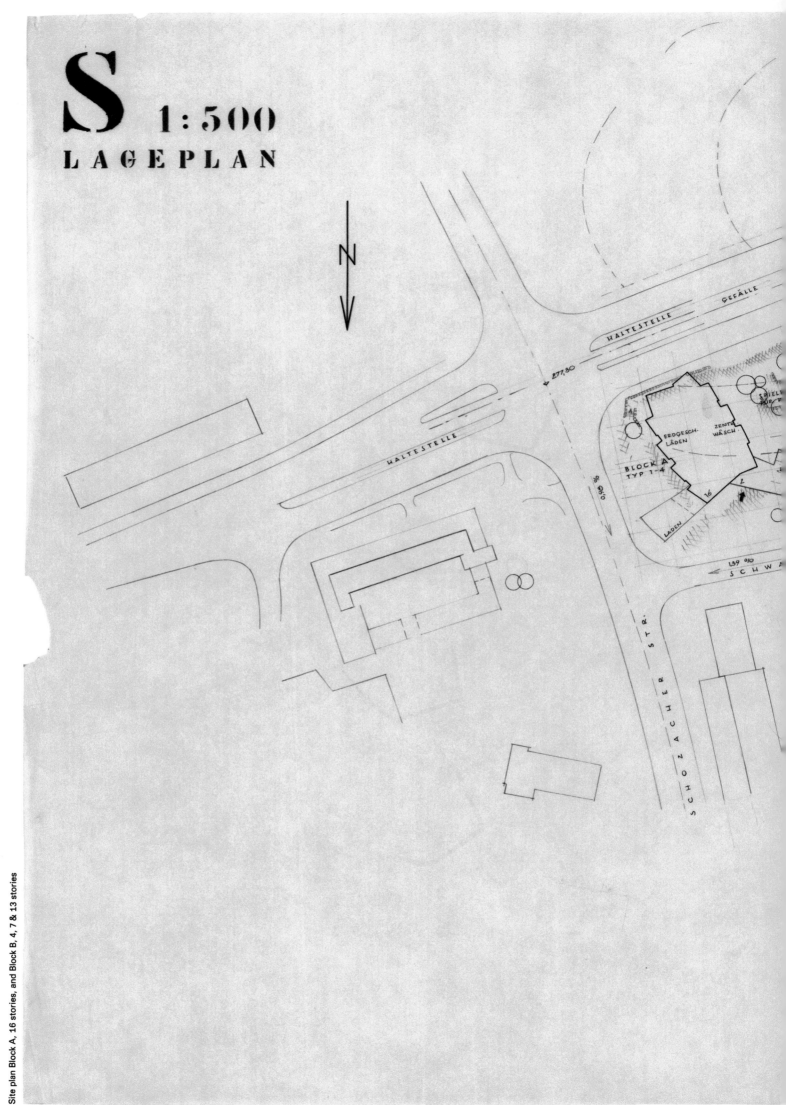

S 1:500
LAGEPLAN

N

Site plan Block A, 16 stories, and Block B, 4, 7 & 13 stories

HALDENRAIN STR.

274.26

BRÜCKE

PERGOLA

EINFAM.
HAUS

274

275

276

277

8 GARAG.
MIT TERRASSEN
SPIELPLATZ
FÜR KLEINK.

277.00

BLOCK B
TYP 1-3

13

10

7

5 GARAG.
MIT DACH

PERGOL

SPIELPLATZ
FÜR KINDER

10 GARAG.
MIT DACH

1

HAUSMSTR. WOHN.

FAHRRÄDER

SCHULE

P

MAUER

278.10

P

ER STR.

HOCHSPANNUNGSLEITUNG

37

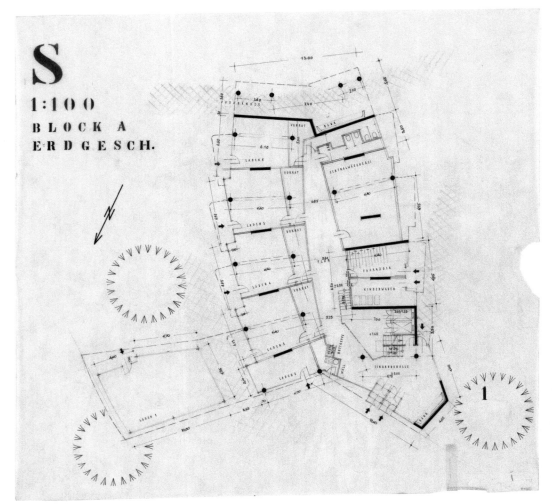

Block A, ground floor

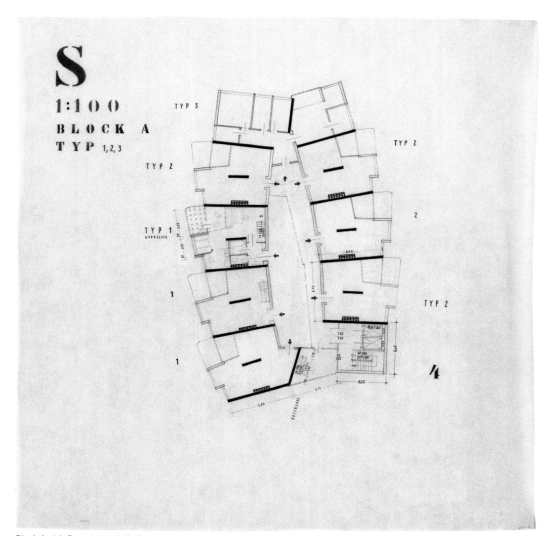

Block A, 4th floor, types 1, 2, 3

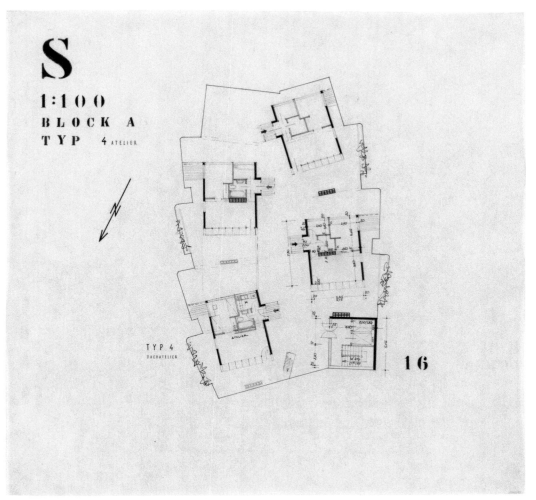

Block A, 16th floor, type 4 rooftop studios

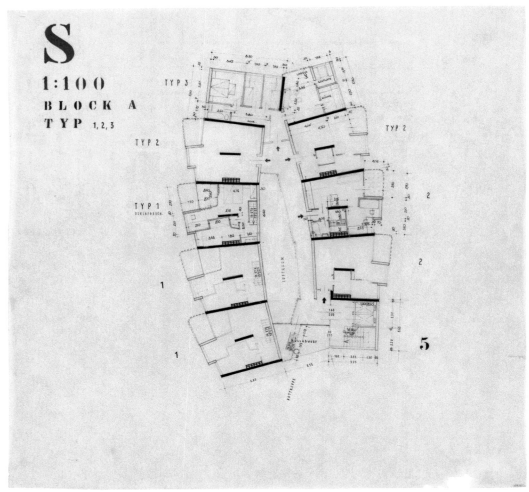

Block A, 5th floor, types 1, 2, 3

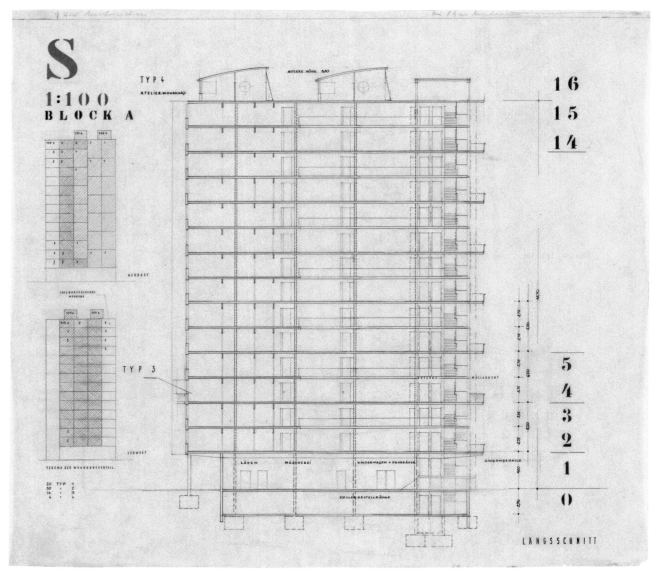

Block A, longitudinal section

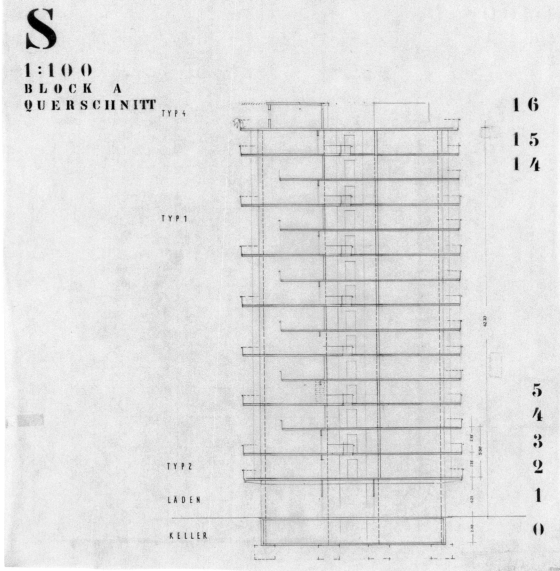

S

1:100
BLOCK A
QUERSCHNITT TYP 4

TYP 1

TYP 2

LÄDEN

KELLER

16
15
14

5
4
3
2
1
0

Block A, cross section

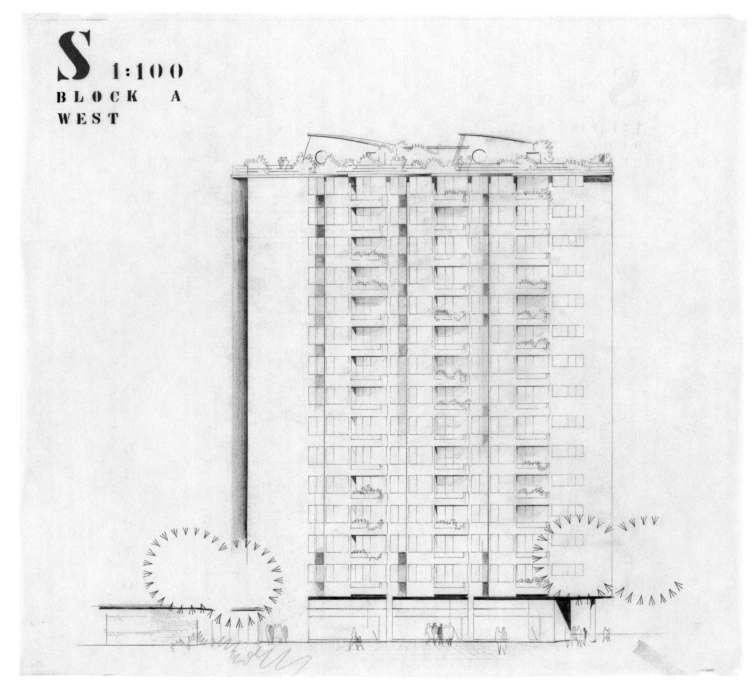

S 1:100
BLOCK A
WEST

Block A, west façade

Block A, east façade

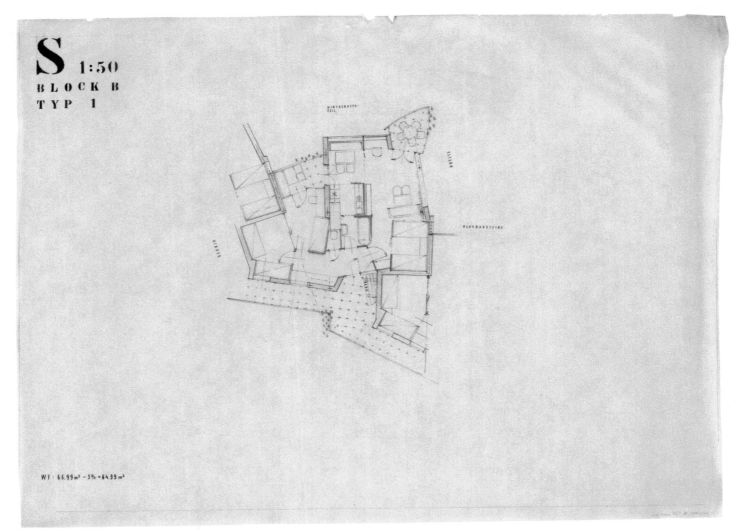

S 1:50

BLOCK B
TYP 1

WF: 66.99 m² − 3% = 64.99 m²

Block B, type 1, 64.99 m²

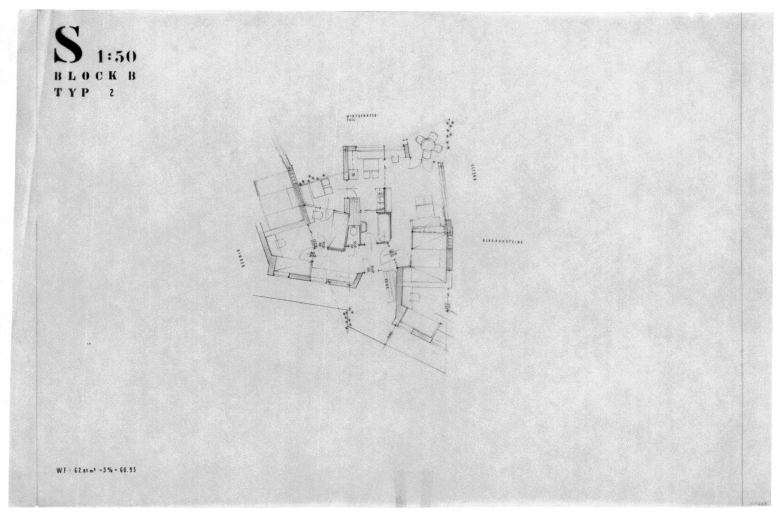

S 1:50
BLOCK B
TYP 2

WF : 62.81 m² -3% - 60.93

Block B, type 2, 60.93 m²

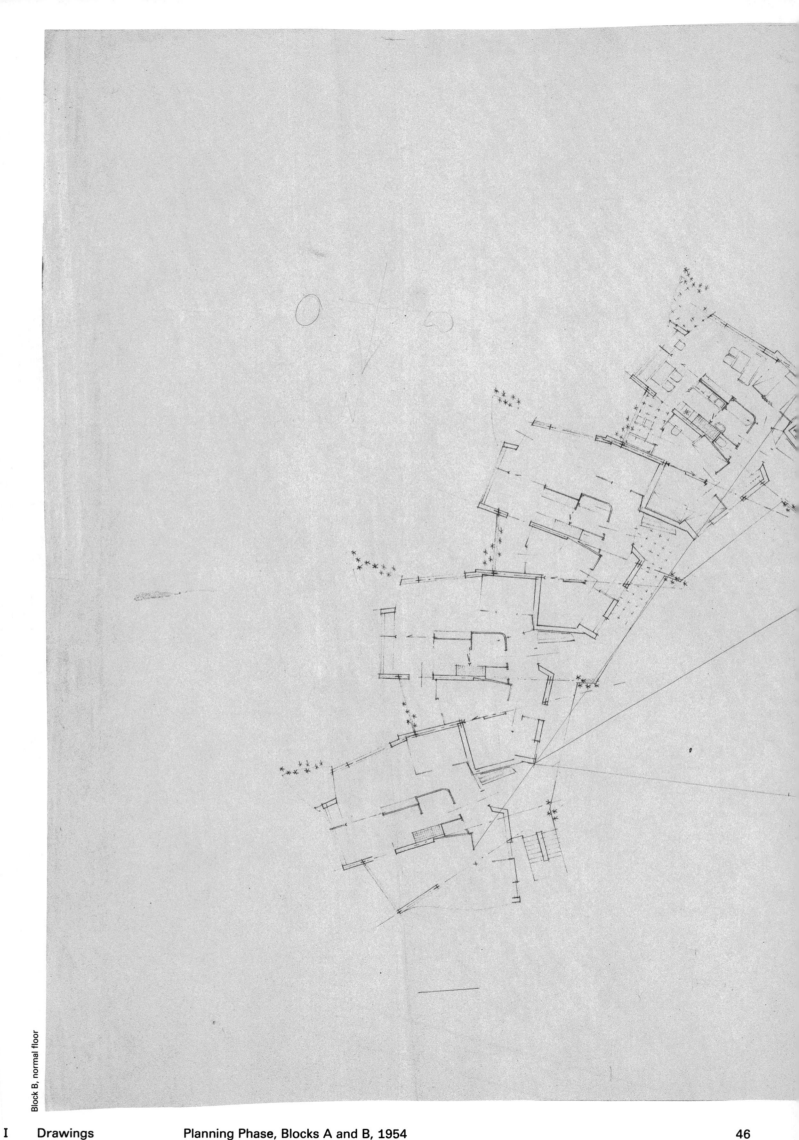

Block B, normal floor

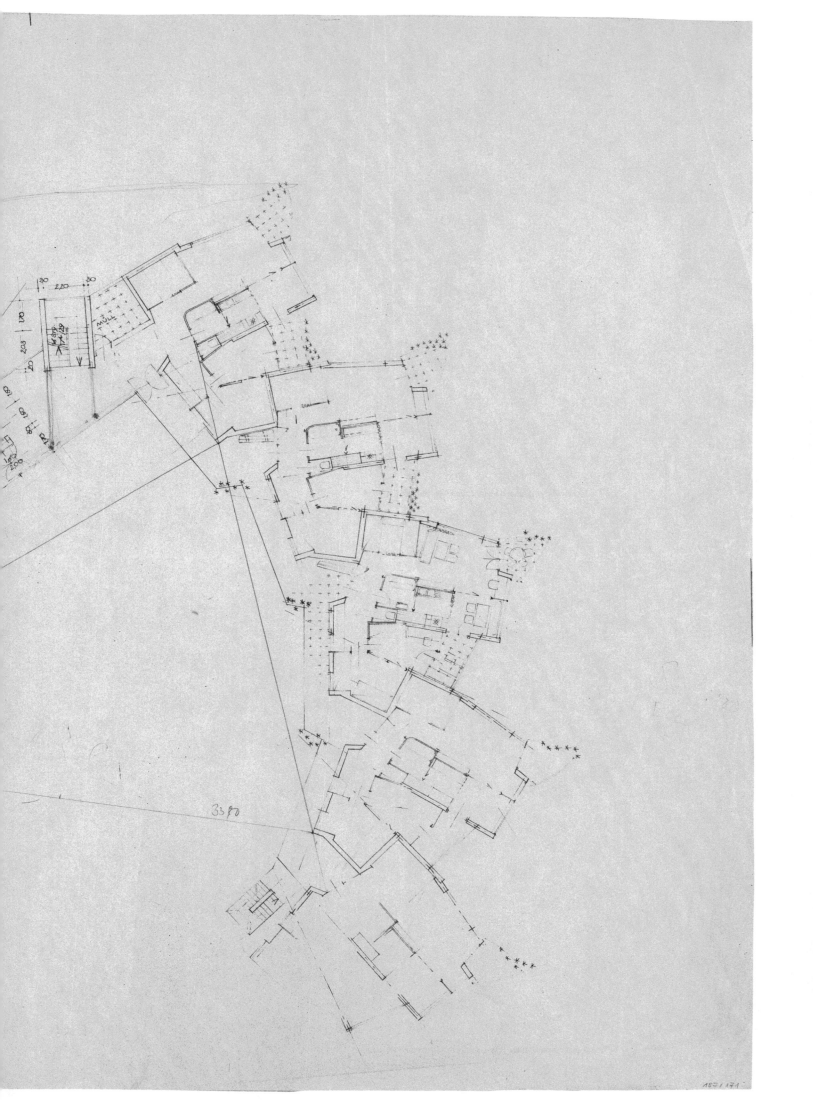

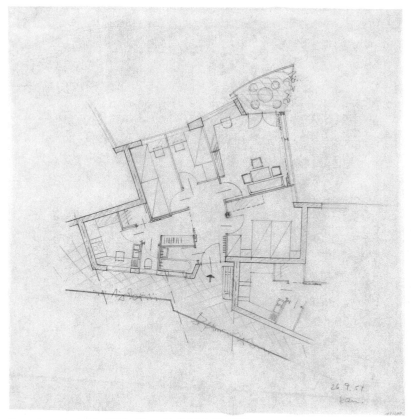

Floor plan variant Julia, 5 ½-bed type, September 26, 1954

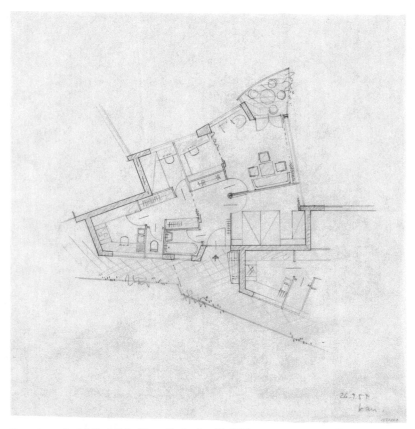

Floor plan variant Julia, 3 ½-bed type, September 26, 1954

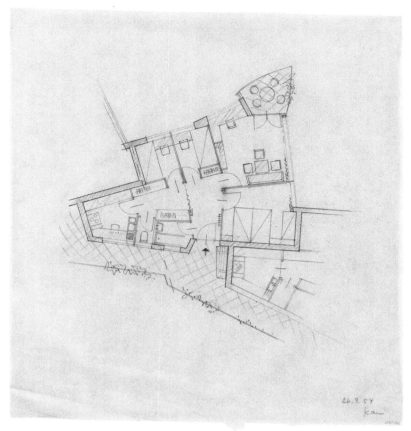

Floor plan variant Julia, 4 ½-bed type, September 26, 1954

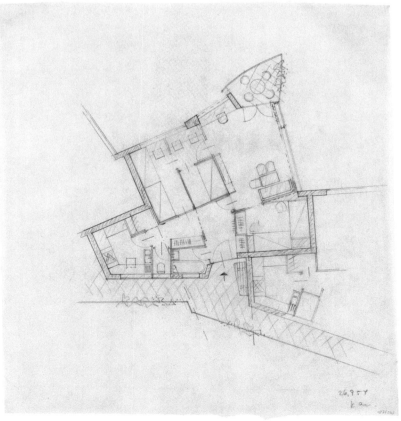

Floor plan variant Julia, 5-bed type, September 26, 1954

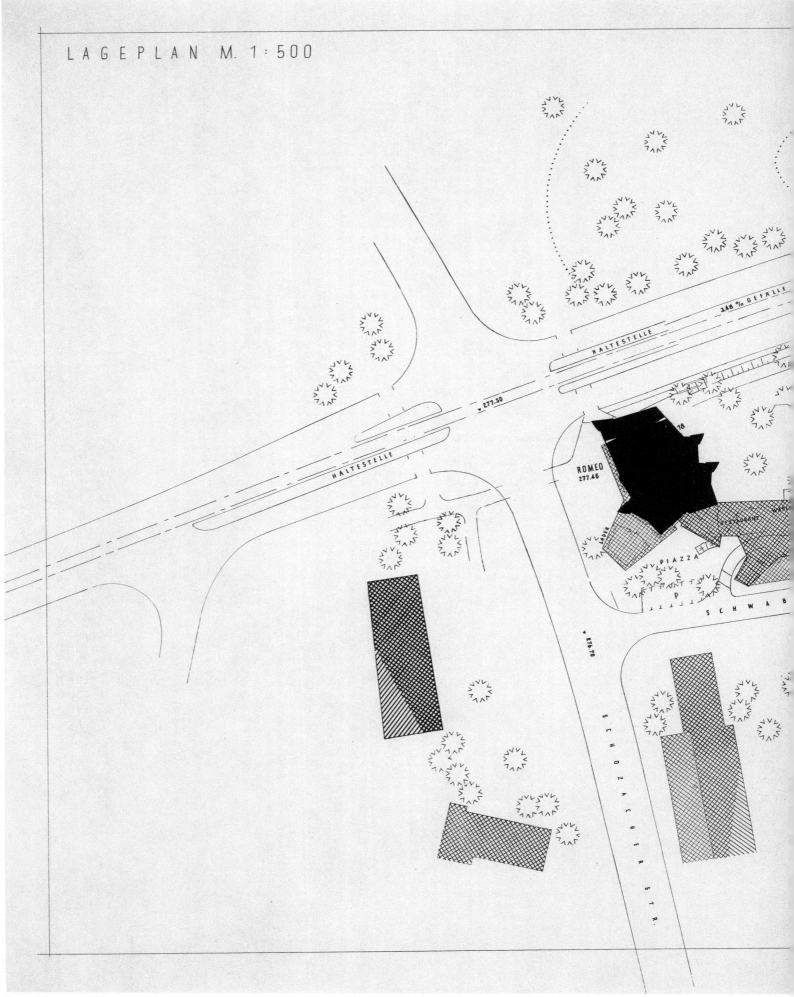

LAGEPLAN M. 1:500

Site plan Romeo and Julia

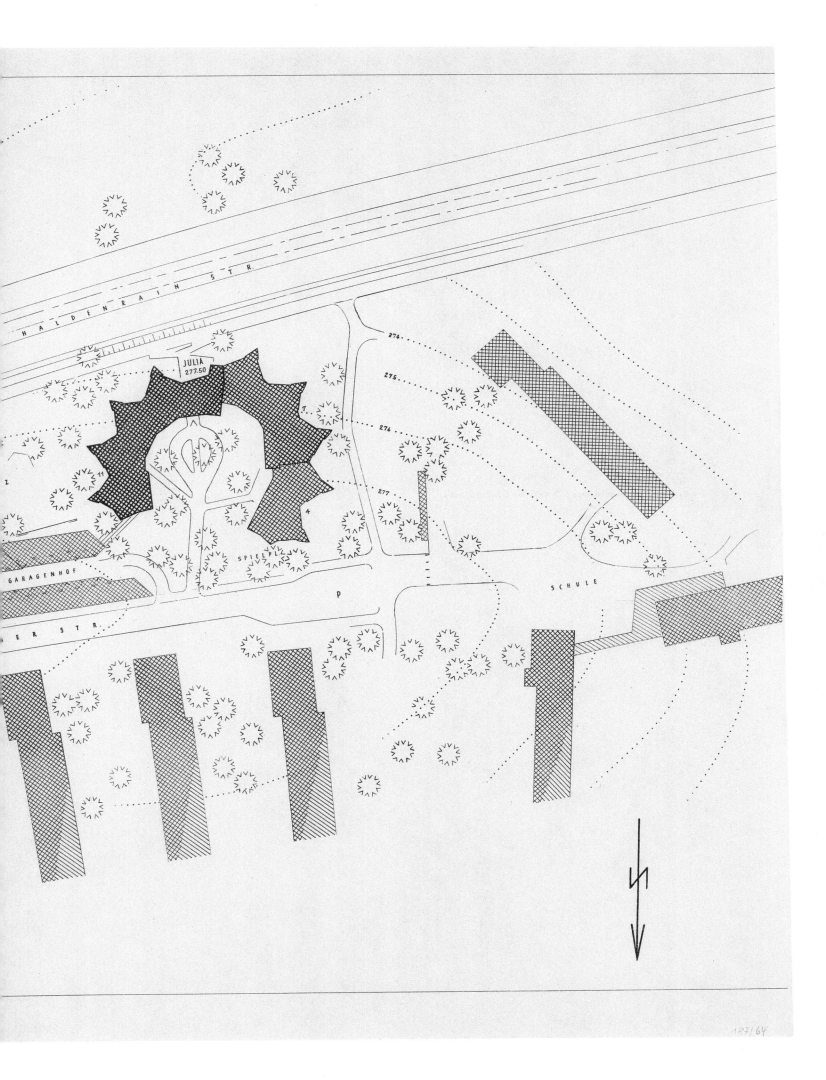

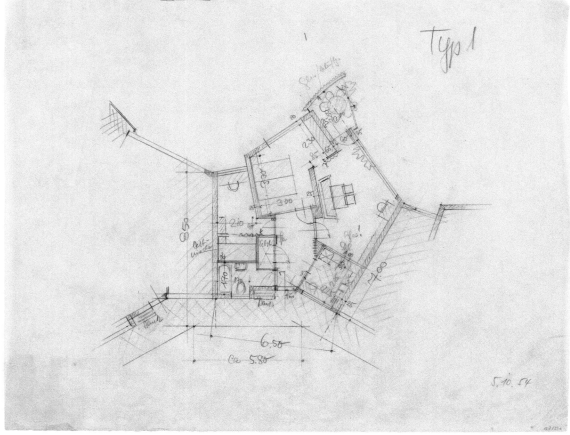

Floor plan variant Julia, type 1, 3-bed type, October 5, 1954

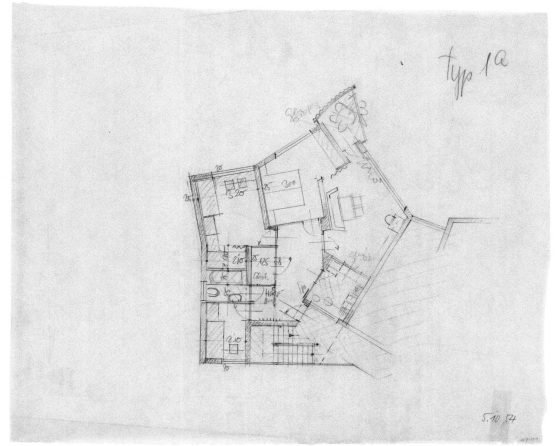

Floor plan variant Julia, type 1a, corner variant, 4-bed type, October 5, 1954

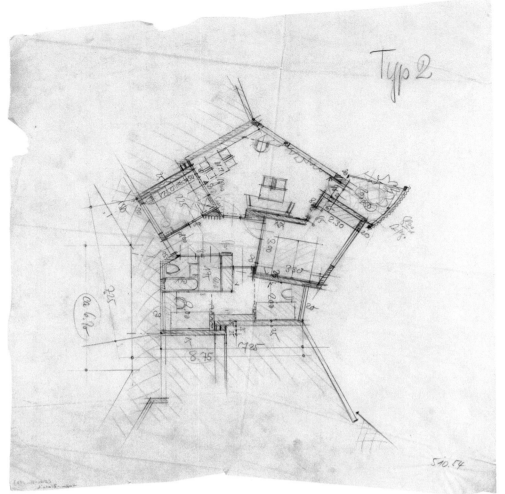

Floor plan variant Julia, type 2, 4-bed type, October 5, 1954

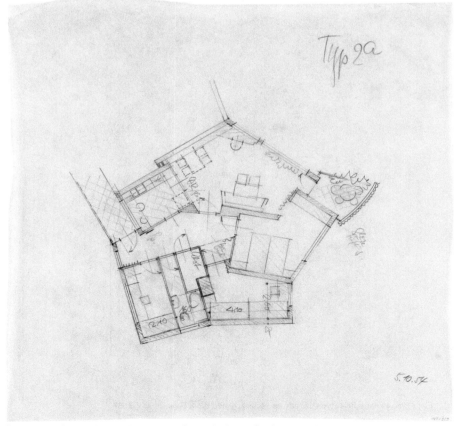

Floor plan variant Julia, type 2a, corner variant, 5-bed type, October 5, 1954

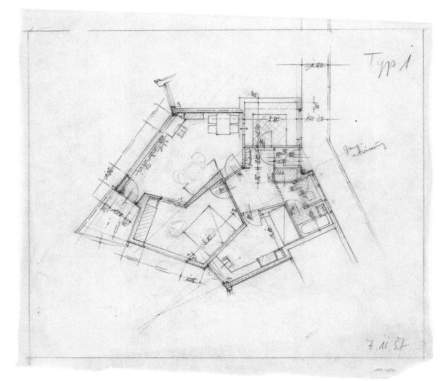

Floor plan variant Julia, type 1, 3-bed type, November 7, 1957

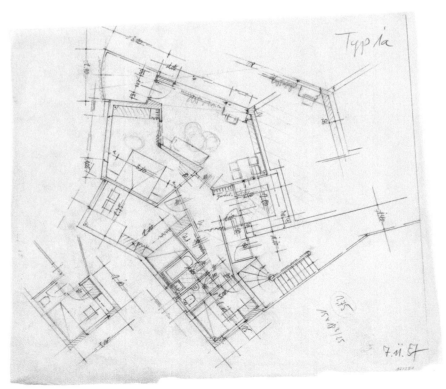

Floor plan variant Julia, type 1a, corner variant, 4-bed type, November 7, 1957

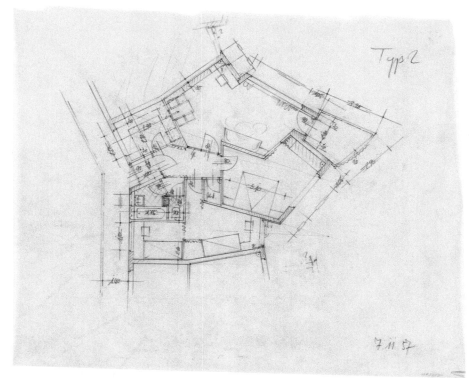

Floor plan variant Julia, type 2, 4-bed type, November 7, 1957

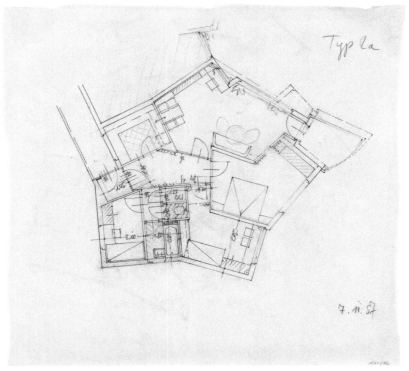

Floor plan variant Julia, type 2a, corner variant, 4-bed type, November 7, 1957

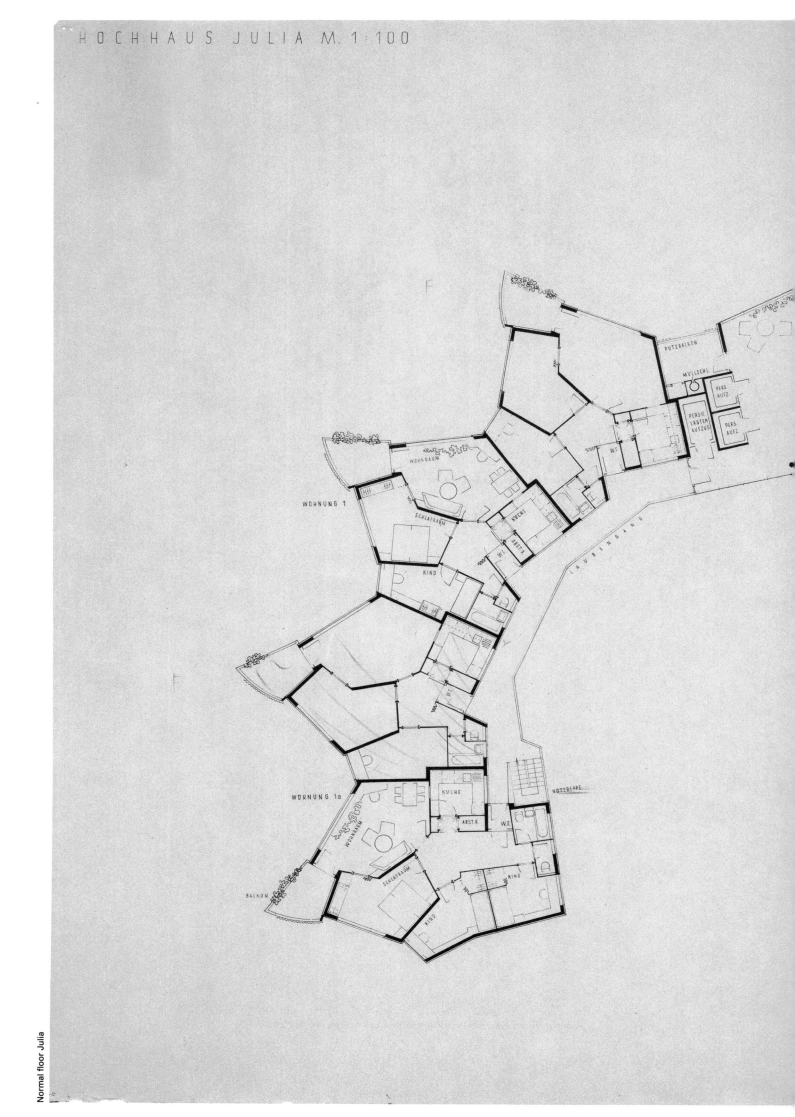

PUTZBALKON

MÜLLSCHL.

PERS.
AUFZ.

PERS.
LASTEN
AUFZUG

PERS.
AUFZ.

W.C.

WOHNRAUM

WOHNUNG 1

SCHLAFRAUM

KÜCHE

ABSTR.

W.C.

LAUBENGANG

KIND

WC

WOHNUNG 1a

KÜCHE

NOTTREPPE

ABSTR.

W.C.

WOHNRAUM

BALKON

SCHLAFRAUM

KIND

KIND

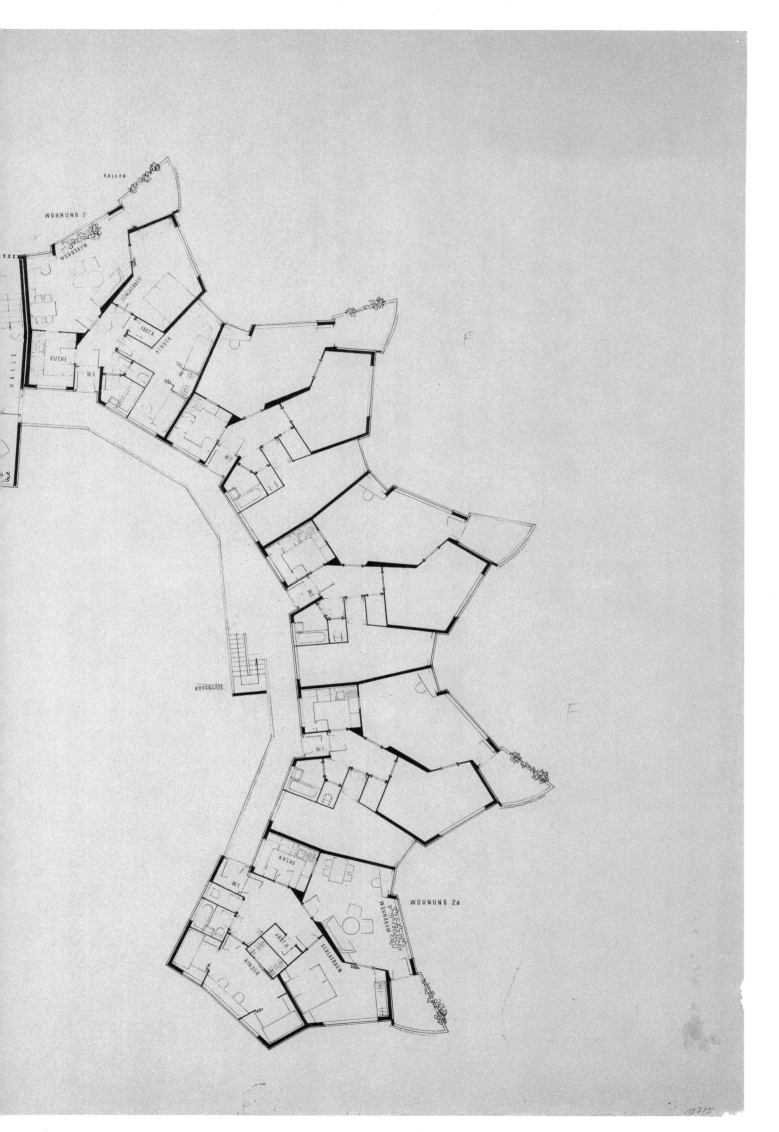

WOHNUNG 2

BALKON

WOHNRAUM

SCHLAFRAUM

ABST.R.

KÜCHE

KINDER

W.R.

HALLE

NOTTREPPE

W.R.

W.R.

W.R.

KÜCHE

WOHNUNG 2a

W.R.

WOHNRAUM

ABST.R.

KINDER

SCHLAFRAUM

57

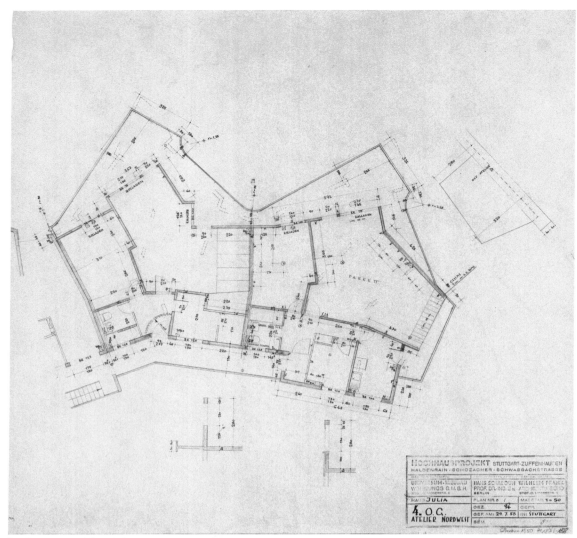

Studio apartment Julia, 4th floor, northwest, July 29, 1958

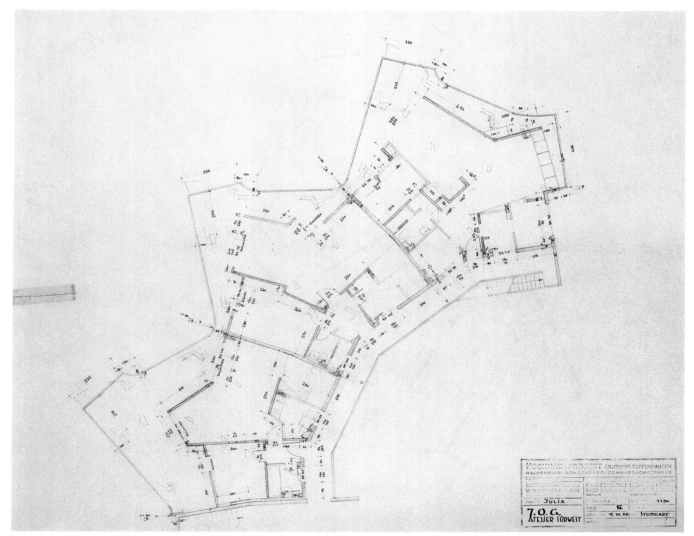

Studio apartment Julia, 7th floor, southwest, October 9, 1958

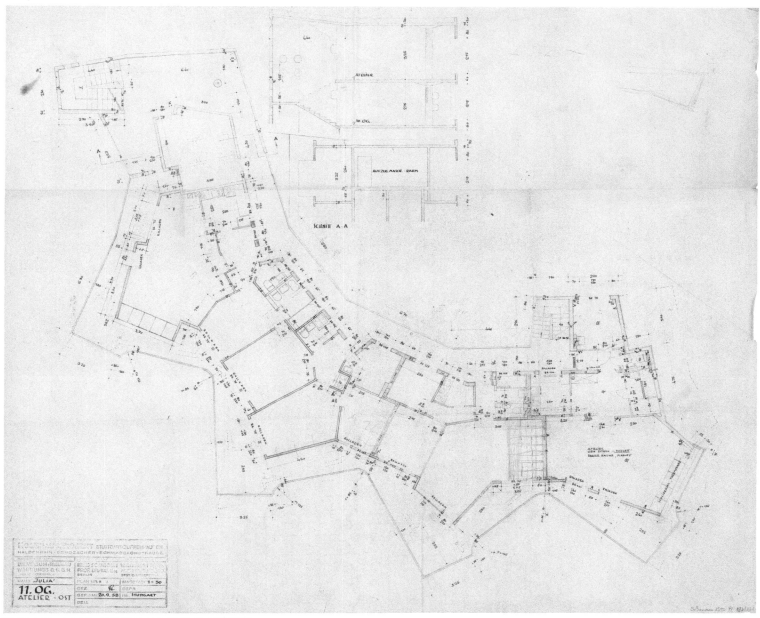

Studio apartment Julia, 11th floor, east, September 20, 1958

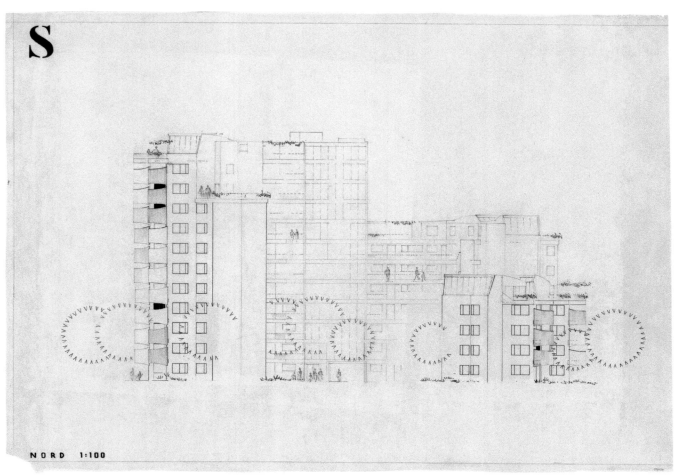

Julia, elevation of north façade

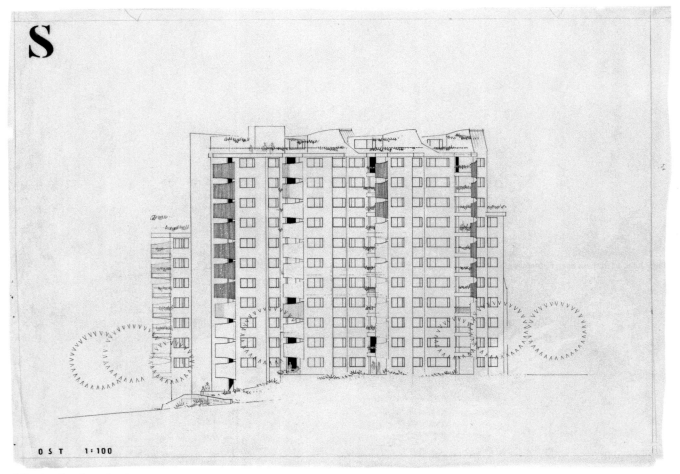

Julia, elevation of east façade

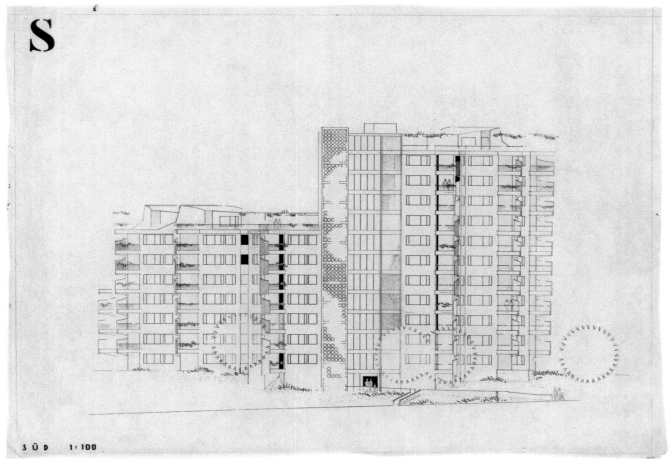

SÜD 1:100

Julia, elevation of south façade

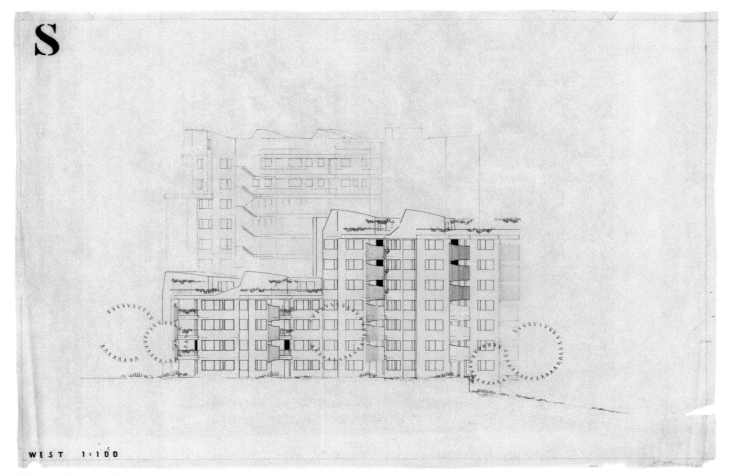

WEST 1:100

Julia, elevation of west façade

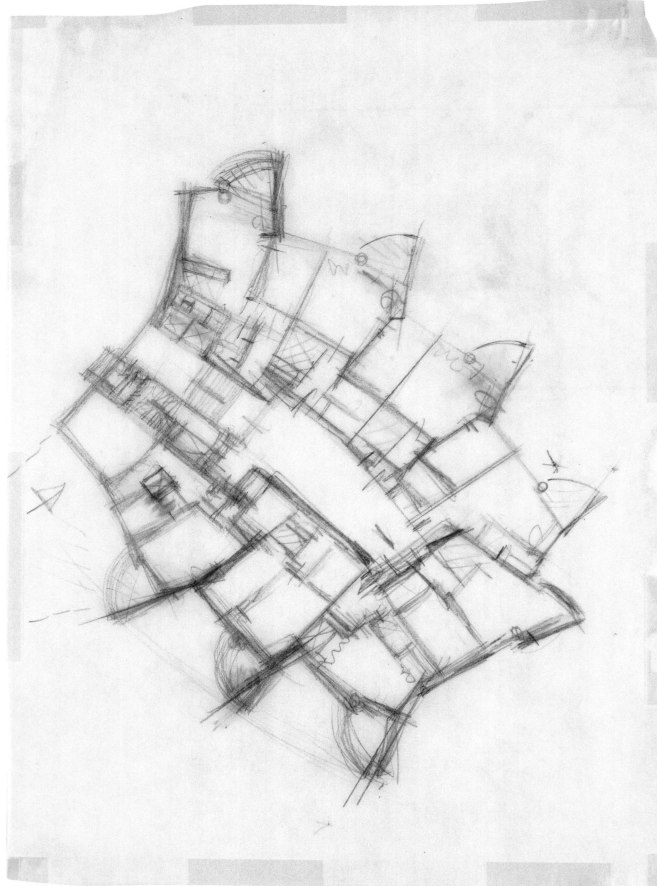

Sketch of Romeo

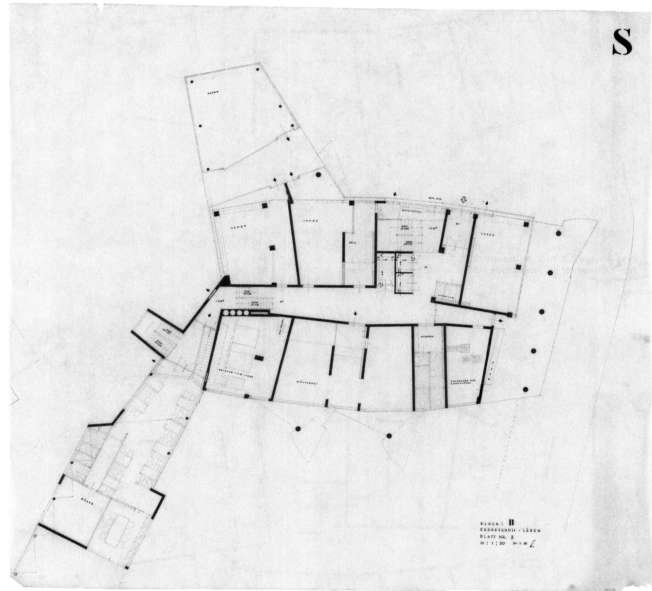

Block B, ground floor with stores, January 30, 1955

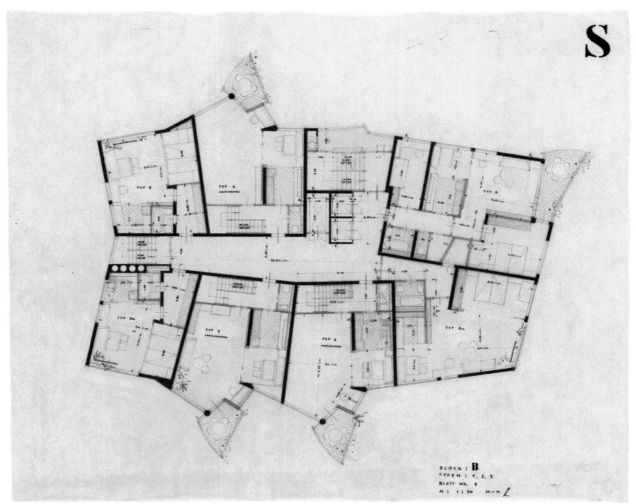

Block B, types 1, 2, 2a, 3, 3a, January 28, 1955
Type 1 (upstairs of the duplex), type 2 (2 Rooms (R)), type 2a (2 R), types 3, 3a (1.5 R)

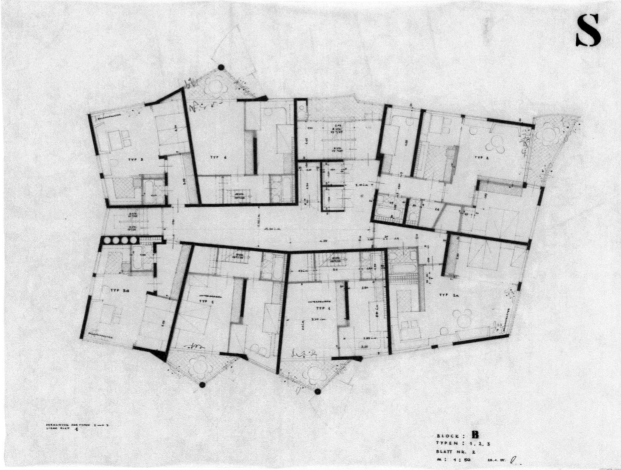

Block B, floor plan types 1, 2, 2a, 3, 3a, January 28, 1955
Floor plan type 1 (downstairs of the duplex), type 2 (3), type 2a (2 R), types 3, 3a (1.5 R)

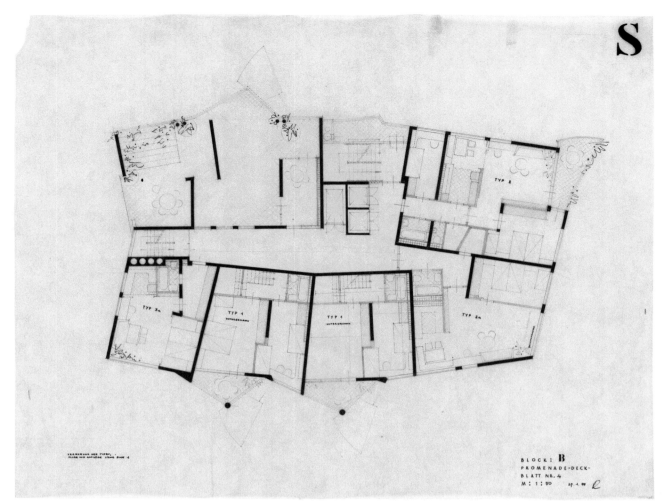

Block B, "Promenade Deck," January 29, 1955

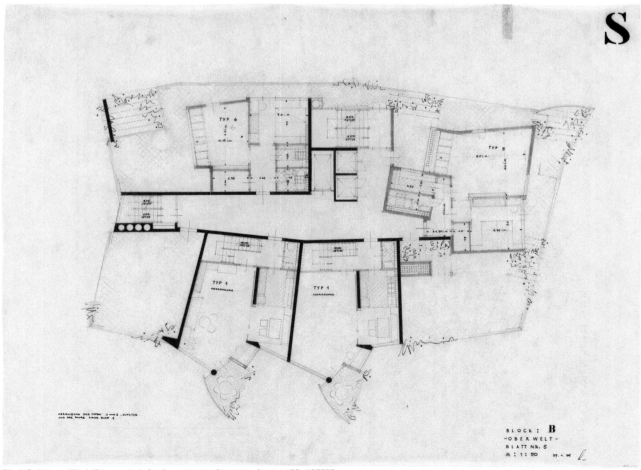

Block B, "Upper World," types 1, 2, 2a, 3a, communal terrace, January 29, 195555
Type 1 (downstairs of the duplex), type 2 (2 R), type 2a (2 R), type 3a (1.5 R)

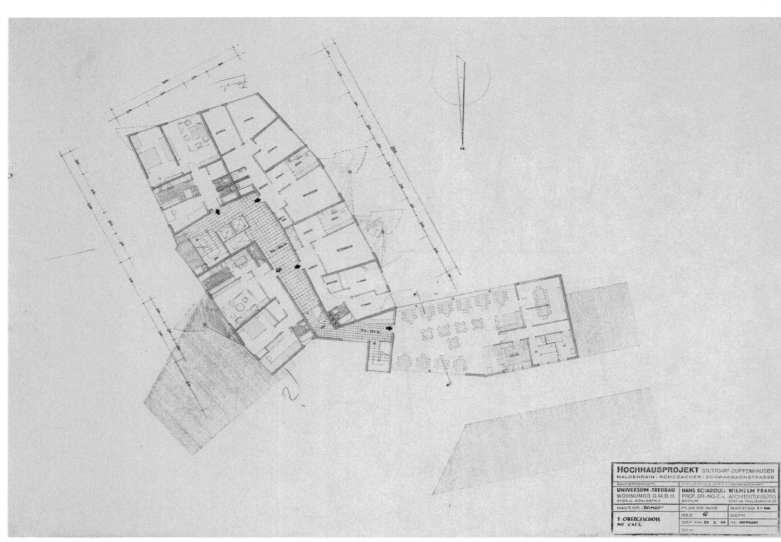

Romeo, 1st floor with café, February 25, 1955

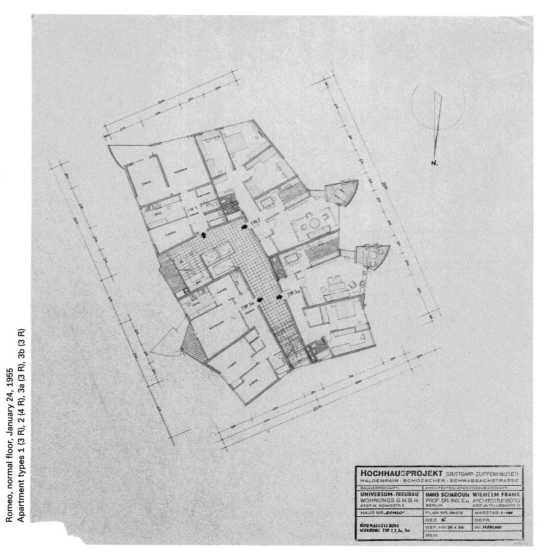

Romeo, normal floor, January 24, 1955
Apartment types 1 (3 R), 2 (4 R), 3a (3 R), 3b (3 R)

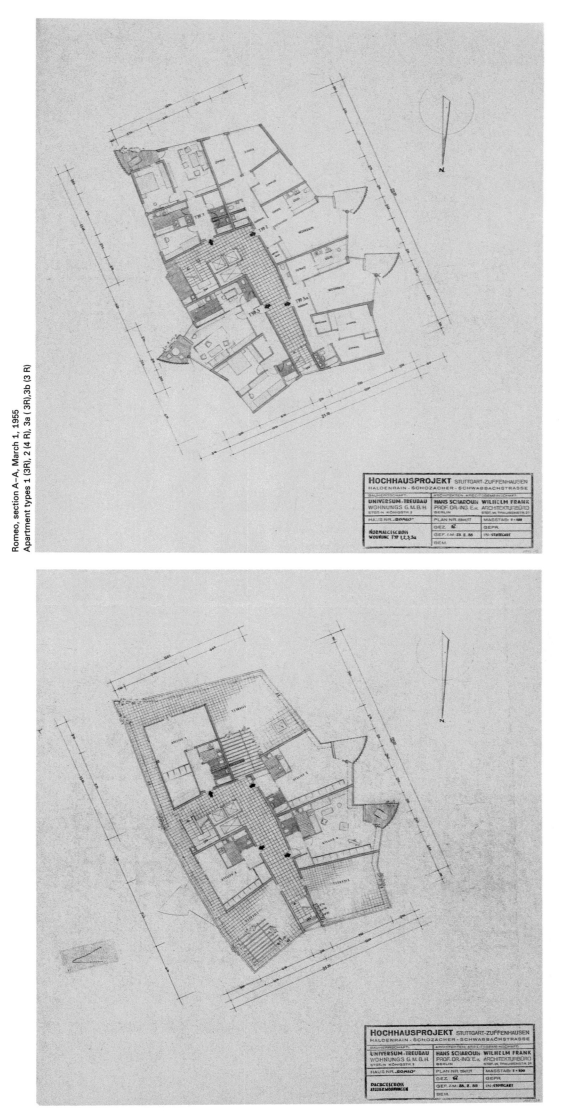

Romeo, section A–A, March 1, 1955
Apartment types 1 (3R), 2 (4 R), 3a (3R),3b (3 R)

Romeo, normal floor, apartment types 1, 2, 3, 4, 5, 6
Type 1 (3 R), type 2 (2 R), type 3 (2 R), type 4 (2 R), type 5 (1.5 R), type 6 (4 R)

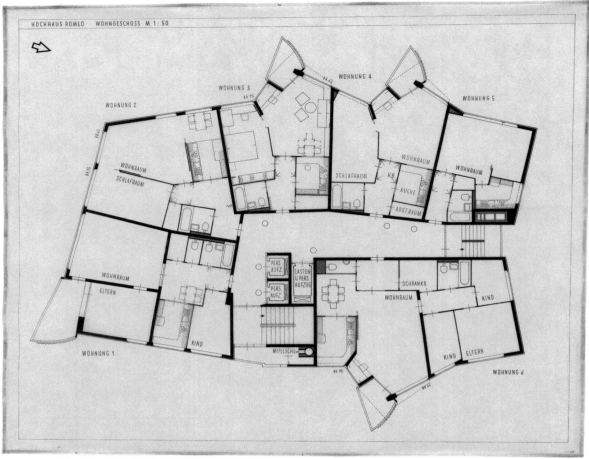

Romeo, normal floor, apartment types 1, 2, 3, 4, 5, 6
Type 1 (3 R), type 2 (2 R), type 3 (2 R), type 4 (2 R), type 5 (1.5 R), type 6 (4 R)

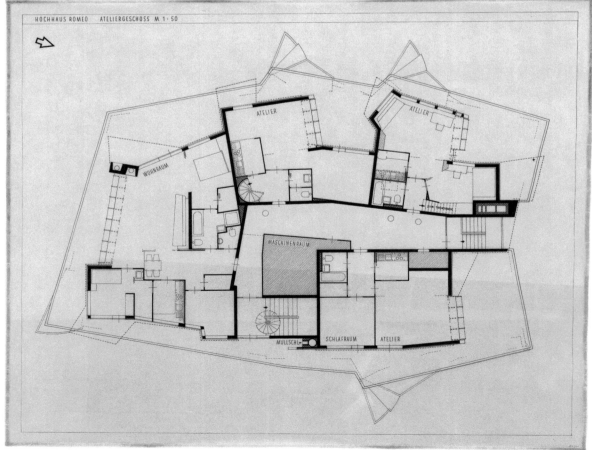

Romeo, top floor, 4 apartments

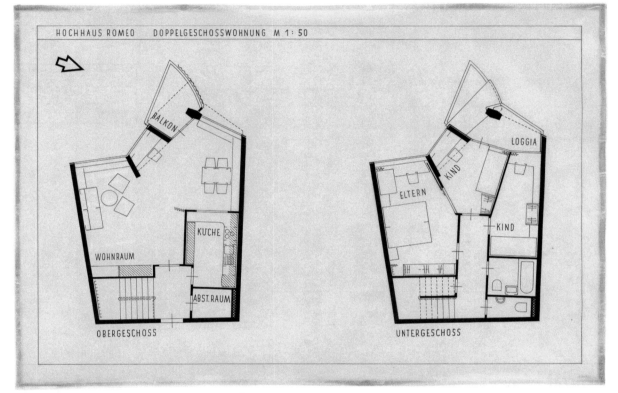

HOCHHAUS ROMEO   DOPPELGESCHOSSWOHNUNG   M 1: 50

BALKON

WOHNRAUM

KÜCHE

ABST.RAUM

OBERGESCHOSS

LOGGIA

KIND

ELTERN

KIND

UNTERGESCHOSS

Romeo, floor plan of the duplex apartment on the 16th floor

Romeo, north elevation, March 2, 1955

Romeo, east elevation, March 1, 1955

Romeo, south elevation, March 1, 1955

Romeo, west elevation, March 2, 1955

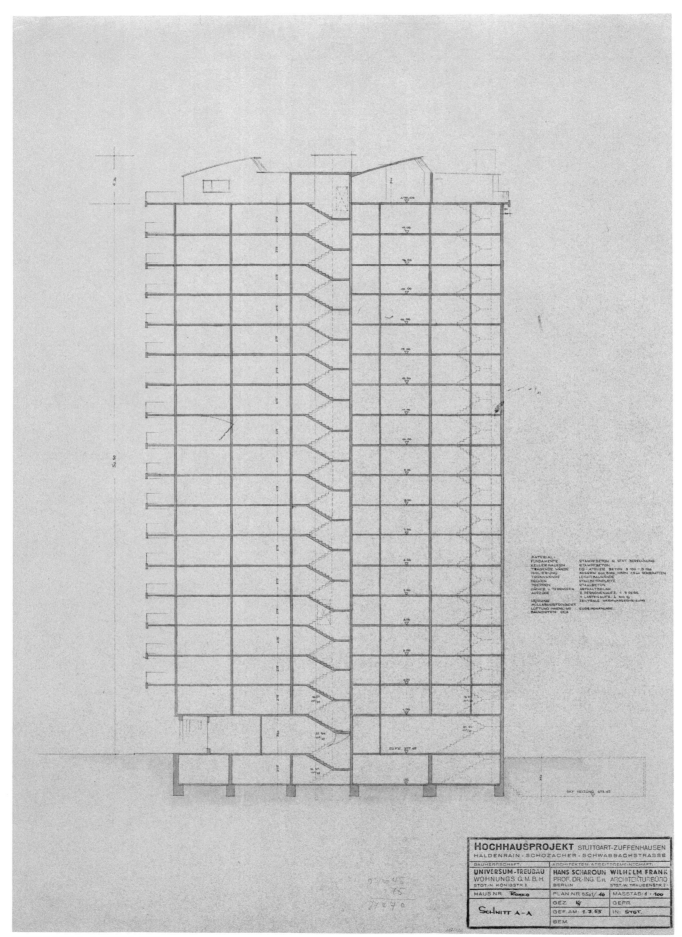

Romeo, section A–A, March 1, 1955

II   The Planning Process

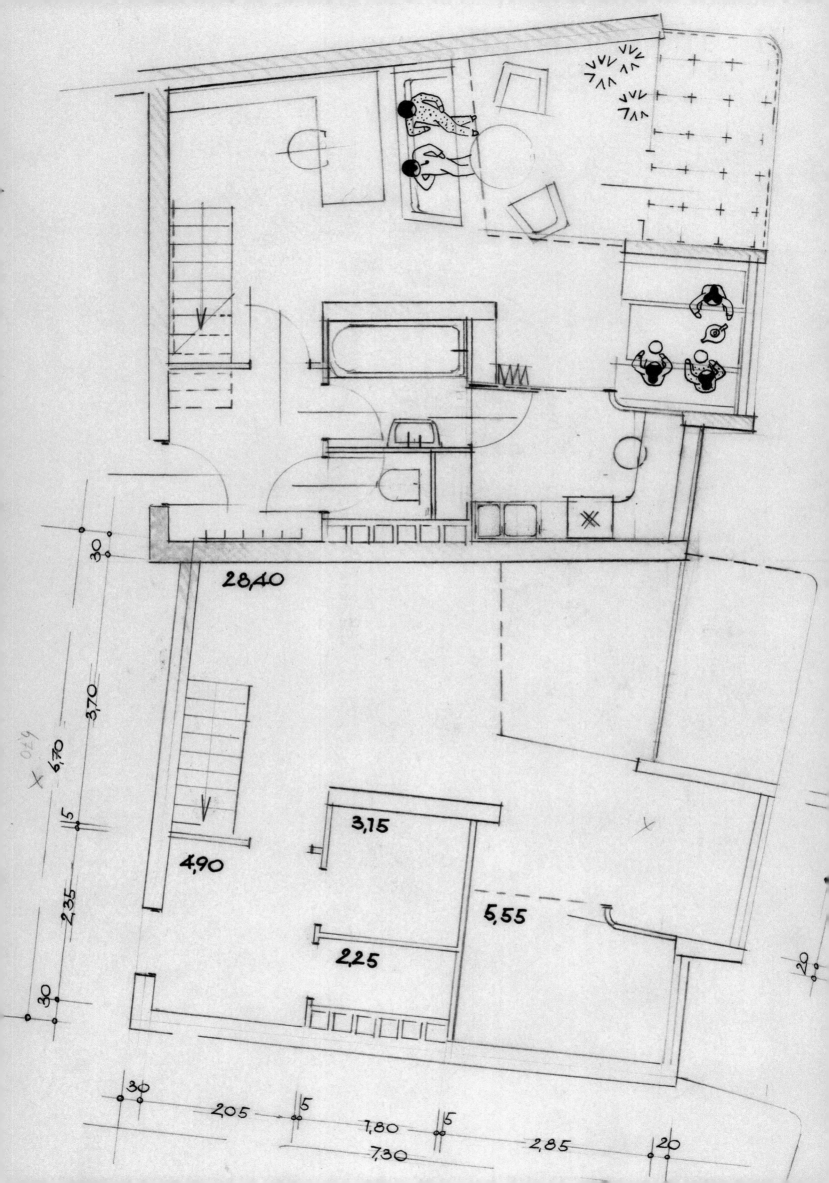

28,40

3,70

6,70

5

2,35

30

4,90

3,15

5,55

2,25

30

2,05

5

1,80

5

2,85

20

7,30

> "If we are to forge ahead to new things, the system must be destabilized—though without prior stabilization, it produces only noise."

Hans-Jörg Rheinberger, "Augenmerk," 2005[1]

When Hans Scharoun took over as director of the Institut für Bauforschung after the war, he also worked feverishly on expanding his own design work to the whole of the fledgling Federal Republic. His prize-winning design for the new Liederhalle in Stuttgart in 1949 was the first in a seemingly endless series of competition entries that garnered plenty of acclaim and prizes, but were never actually built.[2] Scharoun had previously met Richard Döcker, an erstwhile member of Der Ring, an artists' society, who had overseen the construction of the Weissenhof Estate in Stuttgart and who had discussed Germany's reconstruction with Hugo Häring at some length even while the war was still raging. Another important link to Stuttgart came about through Manfred Pahl, a painter, draftsman, and graphic artist, and until 1946 a resident of Berlin. Pahl was an exponent of Expressive Realism whom the Nazis had forbidden from working as an artist and declared a forced laborer, as which he found work in the offices of landscape designer Hermann Mattern and Scharoun himself. It was Scharoun who saw to it that Pahl was appointed head of the design office for the planning of Berlin's parks and gardens so that this would be his remit in the reconstruction, too. He collaborated with Scharoun right up to the exhibition *Berlin plant—erster Bericht* in August 1946.[3] After returning to Stuttgart, Pahl was employed in the Central Office for the Rebuilding of the City of Stuttgart, where he was again placed in charge of parks and gardens. It was Pahl, who from 1956, developed proposals for the color schemes of the high-rises, created the mosaic for the foyer of Julia, and planned the grounds. Döcker, meanwhile, was Stuttgart's first general director of buildings from May 1, 1946, but on being appointed professor of design and urban planning at the Technical University of Stuttgart in early 1947 handed over the reins to Walther Hoss, with whom he had headed the planning team for the reconstruction of Lorraine and Saarbrücken during the war.[4]

From mid-1947, Scharoun was regularly in touch with both Hoss and Stuttgart's governing mayor, Arnulf Klett, as the three of them prepared a congress and exhibition on the development of architecture and modern building methods in various countries. The possibility of a meeting with the CIAM group on the same occasion was also discussed. Döcker and Häring were consulted, but were both critical of the plan, not least on account of Hoss.[5] Häring was dismissive on the grounds that what Hoss really wanted from the congress was an opportunity "to showcase his development plan for Stuttgart. He has made contact with Congrès internationaux d'architecture moderne (CIAM) people through Swiss circles. What kind of a figure are we going to cut in such company? It's bound to misfire."[6] The planned congress never came about. What did materialize was a rather different kind of event that we find listed in the Association of German Architects (Bund Deutscher Architekten, BDA) calendar of events for November 7, 1953 as follows: "Planning and Reconstruction of the City of Stuttgart headed by Prof.

Walther Hoss."[7] The said plans were published retroactively in the official gazette of 1954[8] and served as the basis on which Romeo and Julia would be built. They are essential urban planning studies dating back to the general development plan debated by Stuttgart's Municipal Council in May 1948. They show the infrastructure needed for a new industrial base and transport hub, and they earmark the whole of northeast Stuttgart, that is to say, the area between the historical town center of Zuffenhausen and Münster, for new development on a grand scale. The residential districts of Rot, Mönchfeld, and Freiberg were built one after another on a comparatively narrow, three-kilometer-long strip of land. The foundation stone for the Rot development in Zuffenhausen was laid in 1949[9] and, as the 1950s progressed, it became a residential district consisting of three- to five-story apartment blocks, the majority of which faced east. Two-story single-family dwellings and row houses were erected along the central green space and facing onto the surrounding countryside. Scharoun's familiarity with the facts on the ground in Stuttgart is evident from his lecture on "Regional Planning" of 1948, in which he described the building boom already under way there as dominated by individualism and egotism, so that the "initially circumspect and generous remodeling of the urban fabric" had had to be repeatedly modified with the result that ultimately, it had been impossible to make any "fundamental changes to the underlying structures."[10] In the course of the same lecture, he defined the "Lex Hoss" as a planning tool for grouping landowners together with the aim of enabling the large-scale development of several contiguous properties at once.

The unusual contract for a residential high-rise was awarded to Hans Scharoun by Universum Treubau-Wohnungs-GmbH, a Stuttgart-based limited liability company established in 1951, whose first Y-type high-rise proj-

1   Hans-Jörg Rheinberger, "Augenmerk," in idem, *Iterationen*, Berlin 2005, pp. 51–73, here p. 68.
2   By 1956, Scharoun had won four competitions, none of which prize-winning entries was ever built. They include the aforementioned Liederhalle in Stuttgart (1949), a new theater in Kassel (1952), a senior citizens' home for Berlin-Tiergarten (1952), and an urban planning competition in Bremen (1956), (in the second round of which, Scharoun's design for a new Stadthalle won second prize.) The first of his prize-winning designs to be built was the Berlin Philharmonie of 1956 (built: 1956–1963).
3   This information was taken from the unpublished personal records of Manfred Pahl.
4   Durth, *Deutsche Architekten*, 1986, p. 344.
5   This is what Scharoun discussed in his correspondence with Hoss, Gropius, Hildebrandt, Döcker, Giedion, Häring, and Boettcher, among others, HSA 3249.
6   Hugo Häring to Hans Scharoun, December 27, 1947, HHA 1055.
7   Hoss was head of the "Zentrale für den Wiederaufbau in Stuttgart" (Office for the reconstruction of Stuttgart).
8   *Amtsblatt der Stadt Stuttgart*, No. 42 (1954), pp. 1–8.
9   Map 4.12: "Großstadtentwicklung im Industriezeitalter I: Stuttgart, Bebauung (1862–1977) und funktionale Gliederung (1977)," edited and annotated by Kuno Drollinger, in *Historischer Atlas von Baden-Württemberg. Erläuterungen,* edited by the Kommission für geschichtliche Landeskunde in Baden-Württemberg, 1982 (https://www.leo-bw.de/detail-gis/-/Detail/details/DOKUMENT/kgl_atlas/HABW_04_12/Gro%C3%9Fstadtentwicklung+im+Industriezeitalter+I+Stuttgart+Bebauung+%281862-1977%29+und+funktionale+Gliederung+%281977%29): accessed: February 3, 2019.
10   Scharoun, "Landesplanung," Lecture I/21, n.d.

ect had come to nothing after the necessary land swap proceedings broke down. Managing director Willi Oppenländer nevertheless insisted that high-rise was the way to go, for as he explained in his memoirs, "Stuttgart's west end cries out for one or two dominant landmarks and for decongestion."[11] Universum Treubau thereupon acquired the strip of land in Stuttgart-Zuffenhausen sandwiched between Schwabbacher Strasse to the north, Schozacher Strasse to the east, and Haldenrainstrasse to the south. It lies at the highest elevation in the entire area on the main feeder road to Zuffenhausen-Rot. Right from the start, Scharoun's contract was tied to the proviso that he work hand in hand with Wilhelm Frank, proprietor of an architect's office in Stuttgart and Dortmund, who was also a Universum Treubau shareholder and the architect of its first linear buildings. Frank candidly acknowledged the internal friction to which this collaboration with Scharoun gave rise in a letter to the same dated September 11, 1954. He also made it clear "that if the project is to proceed without friction and without financial surprises, the plans must be aligned with the working methods of the local contractors eligible to execute it, which in turn makes it necessary that the detailed planning be done in Stuttgart and not in Berlin, as originally intended."[12] Shortly after completion of Romeo and Julia, Scharoun took stock of their successful teamwork in a letter to the Swedish architect Hakon Ahlberg, who at the time was head of Stockholm's planning department. He had been working together with a "small but courageous developer," Scharoun explained, "which has gotten used to me and is even fighting for my ideas." Its managing director, Andreas Hastenteufel, had been "expelled from his home" and had made "his second home Stuttgart and the building of owner-occupied dwellings. Now that the battle for the 'Romeo' and 'Julia' apartment blocks (with some 200 owner-occupied apartments) has been fought and won and the objects themselves are proving their worth in practice, there are plans for a new residential high-rise to be called 'Salute' near the airport."[13]

The planning of Romeo and Julia began with urban planning studies in which Scharoun, working according to the principle of a combination of variously dimensioned volumes, including high-rise, medium-rise, and slab-type buildings, proposed four alternative site plans, each on a scale of 1:500 (figs. pp. 18–21). The plans envisage two high-rises of eight, ten, or twelve stories each at the eastern and western ends of the site, flanking a low-rise carpet of one- or two-story single-family dwellings and four- to six-story linear buildings. The buildings grew out of the floor plan repertoire developed at the Institut für Bauwesen in Berlin for the Wohnzelle Friedrichshain in 1949–1950, a stock of nine basic types for one- to twelve-story buildings that Scharoun modified and enlarged (figs. pp. 22–26). Alongside the saw-tooth type and the single-family dwellings, the layouts actually applied were again those for two and four apartments per floor. The four-apartment model was enlarged to a type with both single-story apartments and duplexes. The Y-shaped high-rise in site plan 3 took up a standard type of the 1950s that Universum Treubau had applied for its very first high-rise project. The floor plan of apartment type 7 in site plan 1 is repeated to produce a symmetrical, horseshoe-shaped building, whose units are accessed via a curved access balcony (fig. p. 23). This access balcony typology is structured so that it does not form an endless line, but rather can be pieced together to form a broken ring figure. The elastic determinants of this figure became apparent

later on during the work on the curved access balcony of Julia, which Scharoun himself corrected: "While working on the detailed plans it transpired that the curvature would have to be somewhat flatter."[14] The layout of the apartment which envisaged its division into separate zones, later called the "Children's world" and "Parents' world," the concentration of the dwelling functions in an inner core consisting of kitchen and bathroom, the two balconies, and the extension of the façade introduced the type that was to prove crucial to the development of Julia.

At the eastern end of the site, which was also its highest point, there was to be a sixteen-story high-rise with an expansive, two-story-high inside corridor (figs. pp. 30–31). Forty-eight duplexes (77 m²) and just two single-story apartments (42.65 m²) were to be lined up along the east and west side of this. At the southern end there was to be one three-room apartment per floor (fourteen times 75.10 m²), while on the roof there were to be four studio apartments (35.40 m²). The duplexes were divided into a downstairs living area and an upstairs sleeping area, which were connected by an open space giving onto the balcony. Because the inside bathroom could be accessed from two sides, the entrance area, living area, and kitchen formed a spatial continuum. This in turn gave rise to spatial relations transcending the apartment's division into separate functional zones, ensuring that it was experienced as a coherent whole. The upstairs housed the parents' bedroom and the two children's bedrooms. The former was conceived as an open gallery facing onto the open space. Only one of the children's bedrooms could be accessed directly, while the other had to be accessed via the parents' bedroom.

Block 2 takes up floor plan type 7 from the preliminary project and with it the idea of separate living areas for parents and children (figs. pp. 32–35). A slightly modified version of the small, three-room type 2 (51.92 m²) was adopted, as was a further development of the larger type 1 (74.23 m²). Both floor plans possess an inner core consisting of bathroom and kitchen so that circulation would be through the living areas, including the loggia, arranged around it. The two-door bathroom and kitchen of type 1 permitted circulation inside the inner core as well. Each room in the apartment could be accessed in two ways. The parents' bedroom was conceived as a cabin positioned again the outside wall. Its location within the apartment was exposed but functionally separate from the general living area consisting of loggia, kitchen, dining area, and living room with balcony. The attic studios (type 3, 35.40 m²) were divided into a large main room facing north (19 m²) and an extremely small bathroom, kitchen, and bedroom.

Scharoun was in Stuttgart to discuss the high-rise project from June 17–19, 1954 and took the opportunity to visit Richard Döcker. A short time later Frank reported "that the Municipal Council has approved the development proposals for the above construction project," although the review of the application for a building permit of November/December 1954 talks of a "preliminary project," that "the Tech. Dept. approved in principle on 7.7.54." Frank pushed for further steps to be initiated, including "the drafting of detailed plans to be submitted in support of the application for a building permit and based on these the drawing up of

11 Willi Oppenländer, *Bauen in die Zukunft. Lebendiges Bauen in Stuttgart*, Stuttgart 1962, p. 15.
12 Wilhelm Frank to Hans Scharoun, September 11, 1954, HSA WV 187, I, Correspondence 1954.
13 Hans Scharoun to Hakon Ahlberg, December 7, 1960, HSA 417.
14 Hans Scharoun to Wilhelm Frank, October 5, 1954, HSA WV 187, I, Correspondence 1954.
15 Wilhelm Frank to Hans Scharoun, July 8, 1954, HSA WV 187, I, Correspondence 1954.

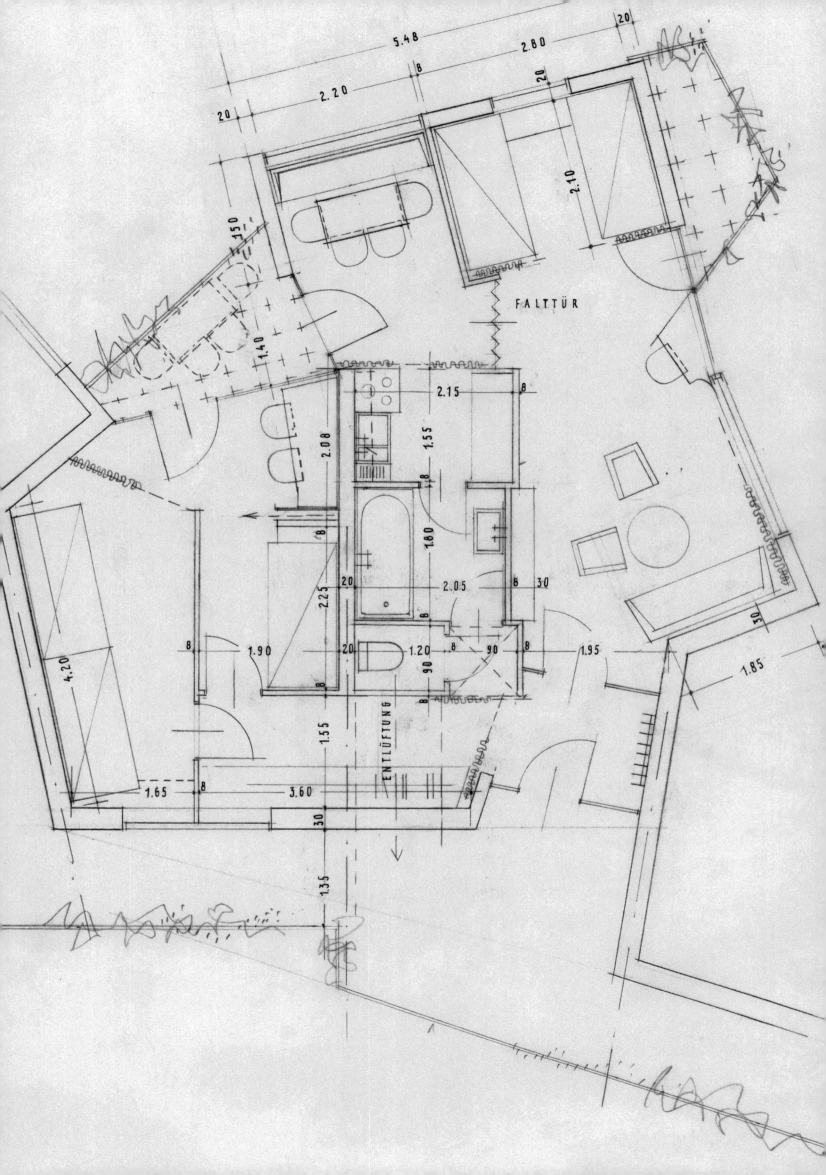

FALTTÜR

5.48
2.80
2.20
20
20
20
20
2.10
1.50
1.40
2.15
8
2.08
1.55
8
1.80
8
2.25
20
30
4.20
8
1.90
20
1.20
90
90
8
2.05
8
30
1.95
1.85
8
8
1.55
ENTLÜFTUNG
1.65
8
3.60
30
1.35

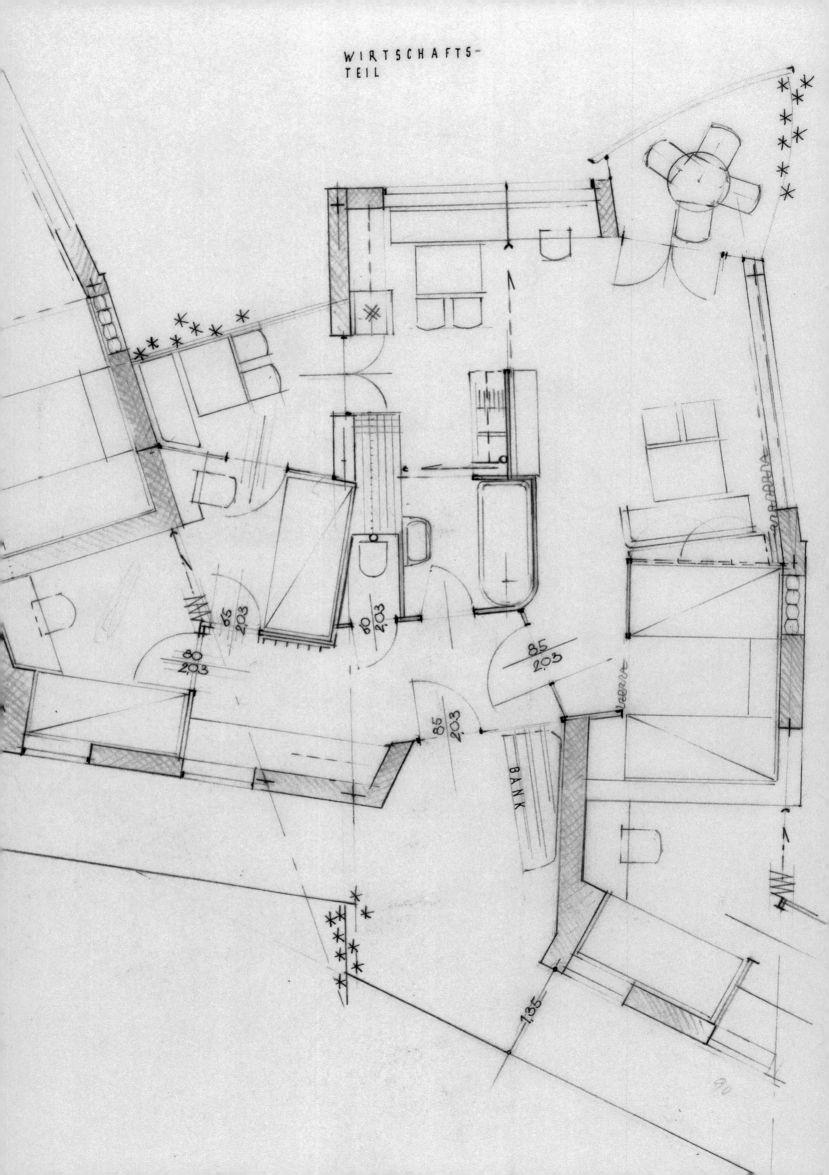

WIRTSCHAFTS-
TEIL

WIRTSCHAFTS-
TEIL

BANK

65
203

60
203

80
203

85
203

85
203

1.35

a detailed budget and financing plan."[15] On July 23, 1954 he received a call from the Stuttgart's Planning Office alerting him to objections to the density of the proposed development generally, and to the single-story dwellings in particular.[16] Unaware of these objections, Scharoun's office in Berlin sent its drawings of Block 1 and Block 2 as well as the single-family dwelling types to Frank's office in Stuttgart in late July 1954.[17] Four weeks later, Scharoun submitted revised variants of the same plans, which he now called Block A and Block B[18] (fig. pp. 35–36). Here, the critique of the building density that Frank had been warned of had been noted and the site plan stripped of all single-family dwellings. Block A was still sixteen stories high, while Block B was now stepped from seven to ten to thirteen floors. Except for the apartment key, Block A had remained virtually unchanged (figs. pp. 38–41). The duplexes (20) were scaled back in favor of smaller, single-story apartments (58). The duplex bathroom lost its second door and the doorway connecting kitchen and bathroom was walled up. During the work on the plans for Block B, the principle of circulation around an inner core was retained (figs. pp. 44–47). This idea and the partitioning and connecting options on which it was premised necessitated an inordinate number of doors, sliding doors, and curtains. The most significant change was that to the parents' bedroom, which was moved from the outside wall to the access balcony side of the apartment. The balcony proper now projected further out and its hallmark arrowhead shape is clearly visible. The small four-bed type 2 is now 60.93 m² in size and the larger version 64.99 m²; Scharoun, moreover, had begun using the terms "Parents," "Children," and "Housekeeping."

The "Minutes of the meeting to discuss the building project of Prof. Scharoun—Arch. Frank, Schwabbacher/Schozacher Strasse Zuffenhausen-Rot" on January 5, 1955 with representatives of the Central Office for the Reconstruction of the City of Stuttgart (headed by Hoss), the Building Regulations Office (Scholl), the Planning Office (Heyer), and the Housing Authority (Heckmann), notes that the application for a building permit "deviates from the preliminary project in certain key points, especially total land use."[19] The following corrections had been agreed: "The circular corpus shall be set further back from Schwabbacher Strasse to reduce the shade on the buildings on the north side of Schwabbacher Strasse. As a transition to the highest structure on the corner, the corpus shall be two stories lower throughout.[20] [...] The tower-like corpus [...] as the dominant landmark of the residential town, shall be raised by two stories to an overall height of 50 m." The last recommendation concerned the overall layout of the development. There was "a strong desire," the minutes said, to see "the ten-story residential block to the east of Schozacher Strasse lowered by one story to an overall height of ca. 29 m."[21] To the west, the figure of Romeo and Julia that seems to spiral upward and at its lowest point is just four stories high referenced the nearby Silcher School designed by Günter Wilhelm. Inaugurated in December 1953, this was one of the first schools to be built as part of the City of Stuttgart's postwar school-building program.[22]

Willi Oppenländer chose not to mention the resistance and opposition to the project in his memoirs written over a decade later, and erroneously dated the submission of the plans for Romeo and Julia and their unveiling to the public at large to 1952. What he did remember rightly was that they sparked "both enthusiastic approval and genuine shock."[23] The seriousness of the obstacles that the Planning Office had to overcome is evident from a memorandum from the Stuttgart Building Regulations Office of May 26,

1955, which lists in great detail the various ways in which the plans infringed the directive of July 14, 1953 of the development plan authorized by the Stuttgart-Zuffenhausen Building Regulations: "1. Art. 37, Para. 1 BauO., because the height of the building on Schwabbacherhochstrasse and Schozacherstrasse exceeds by far the width of the street, including front gardens; 2. Art. 37, Para. 8 BauO., because the building, which is primarily for residential purposes, is more than 20 m high; 3. Art. 41, Para. 2 BauO., because most of the toilets receive neither light nor air from windows or similar fixtures connecting them directly to the outside; 4. Section 60, Para. 1, OBS [...] because the outside walls do not meet the thickness required of firewalls."[24]

But the real threat to the project was that mounting on the financial side. In a letter dated September 11, 1954, Frank told Scharoun of the bankruptcy of a large housing developer, and of a recent directive that would impact directly on the high-rise project since it insisted that any housing project that "laid claim to public funds has to meet the requirements laid down in the laws governing new housing. This means that I will not be able to mortgage the high-rises based on the plans as they stand at present, since they do not comply with the regulations applicable to the building of social housing."[25] Even after extensive reworking, the floor plan type that Scharoun designed for Julia was no longer in a position to fulfill the DIN 18011 standards for furniture space, clearance, and circulation, as required by the legislation on subsidized housing. The parents' bedroom had been inflated to the second-largest room in the apartment. What this meant for the floor plan of Julia was that both the central core and the second balcony had to be abandoned; the rooms would henceforth be accessed from a hall rather than from each other; and the bathroom and kitchen were moved to the access balcony side.

Connecting the front rooms was a last-ditch attempt to retain the idea of circulation; as the main room, the combined living room-bedroom was planned with the sofa in the middle facing a window full of indoor plants, a workspace at the window, and a dining area adjoining the kitchen. All these changes were made without changing the overall shape of the building. After various versions had been developed to play through the various ways of accommodating the necessary number of beds, albeit without resolving the problem of clearance (figs. pp. 48–49), the solution for Julia that would ultimately be built was at last presented in late September 1954. In a letter dated October 5, 1954 (figs. pp. 52–53), Scharoun explained that he believed he had found in these new types "a healthy compromise between my original solution and the definitive one". "The two separate points of entry to the parents' bedroom allow it to be incorporated into the living area, if so desired. Rapid access to the bathroom and toilet is thus also assured. The parents' bedroom seems less cramped in this new version." The chil-

16 Wilhelm Frank to Hans Scharoun, July 29, 1954, HSA WV 187, I, Correspondence 1954.
17 Hans Scharoun to Wilhelm Frank, July 30, 1954, HSA WV 187, I, Correspondence 1954.
18 Hans Scharoun to Wilhelm Frank, September 1, 1954, HSA WV 187, I, Correspondence 1954.
19 As already mentioned, this preliminary project was approved on July 7, 1954.
20 In fact, the two lower sections of Julia were reduced by three stories.
21 Copy of the minutes, HSA WV 187, I, Correspondence 1955.
22 Wolf Reuter, "Stuttgart: Kessel, Klima, kleine Türme—vom Einzelfall zur Hochhauspolitik," in Marianne Rodenstein (ed.), Hochhäuser in Deutschland: Zukunft oder Ruin der Städte? Stuttgart/Berlin/Cologne 2000, pp. 214–230.
23 Dorn, Hastenteufel, and Oppenländer, Hans Scharoun, 1968, p. 12.
24 Copy of the directive, Regierungspräsidium Nordwürttemberg, July 4, 1955, copy of the letter from Wilhelm Frank to Hans Scharoun, June 30, 1955, HSA WV 187, I, Correspondence 1955.
25 Wilhelm Frank to Hans Scharoun, September 11, 1954, HSA WV 187, I, Correspondence 1954.

dren's room with its two light sources, moreover, allowed "boys and girls to be separated or the use of one niche (poss. with bunk beds) as a bedroom and the other niche as a playroom and study."[26]

Yet even this new solution was rejected by Dr. Heckmann, who as the head of Stuttgart's Housing Authority conjectured that the "idiosyncratic floor plan and design will make compliance with the prescribed binding standards impossible as well as raising the construction costs by at least 20 percent,"[27] which the Landeskreditanstalt would not approve. Frank told Scharoun that in his view, "the best thing would be for [Universum Treubau] to build owner-occupied apartments rather than rental apartments. For this I need you to send me the documents relating to Romeo (1 floor plan)."[28]

The changes to variant Block A, which on the plans is now called Block B, first appeared in the drawings dated January 28, 1955 (figs. pp. 64–65). The duplexes were now larger (type 1, 89.70 m²) and had lost the open space above the living room, while the bathroom had been moved upstairs into the sleeping area. The block now had one three-room and one two-room apartment (types 2, 71.30 m² and 2a, 60.53 m², no balcony) at its southern end and two small two-room apartments (types 3 and 3a, 33.48 m²) at its northern end. The top floor, moreover, had been remodeled as a "Promenade Deck," part of which was left open as a communal space. The floor above this, labeled the "Upper World" on the plans, now housed two duplex apartments as well as two studios along with still more communal space. The design of the studio apartments mounted on the roof followed a developmental trajectory all its own. As the plans were reworked, the north-facing mini-studio intended for use by an artist or scholar became a special type of dwelling that introduced the as yet embryonic ideal of the individual, urban form of dwelling. Because the studios were built onto a special load-bearing frame surmounting the top story of the block, their geometry was liberated from the dictates to which the apartments below them were subject. Only the stairwell with the two elevators went all the way up, at least in the first draft, and the studios were accessed via the open rooftop terrace. The four studio structures each had 41.40 m² of floor space; the studios themselves were north-facing and had a bedroom and kitchenette adjoining them. The revised plan of Block B of January 29, 1955 showed only two studios, the remaining two having been remodeled as duplexes, and all four apartments with roofed-over access from the elevators. The definitive version of Romeo once again had four studio apartments, one of them a duplex, and one of them with an additional tower room. The only south-facing studio has been relabeled "Living room" to reflect its new function.

Despite Universum Treubau's sales drive, it slowly but surely became clear that the duplexes were unsellable. Scharoun tried to persuade it to keep them in its program since he would regret it very much "if the duplex type were not executed at all, it being fundamental to the concept on which the whole building rests. If larger types are possible at all, it would seem to be merely a question of what we are accustomed to, so that once the other larger apartments have gone, it might still be possible to sell the residue in the form of duplexes. That this 'residue' be preserved—that is my suggestion. With this in mind, could at least the stack of duplexes on the street side (east) be retained? Of the two stacks on the garden side (west), one could be converted into a large apartment (northwest corner) and the other into

single-story apartments."[29] The later variants, however, no longer feature any duplexes at all, and in the end, only one duplex was actually built (fig. p. 69).

All further work on the plans was focused on the inner façade, which was broken up into single sections of varying geometry and depth. This was decisive, since the unilateral orientation of the smaller apartments arranged along a central corridor combined with their considerable depth reduced the outside space available to each unit to the barest minimum. Scharoun not only folded the façade until the inner corridor had almost doubled in length, but he proposed "inside bathrooms and inside toilets and for the most part inside kitchens" on the grounds that "where housing is exceptionally dense, every meter of façade is precious and should be assigned weightier purposes."[30] The geometric operations had the effect of setting apart the workspace that was so important to Scharoun.

The revised application for a building permit was submitted on March 3, 1955, and won the approval of the Building Regulations Office on July 4, 1955[31] (figs. pp. 66–67). In the latest variant, the duplexes were missing altogether. In a letter of March 4, 1955, Frank explained to Scharoun what had happened: "We took account of your wishes that the concrete posts on the eastern side remain visible. No buyers could be found for the apartments from the first application that we had also finished (the duplexes). The apartments in their current version, by contrast, are much sought-after and around twenty of them and a store have been sold."[32] The high-rise Romeo apartment block was built in 1957 and on its completion was widely acclaimed in the press.

As "the source of the necessary capital," the advance sales made possible by the Property Ownership Law that came into force on March 20, 1951 were the crucial factor in determining whether or not the project could go ahead. The price was set at 529 Deutschmarks per square meter with "apartment owners contributing around one third of the total construction costs."[33] "We were able to meet the condition that at least forty apartments in Romeo be sold before construction could go ahead only by persuading our workmen, our family members, our architects, and our staff to buy one or other of them," explained Oppenländer.[34]

"The New Dwelling Awareness"—to quote the title of Scharoun's introduction to a Festschrift marking the tenth anniversary of Universum Treubau-Wohnungs-GmbH—combined "both concepts, that of the owner-occupied dwelling and that of the high-rise."[35] In his passionate defense of the residential high-rise, he demonstrates the virulence of the model and redefines the concept of property ownership. What counted, he argued, was no longer the owner's personal ties to the land, "since time immemorial typified by the single-family dwelling, arranged either in clusters or in rows." The new form was "the high-rise apart-

26 Hans Scharoun to Wilhelm Frank, October 5, 1954, HSA WV 187, I, Correspondence 1954.
27 Dr. Heckmann to Wilhelm Frank, January 14, 1955, HSA WV 187, I, Correspondence 1955.
28 Wilhelm Frank to Hans Scharoun, January 15, 1955, HSA WV 187, I, Correspondence 1955.
29 Hans Scharoun to Wilhelm Frank, February 15, 1955, HSA WV 187, I, Correspondence 1955.
30 Scharoun, Lecture IX/16, February 27, 1956.
31 Date of the copy of the directive; the Building Regulations Office in Stuttgart dates the decision on the provisional building permit to August 1, 1955.
32 Wilhelm Frank to Hans Scharoun, March 4, 1955, HSA WV 187, I, Correspondence 1955.
33 "Einweihung mit Shakespeare," in Stuttgarter Nachrichten, September 12, 1959.
34 Willi Oppenländer, Bauen in die Zukunft. Lebendiges Bauen in Stuttgart, Stuttgart 1962, p. 20.
35 Scharoun, "Das neue Wohnbewusstsein," 1962, p. 7.

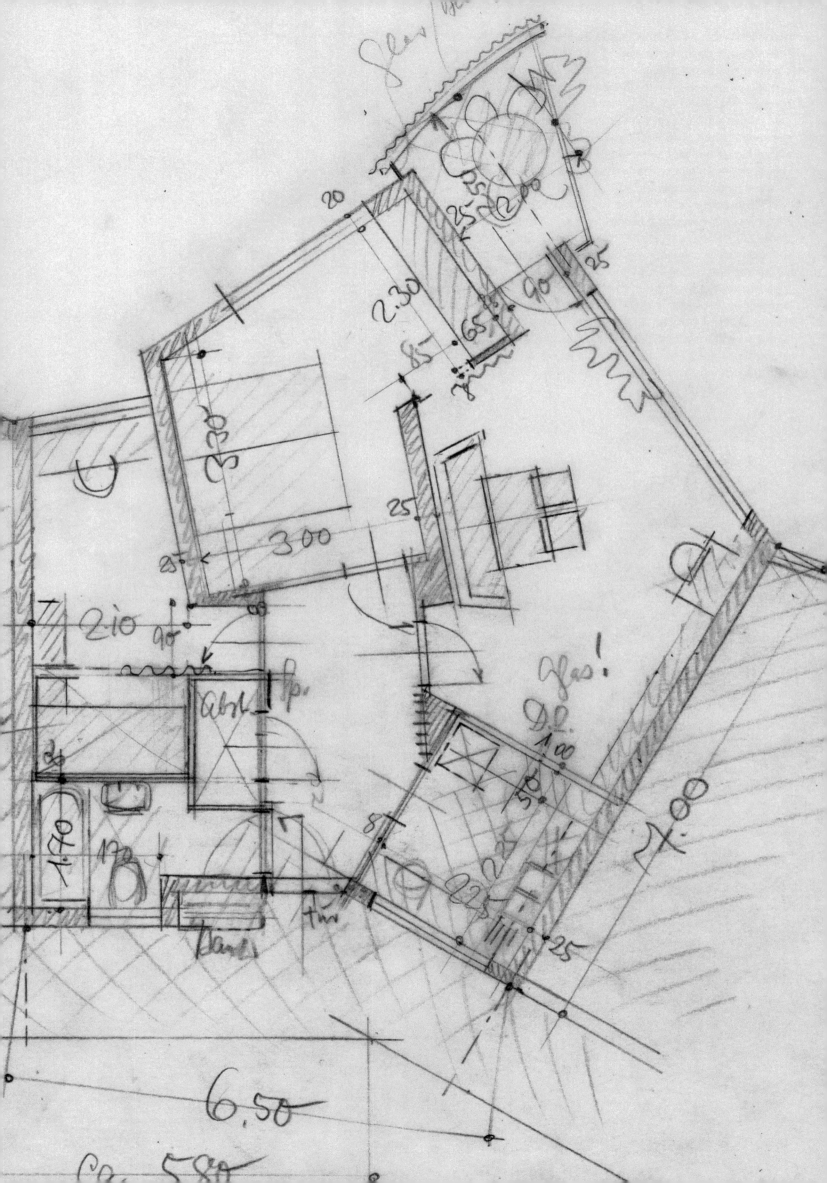

ment block by which the residential community was defined, and if possible named."[36] Not only could "the floor plans of the individual apartments be varied as required, but if owner-occupied high-rises were properly thought through, 'flexible' but economically viable dwellings would also be possible. The progressive solution to the problem of the sensible and purposeful owner-occupied dwelling is the slab building, which can be extended or raised, or the high-rise apartment block, the technical construction of which enables flexible dwellings."[37]

The construction of the high-rise Romeo apartment block was approved at a Municipal Council meeting held on June 29, 1955; just a short time later, Stephan Heise, Scharoun's site manager, reported that the excavation work at the site had begun on August 31, 1955. Julia, meanwhile, was put on hold and postponed until 1959. The floor plan options of 1954 were revised, but not drastically altered (figs. pp. 54–55). After further lobbying by Scharoun, the Landeskreditanstalt in March 1958 raised the prospect of a grant for Julia.[38] The parceling plans were submitted to Stuttgart Buildings Office on February 25, 1958. ●●

36 Scharoun, "Zum Begriff der Eigentumswohnung," 1960.
37 Ibid.
38 In a letter of February 14, 1958, Scharoun tried once again to persuade the president of the Badische Landeskreditanstalt, Dr. Hagmann, of the soundness of the project. One "Herr Dertinger" also received a letter dated February 21, 1958 in his capacity as director. A letter of March 12, 1958 holds out the prospect of a definitive review of the project. Correspondence, HSA WV 187, I, Correspondence 1958.

III Genealogy of the Dwelling

Romeo, duplex apartment

"Always getting to the bottom of things, we drown."

Friedrich Nietzsche, *Nachgelassene Fragmente*, 1887–1889[1]

On February 24 and March 3, 1950, Hans Scharoun gave two lectures at the Technical University of Berlin called "Wandlung der Wohnung"[2] ("The Transformation of the Dwelling") and "Entwürfe des Wohnungsbaus—heutiger Wohnungsbaus,"[3] ("Housing Designs Today") in which he revisited subjects from his earlier urban planning lectures. In a general discussion of the "development of the dwelling in the Western world," he pinpointed its origin in the "grouping of the functions of the house and dwelling around a religiously defined center—the hearth or fireplace."[4]

of workers' houses ran from north to south and so protected the remainder of the city from the hot winds blowing in from the west. One of his examples from the present was the row of houses that J.J.P. Oud built for the Weissenhof Estate in Stuttgart in 1927. For Scharoun, these were all examples of a development toward the townhouse, which in a departure from the "Sphäre von Lebensbau und Wirtschaftsbau," that is, the practice of accommodating living and working quarters under one roof, kept the increasingly specialized domains of working and dwelling sepa-

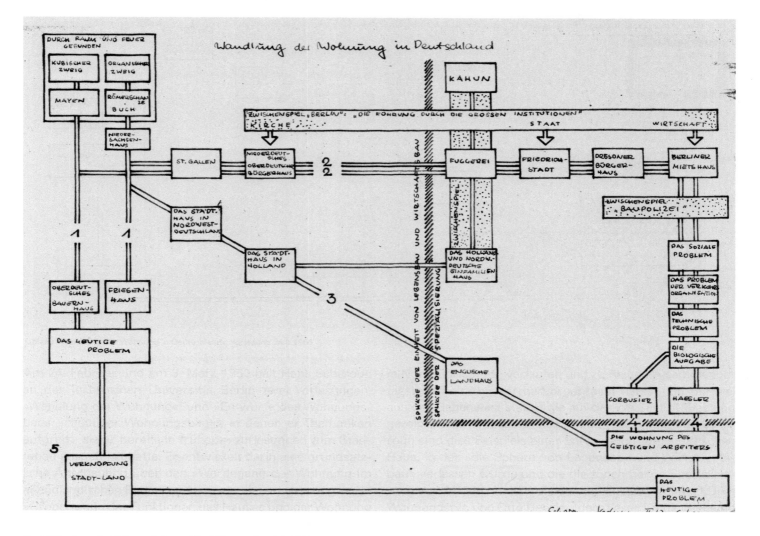

Chart "Wandlung der Wohnung in Deutschland," lecture June 24, 1950

Starting with a Nietzschean "In the beginning was …,"[5] a genealogy in which everything begins with the glorification of its *Entstehung* or emergence, with the metaphysical contemplation of history, Scharoun developed a meticulous interpretation of the *Herkunft* or origin and development of the dwelling in Germany in the form of a synoptic chart.

The vertical coordinates trace the history of peasant dwellings, the horizontal that of urban forms of habitation. Scharoun supplemented his diagram with floor plans and perspectival sketches in which we find countless topoi of German dwelling studies: the Neolithic pile dwellings (long houses) in Mayen, the Fuggerei in Augsburg as the world's oldest social housing development still in use today, and the floor plans of Berlin's tenements. Venturing even deeper into the past, Scharoun mentioned the "row houses" of El Lahun in Egypt, the Pyramid City of Senusret II (12th Dynasty, ca. 1890 B.C.), whose broad streets lined with rows

rate.[6] The dwelling type that Otto Haesler developed for the subdivision in Rathenow, explained Scharoun, had "given precedence to the living area" by reducing the bedrooms to little more than sleeping alcoves and had reintroduced the "tradition of the conciliatory living space" by combining the living area with a kitchenette.[7]

This turn to the "original and unambiguously inclusive"[8] in the field of genealogies, which being all but unknown and hence something of a surprise in modern dwell-

1   Friedrich Nietzsche, *Nachgelassene Fragmente 1887–1889*, KSA 13, Munich 1999, p. 330.
2   Scharoun, Lecture II/9, February 24, 1950.
3   Scharoun, Lecture II/7, March 3, 1950.
4   Scharoun, Lecture I/15. n.d.
5   Friedrich Nietzsche, *Menschliches, Allzumenschliches I und II*, KSA 2, Munich 1999, p. 540.
6   Scharoun, Lecture II/9, February 24, 1950.
7   Ibid.
8   Ibid.

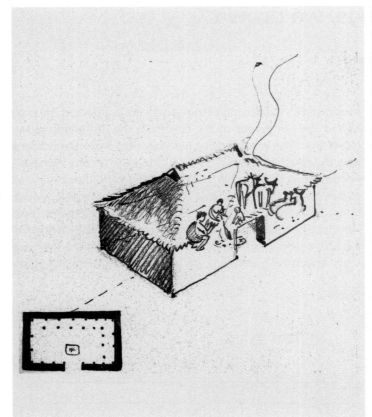

"Mayen," sketch for the lecture "Wandlung der Wohnung"

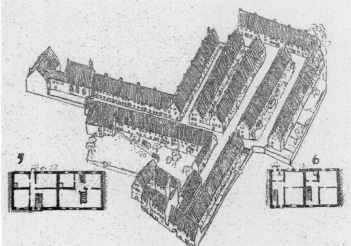

"El Lahun (Egypt)," sketch for the lecture "Wandlung der Wohnung"

"Fuggerei," sketch for the lecture "Wandlung der Wohnung"

"Low German Farmhouse," sketch for the lecture "Wandlung der Wohnung"

"J.J.P. Oud (Weissenhof Estate)," sketch for the lecture "Wandlung der Wohnung"

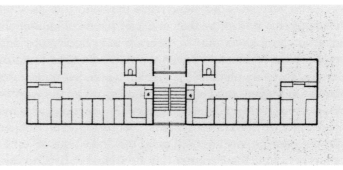

"Haesler" floor plan, sketch for the lecture "Wandlung der Wohnung"

Louis Ude's smithy at the back of Bardowicker Mauer 12, Lüneburg (ca. 1915)

ing studies, was to lead to new findings in the study and development of floor plans.

Scharoun's chart, or so he claimed, not only revealed how the dwelling had changed in material respects, but even more importantly, it exposed its "existential spiritual basis." To support this assertion, he had to push the boundaries and stretch the category of culture to the limit: culture, he opined, comprised "the totality of the structures, equipment, symbols, and ordering systems which as tools, settlements, forms of commercial activity in part serve human life and in part express its spiritual meaning in a way that can be understood, e.g. in the work of art."[9] The cultural also supplied the underpinning for Scharoun's further inquiries into the "heterogeneity" of cultural spaces spoken of by Leo Frobenius, the founder of the Institute for Cultural Morphology. His referencing of Frobenius's *Paideuma*[10] was thus part of his attempt to explain that every human culture constitutes a kind of organism. It also showed that a culture is more than just an accumulation of art works or craft techniques, being at the same time the manifestation of a distinct "cultural soul" shaped by its surroundings and by its own self-education, for which Frobenius coined the term *Paideuma*.

Following his intellectual mentor Hugo Häring, Scharoun divided his genealogical lines of development into

a cubic and an organic lineage, "two art-nature forces"[11] that would be pitted against each other in Häring's late works, just as the picture that emerges when art history is viewed as a succession of stylistic periods is one of a constant back and forth between the geometric and the organic. The trajectory that starts with the first geometric figures, such as the cube in the ancient cultures of Mesopotamia, leads eventually to the Gothic, into whose structural world the organic returns. In this genealogy, as in Frobenius and in Nietzsche's dichotomy of the Apollonian versus the Dionysian,[12] the place of descent and rank is taken by powerful opposing forces, and the value of the *Ursprung*—the source or origin—is subjected to a process of "denaturing."[13]

9   Scharoun, Lecture IA/22, n.d.
10   Frobenius, *Paideuma*, 1921.
11   Friedrich Nietzsche, *Nachgelassene Fragmente 1885–1887*, KSA 12, Munich 1999, p. 224.
12   The library in Hugo Häring's estate contained the following works: Leo Frobenius, *Das sterbende Afrika. Veröffentlichung des Forschungsinstitutes für Kulturmorphologie,* Vol. 1. Munich 1923; Leo Frobenius, *Kulturgeschichte Afrikas. Prolegomena zu einer historischen Gestaltlehre,* Zurich 1933; Ernst Seillière, *Apollo oder Dionysos? Kritische Studie über Friedrich Nietzsche,* Berlin 1906; see also Häring, "athene apollo dionysos," June 3, 1949.
13   Michel Foucault, "Nietzsche, Genealogy, History," in Paul Rabinow (ed.), *The Foucault Reader,* New York 1984, pp. 76–100, here p. 16.

Häring's, and hence Scharoun's, entelechic view of history is steeped in the "ethnopsychological antithesis" of the Nordic-organic and the Mediterranean-geometric and consequently goes right to the heart of modern architecture's battles over interpretation. In his last publication, Über *das Geheimnis der Gestalt,* Häring argues that this historic dualism legitimizes the future of organic architecture and prophesies that "the north will understand the house as an organ of dwelling whereas in the south it will still be a machine for living in."[14]

Scharoun's real interest was in the medieval townhouse, especially the house in Lüneburg that he had discovered as a child and that he repeatedly and demonstratively presented to his students as an example of the same.[15] What was decisive about this type of house was the collective way of life of the Middle Ages that it was built to serve; hence the overlapping of living and working that in the floor plans resulted in cavernous *Dielen* or halls. "The *Diele* that grew out of the central space of the Low German farmhouse was both somewhere to live and somewhere to work," explained Scharoun.[16]

This led him into another field of relevance to the history of residential architecture, namely the discipline of anthropology and ethnography, whose beginnings can be dated to 1860 or thereabouts. Of particular interest to anthropologists, alongside the meticulous study of structures and their role in the history of a given people, was the emergence of dwelling types and their respective urforms. Unusually for a Modernist architect, Scharoun was fascinated by the *civilisation matérielle*[17] and the slow rhythms of history by which the dwelling was shaped. The medieval historian Jacques Le Goff once argued that contemplating history over long periods has the effect of bringing it closer to those humanities that are dedicated to the study of societies that have "barely moved" at all, i.e. ethnography or anthropology.[18] Then the object of study becomes "material culture," or what German anthropologists call *dinglicher Kulturbesitz* (material cultural heritage).[19] The results of the genealogical approach to the history of residential architecture in Germany with its attributions to certain classes and races were nevertheless controversial right from the start. In his handbook of architecture of 1927, for example, Herman Sörgel devoted a whole chapter to the "physiognomy and origin of today's dwellings" in which the section on houses contained the following assertion: "the development of the dwelling belongs less to the field of art history than to that of cultural and racial history"—as grounds for which he cited its proximity to the farmhouse as one of the constants of building history.[20]

Among the buildings included in the "History" section of the list of photographs and sketches that Scharoun used as material for his lectures of the spring semester of 1950 were the Nuremberg House, the Hamburg House, a Townhouse in Northwest Germany, and the Low German Farmhouse. This reference to one of the paradigmatic discoveries in the history of German residential architecture turned the spotlight onto the development of the floor plan type of the *Diele* and its origin in the Low German Farmhouse. In Scharoun's genealogy, the "central living area with cooking niche"[21] belongs to the tradition of what was originally a collective living space. How this type evolved in the course of history is described in great detail by Carl Schäfer in his studies of the urform of the farmhouse.[22] He notes, for example, how the last two posts of the timber-frame construction were spaced further apart than the preceding

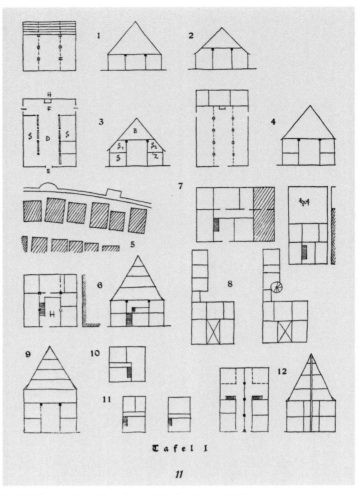

Carl Schäfer, studies of the urform of the farmhouse, 1937

ones. The space inside the elevated central nave—called the *Fleet*—served the inhabitants as daytime living space and contained the hearth, as one would expect of the type of the "single fire house." The Gothic principle of elongation caused this space to overlap with the *Diele,* which as a threshing floor was a work space. The roof is more steeply pitched than the urtype and it is divided into several separate floors by tie beams. Of crucial importance is the metamorphosis of this type, a later developmental stage of which Schäfer sees in the medieval townhouse—the development of the farmhouse being by then more or less complete, its four different types corresponding to the four major Germanic tribes: the Saxons, Franks, Alemanni, and Bavarians. Later studies of the townhouses of Lübeck's merchants, some of whose *Diele* had interiors dating back to the Rococo era, and of the considerably more elaborate Leibniz House in Hanover as an example from the mid-seventeenth century, confirm "the powerful hold of the basic concept of the Old German house on house builders in northern Germany, even under completely different living conditions."[23] The typological continuity was evident not just in the spatial verticality, moreover, but also in the continued presence of large gates and the unchanged location of the hearth. Even more important to Schäfer, however, were the ways of life and the social fabric within which the *Diele* still constituted the main living space. Other observations attest to this anthropological view: "To make the rooms of the upper story more accessible, a gallery was installed half way up—perhaps only on two sides—with a staircase leading up to it."[24]

There can be no doubt that Scharoun's specific competence lay neither in archaeological excavations nor in his systematization of historical developments, but rather in his capacity for appropriating history for contemporary discourses. The medieval townhouses of northern Germany, "as habitations that had developed out of, and been shaped by, the dwelling and working process,"[25] to him rep-

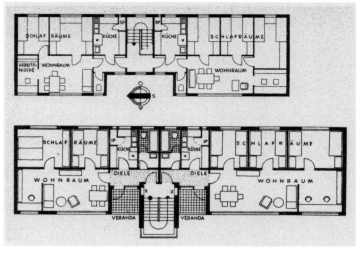

Otto Haesler, floor plans for Celle-Blumlägerfeld (1930–1931) and Kassel Rothenburg (1929–1931)

Inside view of Otto Haesler's experimental house in Celle-Blumlägerfeld (1928–1929)

resented the social ideal of his times. It was against the backdrop of these reflections that his metaphor of the "space in the middle" developed.[26] What he found described in the various studies of residential architecture was not only his notion of the house as organism with its productive tensions between high and low, small and large spaces, but also the handling of furnishings and walled-in or built-in fixtures that served the collective tasks of dwelling for the whole household—a household consisting of the master and his family, as well as journeymen, apprentices, and servants. Scharoun's genealogy of the German house became increasingly pluralistic and multicausal. Now it no longer mattered which of the named origins had once been prescribed; the search for "humble beginnings" replaced the attempt to trace the derivative back to the source. Unlike almost all other historians of residential architecture, Scharoun ultimately succeeded in eschewing what Fernand Simiand described as the famous third idol of the historian: the "idol of chronology."[27]

He sought in the type of the urban tenement in line four of his genealogical chart the "technical and biological" standards for the minimum dwelling, and it was this quest that culminated in the "dwelling of the intellectual worker." Only at first glance is the appearance of the aforementioned floor plan by Otto Haesler in this line surprising. While for Scharoun it provided the dimensions which—"rationally speaking"—were necessary to a minimum dwelling, the floor plan is organized according to the law of the dominant living area with subordinate sleeping alcoves. Otto Völcker's encyclopedic *Grundrisswerk* contains Haesler's floor plan for a minimum dwelling in the Celle-Blumläger-

feld (1930–1931) development as well as the types that he envisaged for Kassel-Rothenberg (1929–1931), whose sleeping alcoves were "accessible only from the living area,"[28] which because of this could be more spacious and even had enough room for a partitioned-off niche in which to sit and work.

But the really crucial line of development in Scharoun's chart is the third, a diagonal that rests on the organizational principle of the *Diele* or large central hall. The "generations" in the line of development leading to the goal defined as the "home of the intellectual worker" are soon covered: pursuing the typological continuum of the Low German Farmhouse and the Townhouse in Northwest Germany with their "two-story, hall-like living space located in the middle of the house and forming its epicenter,"[29] the Dutch Townhouse serves as a springboard to the English Country House, where the hearth metamorphoses into the living room fireplace in the home of the landed gentry. This account is reminiscent of Mackay H. Baillie Scott's calls for a new house plan in which everything turns on a two-story-high central hall. His book *Houses and Gardens* (translated into German and published by Verlag Ernst Wasmuth in 1912), contains countless plans for the ideal country house sketched by Baillie Scott himself. The private rooms in these plans are invariably just compartments or alcoves giving off the main

14 Häring, "über das geheimnis der gestalt," 1954.
15 "I experienced such a household in Lüneburg in the house of my uncle, a master blacksmith. Family, servants, journeymen, and apprentices all gathered around the table together, and in keeping with tradition, the *Diele* at the front was used as a smithy and the rooms adjoining it, spread over two floors, for both individual and communal purposes. The great pride of the house was the spiral staircase in the *Diele* which led to the upper gallery and was highly ornate," (Scharoun, Lecture VI/8, June 30, 1952).
16 Scharoun, Lecture VI/8, June 30, 1952.
17 *Civilisation matérielle* is one of the key concepts of the historians of the Annales School. Fernand Braudel's work *Civilisation matérielle, économie et capitalisme (XVe–XVIIIe siècles)* of 1979 (published in English as *Civilization and Capitalism 15th–18th Century*, Berkeley/Los Angeles 1992), and even before that his *La Méditerranée et le monde méditerranéen à l'époque de Philippe II* of 1949 (published in English as *The Mediterranean and the Mediterranean World in the Age of Philip II*, Berkeley/Los Angeles 1995) depict history as virtually immobile and subject to the *longue durée*. Braudel approaches civilization basically as a geographer, or rather a geohistorian preoccupied with cultural regions. The changes demanded by new furniture, for example, are explained on the basis of the fascinating example of the chair, which traveled from Europe to China, where by the thirteenth century it had become widespread, unlike in Japan. Global connections like this were crucial to his inquiry, which in this respect differs from the local, ethnically defined approach of dwelling studies.
18 Jacques Le Goff, "Neue Geschichtswissenschaft," in Jacques Le Goff, Roger Chartier, and Jacques Revel (eds.), *Die Rückeroberung des historischen Denkens: Grundlagen der Neuen Geschichtswissenschaft*, Frankfurt a.M. 1990, pp. 11–61, here p. 39.
19 Dieter Haller, *Die Suche nach dem Fremden. Geschichte der Ethnologie in der Bundesrepublik Deutschland 1945–1990*, Frankfurt a.M./New York 2012, p. 129; Leo Frobenius, *Auf dem Weg nach Atlantis. Bericht über den Verlauf der zweiten Reise-Periode der Deutschen Inner-Afrikanischen Forschungs-Expedition in den Jahren 1908–1910*, Berlin 1911, p. 217.
20 Sörgel, *Wohnhäuser*, 1927, p. 19.
21 Scharoun, Lecture II/7, March 3, 1950.
22 Schäfer, "Über das deutsche Haus," lecture at the Schinkelfest of the Architekten Verein on March 13, 1883, in Schäfer, *Von deutscher Kunst*, 1910, pp. 221–223.
23 Otto Stiehl, *Der Wohnbau des Mittelalters*, No. 2 of Vol. 4 of the *Handbuch der Architektur, Teil 2 Die Baustile. Historische und technische Entwickelung*, 2nd ed., Leipzig 1908, p. 181.
24 Schäfer, *Deutsche Holzbaukunst*, 1984, p. 14. Schäfer here describes "the townhouse" as the fourth stage in the development of the German farmhouse.
25 Scharoun, Lecture II/7, March 3, 1950.
26 Wen-chi Wang investigates the origins of this notion in great depth in his work on Chen-kuan Lee. He explains the conceptual basis on which it rests and acknowledges that the idea of the "space in the middle" has more to do with sociocultural factors than a purely spatial concept (see Wang, *Chen-kuan Lee* 2010, pp. 167–176). We shall discuss this concept in greater depth in the course of this book.
27 Fernand Simiand, "Méthode historique et Science sociale," in *Revue de synthèse historique*, (1903), pp. 129–157; reprinted in *Annales. Économies, Sociétés, Civilisations*, 15, No. 1 (1960), pp. 83–116.
28 Völckers, *Das Grundrisswerk*, 1941, p. 89.
29 Scharoun, Lecture II/9, February 24, 1950.

"Dutch Townhouse," sketch for the lecture "Wandlung der Wohnung," June 24, 1950

"English Country House," sketch for the lecture "Wandlung der Wohnung"

hall, or are connected to the same by means of sliding doors. The historical hall was henceforth to be not a multipurpose space, but a "room where the family can meet together—a general gathering-place with its large fireplace and ample floor space."[30] The hall could be cured of its "atrophy," as Baillie Scott calls it, only by being planned as the "centre of a solar system," or, as Schäfer put it, the "house middle"[31] in which most of the actual living was done. The central hall with a dining niche that features in many of Baillie Scott's examples is an arrangement we find replicated almost exactly, from the location to the design, in Scharoun's Haus Schminke (1932–1933). Baillie Scott's transference of the principle of the central hall to the single-story apartment took him to the outer reaches of what could possibly be derived from history. "The smaller plan for a flat shows the application of the same principles in a flat [...] Here there is one good-sized sitting-room with ingle fireplace and balcony, adjoining which is a bed-sitting-room, in which the beds can be entirely screened by curtains [...] Besides this bed-sitting room are two other bedrooms at the back, and a servant's bedroom isolated from the family rooms, a bathroom and kitchen premises."[32]

The meticulous work of the anthropologist always begins with the definition of an archetype and a genealogy, even though the study of the emergence of something, such as the floor plans of houses, if anything proves the opposite—namely that such a method actually potentiates the lines of descent, which become increasingly intertwined the closer they come to the present. Michel Foucault, in his essay "Nietzsche, Genealogy, History," sought to arrive at a more far-reaching revaluation of the concept of genealogy itself, which he then used for a frontal attack on any notion of a closed lineage. "The search for descent is not the erecting of foundations," he wrote, "on the contrary, it disturbs what was previously considered immobile; it fragments what was thought unified; it shows the heterogeneity of what was imagined consistent with itself."[33] While Scharoun's interest in objects of interpretation might appear to reflect a concern with the past, what really fascinated him was their constant recycling, in other words their appropriation and use in the present and their meaning in the present. His genealogy of residential architecture, therefore, is about neither revival nor reconstruction, but rather "re-remembering, remembering here meaning not just recalling the past, but inserting it into the present."[34] Scharoun was quick to realize the strategic ambiguity of the genealogical method: to the extent that *Herkunft,* in the sense of descent, is declared a value, this method at once determines, and has recourse to, the values of *Herkunft.*

M.H. Baillie Scott, hall of the "house of an art lover," 1912

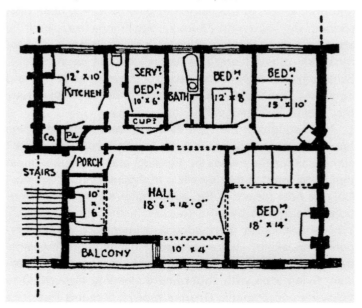

M.H. Baillie Scott, example of a floor plan, 1912

III   Genealogy of the Dwelling

Hall of Landhaus Schminke, Löbau/Saxony, 1933

The "dwelling of the intellectual worker" at the lower end of the third line of development, where the various strands come together again, is actually the true telos of the whole chart. The small perspectival sketches flanking the genealogical map visualize the "dwelling of the intellectual worker," which thanks to its huge slanting skylight takes on the air of a studio. On closer scrutiny, we recognize it as the studio of an artist-architect armed with a T-square, set-square, brush, and canvas. Scharoun's own attic apartment, to which he relocated from Siemensstadt upon completion of the Charlottenburg-Nord development in 1961, ema-nated just such an atmosphere. Such studio apartments, "which starting in 1900 became ever more widespread in big cities," Scharoun opined, liberated people from "all the burdens resulting from the striving for ostentation and the repurposing of the dwelling as a demonstration of socio-economic status." The will to make it accessible primarily to those "intellectual powers who were not economic powers and who did not have substantial means at their disposal [...] led to a drastic curtailment in scope [...] and to the allo-cation to it of multiple purposes—as study, reception room, bedroom etc.—which in turn led to an engagement with the products of furniture manufacturers. (Flexible furniture)."[35]

The figure of the "intellectual worker" was to be found in the countless professional associations in the fields of law, education, medicine, and especially music, litera-ture, and journalism that had proliferated in Wilhelmian Germany. And it was always identified with the capacity for culturally creative intellectual work. Applying Häring's no-tion of "intellectual landscapes," the theological, philosoph-ical, and biological discourses on intellectual work intersect with those of the popular demiurge. But the term has phys-iological and vitalistic connotations, too. For both Häring and Scharoun, the "intellectual workers" laboring away at the "work of creation," at the work "of our age and of our

workspace"[36] are key figures in the quest for forms of work from which the worker is not alienated. Those who "seek to liberate themselves from traditional concepts" as they be-come fully rounded personalities, argued Häring, are also the first to succeed in building and furnishing their homes "in keeping with a new way of life."[37] In the immediate af-termath of the war, Häring developed the figure of the "in-tellectual worker" in opposition to the figure of the engi-neer, then more in demand than ever before;[38] and in a broadside against Ernst Neufert, he asked: "But who was it who led Europe to disaster?"[39]

Ironically, Jacques Le Goff used the term "intellectual worker" in a very different way in his book *Intellectuals in the Middle Ages*.[40] For him, it describes the class of those engaged in independent study and scholarship in the liberal arts, the formation of which he sees as tied to the emer-gence of cities in the twelfth century and to the process of specialization resulting from the division of labor by the crafts. The arts themselves were an intellectual discipline entailing cognitive activity and production in the field of

30 Baillie-Scott, *Houses and Gardens,* 1912, p. 18.
31 Schäfer, "Über das deutsche Haus,"; Baillie-Scott, *Houses and Gar-dens,* 1912, p. 56.
32 Baillie-Scott, *Houses and Gardens,* 1912, p. 115.
33 Michel Foucault, "Nietzsche, Genealogy, History," in Paul Rabinow (ed.), *The Foucault Reader,* New York 1984, pp. 76–100, here p. 82.
34 Pierre Nora, "Wie lässt sich heute eine Geschichte Frankreichs sch-reiben?" in Pierre Nora (ed.), *Erinnerungsorte Frankreichs,* Munich 2005, pp. 15–26, here p. 16.
35 Scharoun, Lecture VII/1, May 11, 1953. The subject of the studio apartments will be taken up again in the chapter "Multiplication," see pp. 180–181.
36 Häring, "Gelegentlich einer ausstellung moderner kunst," in *Bau. Zeitschrift für Wohnen, Arbeiten, sich erholen* 2, No. 2 (1948), p. 62.
37 Häring, "Wettbewerb zur Förderung des neuzeitlichen Möbelbaus" in which he explains the thinking behind a competition for the promo-tion of modern furniture-making.
38 Häring, "Bemerkungen zum Normierungsbegehren," 1948, pp. 311–312.
39 Ibid.
40 Jacques Le Goff, *Intellectuals in the Middle Ages,* London 1992.

"The dwelling of the intellectual worker," sketch for the lecture "Wandlung der Wohnung," June 24, 1950

grammatical construction, syllogism, and rhetoric. Yet the utopian "dwelling of the intellectual worker" sketched by Scharoun was premised on the eradication of this distinction between material and intellectual work, thanks to which "the joy of work" would "one day overcome today's 'compulsion to work.'"[41] He was especially critical of the distinction drawn between manual work and brain work, which he blamed for the potentially pathological one-sidedness of many individuals. Taking account of the ever finer division of labor and the resulting dissolution of the combined living and working premises, line two of Scharoun's chart traces the transformation of the German townhouse into the Tenements of Berlin whose standardized floor plans were developed under the financial pressure to make maximum use of minimum space. The first conscious and planned "intervention in the proliferation" of dwelling forms and the shortage of housing for workers in the aftermath of the First World War was undertaken by the Weimar regime, which began building housing subsidized by a tax on rental income (*Hauszinssteuer*) and founding the first housing cooperatives. The minimum social and hygienic standards required of the new housing were a crucial factor in the formation of the small apartments and minimum dwellings thereupon developed. What Scharoun saw as a predominantly technical way of thinking certainly allowed rents to be lowered; but it also reduced the size of the living area,

which in his view spoke against its use, and its importance, as the epicenter of family life. His answer to this was born of his belief in the potential of intellectual work and drew on Friedrich Engels' ideal of work as a source of pleasure rather than toil, and fulfillment rather than alienation.[42] He read Theodor Adorno's *Minima Moralia* and quoted some of its aphorisms about the human condition in a capitalist and fascist society, which according to Adorno had destroyed the ideal of "dwelling, in the proper sense" and with it that of community. Scharoun's alternative to Ador-

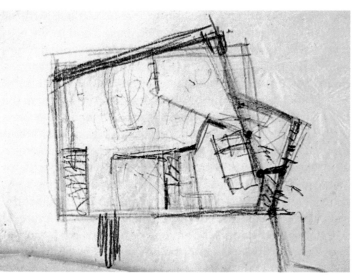

Sketch of the downstairs of a duplex apartment, no date

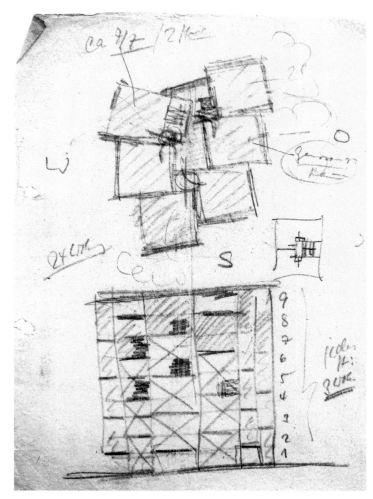

Sketch of a high-rise with duplexes, no date

of sight and constant shifts in the position of the wall panels and polygonal posts inevitably has an effect on the observer's perception of how the space is organized. This putative change in the wall panels and supporting elements against the background of the façade is amplified by the finely staggered heights of the window ledges and lintels. The segmentation, in conjunction with the sharper folding of the façade, enhances the impact of the completely different relationships to the outside. The work niche, which had been a must-have feature for Scharoun even in his Siemensstadt (1930) development, was now boxed into a tiny space between a low lintel, two wall panels fanning out into the room, and another lintel set back at the depth of the façade door. Scharoun, who was inspired especially by Hermann Muthesius's book *Wie baue ich mein Haus*[48], had long been familiar with the country house type and its provision of different spaces for different activities, functions, and habits, and not only had to wrest a different use and a different expression from every kink in the wall, every elongated window seat, every semi-shaded niche, every lintel, every variable partition of his high-rises, but was determined to assign every floor plan, without exception, built-in workspaces, no matter how tiny.

According to his world picture, the development of intellectual "autarky" was a precondition of participation in the larger "Wohnzelle" or "residential cell," and there was "complemented" by the communal facilities—the research center, the special facility of the school, the place of work."[49] This doubling references Scharoun's organic world picture and the connection between dwelling and community, in which the antithesis between community as "genuine enduring life together" and society as "transient and superficial"[50] is not elaborated. Scharoun saw the "intellectual power" at work in the transformation of the dwelling in the ideas of Martin Buber, specifically those laid out in his book *Paths in Utopia* of 1950, in which Buber tried to escape the "utopian socialism" of Marxist critique and to develop an alternative view, which, starting from the early socialists Charles Fourier and Pierre-Joseph Proudhon, would reach beyond Marx and Engels and show how a society free of oppression might be achieved in the here and now. This anti-statist line of thinking resists the subordination of communal forms to strategic power politics. The aim should rather be, Buber argued, to use the material of history to build a genuinely "organic commonwealth—and only such commonwealths can join together to constitute a shapely and ar-

no's labor and concentration camps that "merely proceed as executors with what the immanent development of technology had long decided was to be the fate of houses," and his assertion that the "possibility of residence is annihilated by that of socialist society, which, once missed, saps the foundations of bourgeois life,"[43] was a "socialism of society."[44] Contrary to this "negative dialectic," what Scharoun saw in the ongoing revolution of production was above all a wider range of "elements of enlightenment and progress"[45] through which—with the involvement of science—work itself might be revolutionized over and above the shortening of working hours and easing of the workload. This would not only undermine the age-old distinction between private and professional, but it would also give rise to a new kind of "production intellectual."[46]

The two lines of argument that unite the topoi of intellectual labor and the topoi of dialogue under one roof rose to prominence in the development of the floor plans for the Romeo and Julia project. The barest minimum demanded by Scharoun in a lecture on the floor plans of private dwellings was "the work niche, with preference to be given to the one which, no matter how small, can at least be partitioned off by a curtain. It might even be possible to make a small study of it, which could then have a couch for a family member or a guest to sleep on."[47]

This work niche became all the more important after the duplex apartment in the Romeo high-rise was abandoned. One consequence of the more sharply folded façade was that the trapezoid wall panels and the hexagonal post were now deeper inside the apartment. This in turn allowed Scharoun to multiply the places for reading, resting, conversing, eating, or enjoying the fresh air on the balcony and the loggia. Notwithstanding the spatial overlaps, moving from one such place to another engenders in the viewer a succession of stupendous parallactic effects. A change in the observer's position resulting in the creation of new lines

41 Scharoun, "Von der Wohnung zur Gliederung der Stadt," Lecture II/12, May 30, 1950, June 5 & June 8, 1950.

42 Citing Charles Fourier and Robert Owen, Friedrich Engels in his "Anti-Dühring" identifies the abolition of the old division of labor as crucial to a new form of production: "Its place must be taken by an organisation of production in which on the one hand, no individual can throw on the shoulders of others his share in productive labour, this natural condition of human existence; and in which, on the other hand, productive labour […] by offering each individual the opportunity to develop all his faculties, physical and mental […] will become a pleasure instead of a burden." Friedrich Engels, "Anti-Dühring. Herr Eugen Dühring's Revolution in Science," Part III Socialism, Chapter 3 Production (https://www.marxists.org/archive/marx/works/1877/anti-duhring/index.htm: accessed on July 3, 2019).

43 Adorno, *Minima Moralia*, trans. by E.F.N. Jephcott, London 2005, p. 39.

44 Scharoun, "Die Auswirkung," Lecture V/6, April 20, 1951.

45 Karl Marx and Friedrich Engels, *Manifesto of the Communist Party,* authorized English translation edited and annotated by Friedrich Engels, New York 1908 (http://www.gutenberg.org/files/31193/31193-h/31193-h.htm, accessed: July 6, 2019).

46 Frigga Haug, "Gesamtarbeiter," in *Historisch-kritisches Wörterbuch des Marxismus*, edited by Wolfgang Fritz Haug, Vol. 5: *Gegenöffentlichkeit bis Hegemonialapparat*, Hamburg 2001, pp. 414–427.

47 Scharoun, Lecture IX/16, February 27, 1956.

48 Muthesius, *Wie baue ich mein Haus?* (1915) 1925.

49 Scharoun, "Von der Wohnung zur Gliederung der Stadt," Lecture II/12, May 30, 1950, June 5 & June 8, 1950.

50 Ferdinand Tönnies, *Community and Civil Society*, trans. by Jose Harris and Margaret Hollis, Cambridge 2001, p. 19.

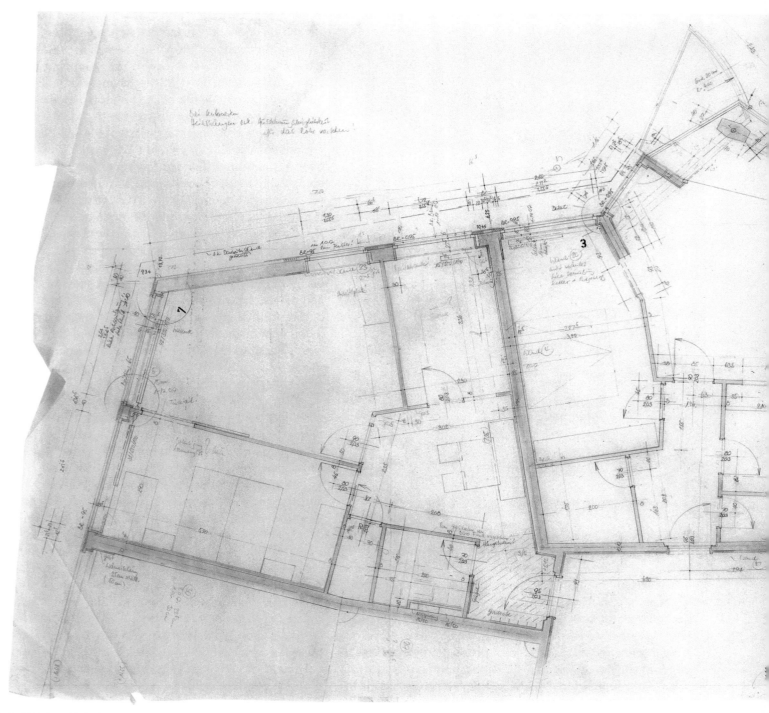

Sketch of a high-rise with duplexes, no date

ticulated race of men." Such a commonwealth, moreover, will never build itself up out of individuals but only out of small and ever smaller communities: a nation is a community to the degree that it is a community of communities."[51] Scharoun countered the division of labor and specialization resulting from scientific and technological advances with the "place of abode," which he defined as a "binding and beaming pivot." Within this structure, he argued, the "space in the middle" served to foster independence even as it was bound by a transcendent whole: "Its centerpiece is the piano or a workbench, the drawing board or discussion corner; it is the germ cell of actively influential friendships on the basis of which every individual, being endowed with his or her own specific creative and intellectual potential, can develop freely—without any leveling down."[52]

For his formulation of a center as a precondition of "community" in Buber's sense of the word, Scharoun used the topical metaphor of the "space in the middle." The metaphor was a product of the creation myth of the formerly united "place of habitation and place of occupation," the "main living space" in which working and dwelling coin-

cided, and which formed a "socially grounded epicenter."[53] In one of his first lectures, Scharoun discovered "this idea of the figure" in George Much's experimental house, which by assigning the leading role to "the central space with the individual functions purposefully grouped around it" to his mind succeeded in "lending expression to family bonds."[54] The target of the typological efforts was the "constriction of living space,"[55] the aim being to create an epicenter of the "dwelling process." This was a concept that Häring had developed in his notes on the *Probleme des neuzeitlichen Wohnens,*[56] and that Scharoun immediately adopted in his own theories. In his lectures of June 8, 15, and 22, 1953, for example, he tried "to grasp dwelling from the essence of the dwelling process" and to connect it with the topical metaphor of the "space in the middle." And even years later, in his address on receiving an honorary doctorate, he explained that in Julia, "the configuration rests on the 'dwelling process'."[57] Gustav Wolf had already placed the concept of the "dwelling process" at the heart of the study of floor plans by claiming that the architect should no longer "imagine and design the cavities and skeleton of the house," but should rather let "dwelling as a life form itself" determine the design.[58]

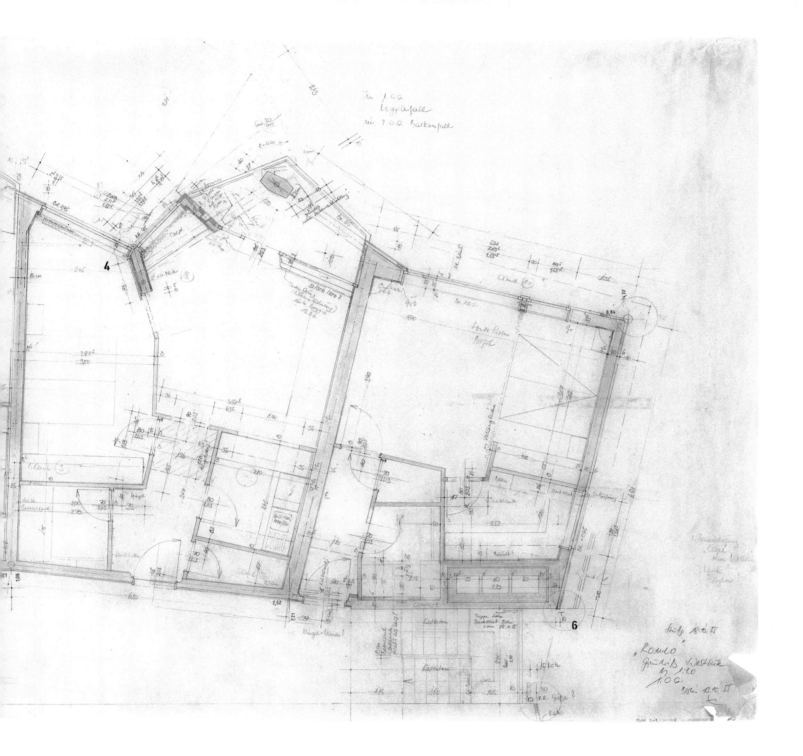

When studying the various types of dwelling with his students, Scharoun called on them to explore how the "space in the middle [might] be emphasized or diminished through references to the other places," whether access from "outside the space in the middle" was desirable, or whether it could be achieved "without burdening the other dwelling functions."[59] On July 7, 1957, he again explained the development of the "dwelling process" as the "raising of experiential possibility within the dwelling. The provision or installation of objects instead of individual items of furniture, especially desk space, closet space, kitchen equipment etc., so that all that the new occupants had to bring with them were tables, chairs, and other such movables" was definitely desirable.[60] In his many different approaches to the concept of the "space in the middle," Scharoun tried to tease out the metaphor's abundance of intentions so as to be able to visualize it as the "germ cell of an organic formation of community."[61]

But the metaphorical and geometrical symbolism of the "space in the middle" eludes the ideal of objectification as the center encompassing all dwelling processes. The metaphor belongs in the tradition of the use of geometrical signs and figures in social contexts without subscribing to the perception of sphere and point as cosmic fundamentals, which since Plato and Aristotle have been synonymous with cosmicity. Scharoun instead used the metaphor to dig down to the substrata of the dwelling process and to translate one of Martin Heidegger's profoundest assertions, that "spaces receive their being from locations and not from 'space,'"[62] into the dwelling process by robbing the "space in the middle" of its topical evidentiality and transferring it to the complex totality of the dwelling process.

Appropriated into urban planning, the "space in the middle" also preoccupied Scharoun as the space with the potential "for structural interlinking with places of work, laboratories, higher education, or even the public realm of

51 Buber, *Paths in Utopia,* Syracuse NY, 1996, p. 136.
52 Scharoun, Lecture I/17, May 24, 1948.
53 Scharoun, Lecture II/9, February 24, 1950.
54 Scharoun, Lecture I/26, November 26, 1948.
55 Scharoun, Notes, Lecture, IX/10.
56 Scharoun, Notes, HSA Lecture XI/10.
57 Scharoun, Address on Receiving an Honorary Doctorate in Rome on June 21, 1965, HSA 2907.
58 Wolf, *Die Grundriss-Staffel,* 1931, p. 23.
59 Scharoun, Lecture, VII/5, June 15, 1953.
60 Scharoun, Lecture, IX/16, February 27, 1956.
61 Ibid.
62 Martin Heidegger, "Building, Dwelling, Thinking," from *Poetry, Language, Thought,* trans. by Albert Hofstadter, New York 1971, n. p.

Perspective sketch of a single-family dwelling for the lecture "Wandlung der Wohnung," June 24, 1950

elementary schools."[63] He sought "the polarity of spaces in the middle to superelevated entities, depending on the density of the social structure at transcendent locations in the urban fabric."[64] And again we note the connection to the ideas of Buber, according to whom the true essence of community, whether it is clearly apparent or hidden, lies in the fact "that it has a center" and that a community emerges "only when its members have a common relation to the center overriding all other relations." Like so much else in Scharoun's texts, this leads straight to the field of architecture, just as the influence of Buber's ideas will again be apparent in his reflections on movement and floor plans discussed in what follows. ●●

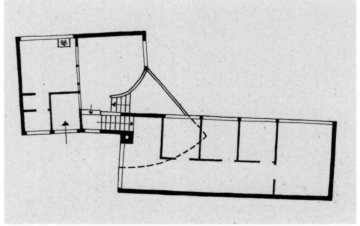

Floor plan of a single-family dwelling for the lecture "Wandlung der Wohnung"

63   Scharoun, Lecture IX/16, February 27, 1956.
64   Scharoun, Lecture X/18, July 15, 1957.

IV   The Physiology of Movement

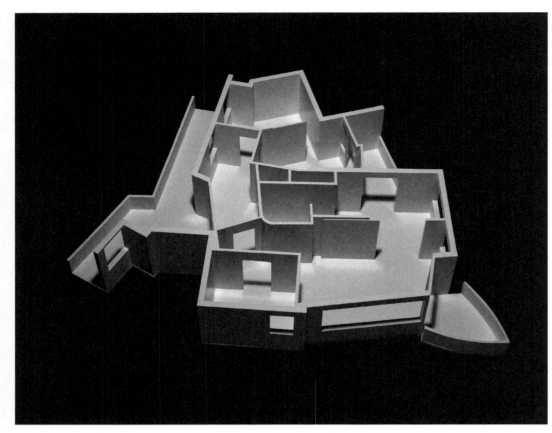

Julia, apartment type 1, 1954

"Problems [...] do not necessarily arise on the same terrain as that on which their solutions are found."

Georges Canguilhem, "La constitution de la physiologie comme science," 1968[1]

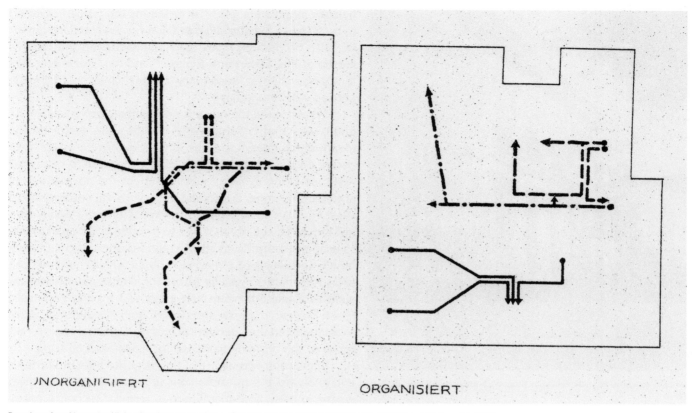

INORGANISIERT   ORGANISIERT

Drawing after Alexander Klein of pathways and lines of traffic for the lecture "Wandlung der Wohnung," June 24, 1950

Hans Scharoun's referencing of Alexander Klein's "Untersuchung zur rationellen Gestaltung von Kleinwohnungsgrundrissen"[2] of 1927 in a lecture of 1950 called "Wandlung der Wohnung"[3] counts as one of those blind but stupendous "cooperations"—in Marx's sense of the word[4]—with which, after twenty years, he resumed his practice of using movement patterns to develop floor plans. A short time later, he elaborated on Klein's paradigms in his manuscript "Normierung und Typisierung im Bauwesen, besonders im sozialen Wohnungsbau."[5] Scharoun saw Klein's objects of study and conceptual lines of argument as "in line with the times," but refrained from judging them or from adopting positions that diverged from Klein's diagrams of pathways and lines of traffic, his plans showing the concentration of the free areas remaining after all the essential items of furniture have been installed, his views of rooms where items of furniture that are higher than half the ceiling height have fragmented the wall space and made the room much smaller, and finally the shadows cast on the floor that would be liable to impair the quality of the hospitality options. Scharoun saw in Klein's analysis of small apartments a productivity that was not derived from standards, but that rather brought forth its own methods that being not so much prescriptive as regulatory allowed for autonomous development.[6]

About a month after his "Wandlung der Wohnung" lecture, Scharoun approached Hugo Häring and asked him in confidence for his opinion of Klein, to whom the Technical University of Stuttgart was intending to award an honorary doctorate. Klein had emigrated to Palestine in 1935, and while Scharoun himself had never met him, Häring almost certainly had.[7] Häring gave him a pointed reply: "He built a palace with an excellent peristyle in the Classical manner for Russian emigrés, just like the palaces they have

in Petersburg; after all, he is himself a Russian emigré and a Jew to boot."[8] Despite their many differences, Häring was not ungenerous, and even as early as 1928 had credited Klein with producing "a measuring device for good floor plans."[9] This verdict was seconded by Max Taut when he, too, was consulted on the question of the honorary doctorate: "I consider the honor well founded, as he was one of the few in the field of residential architecture who approached the search for new floor plans from the point of view of 'dwelling.'"[10]

1 Georges Canguilhem, "La constitution de la physiologie comme science," in *Etudes d'histoire et de philosophie des sciences*, Paris 1968, pp. 226–273, here p. 237; quoted in Hans-Jörg Rheinberger, "Ein erneuerter Blick auf die historische Epistemologie von Georges Canguilhem," in Cornelius Borck, Volker Hess, and Henning Schmidgen (eds.), *Maß und Eigensinn. Studien im Anschluss an Georges Canguilhem*, Paderborn 2005, p. 235.
2 Klein, "Untersuchungen zur rationellen Gestaltung von Kleinwohnungsgrundrissen," 1927, pp. 1350–1367.
3 Scharoun, Lecture II/9, February 24, 1950.
4 According to Karl Marx, "cooperation" is merely a question of form: "When numerous laborers work side by side, whether in one and the same process, or in different but connected processes, they are said to co-operate, or to work in co-operation," Karl Marx, *Capital, Volume 1, Book I: The Process of Production of Capital*, trans. Samuel Moore and Edward Aveling, Moscow 1887, n.p. In the context described above, "production" is taken by epistemologists to refer to scientific cooperation.
5 Scharoun, "Normung und Typisierung im Bauwesen, besonders im sozialen Wohnungsbau," Lecture II/21, May 16, 1950. Scharoun's lecture notes for the summer semester of 1952 include a short piece called "'Verkehrsorganisation in der Wohnung,' Alexander Klein, HSA."
6 Scharoun, "Normung und Typisierung im Bauwesen, besonders im sozialen Wohnungsbau," Lecture II/21, May 16, 1950.
7 Hans Scharoun to Hugo Häring, June 10, 1954, HSA 2836.
8 Hugo Häring to Hans Scharoun, June 14, 1954, HSA 1055, in which Häring cites the development on Ballenstädter Strasse in Berlin.
9 Häring, "Bauen und Wohnen," 1928, p. 760.
10 Max Taut to Hans Volkwart, July 8, 1954, which was enclosed in the letter from the TU Stuttgart, Dept. of Architecture, to Scharoun of July 8, 1954 (HSA 418). Scharoun made a note on it to the effect that he should ask Max Taut about Klein.

Alexander Klein, row of villas on Ballenstedter Strasse 14–16, Berlin-Wilmersdorf, 1923–1924

Scharoun's resumption of Klein's graphical method was a direct response to the threat posed by the kind of narrow, purely technical typologies and standards that reduced floor plans to the sum of the furniture that they were to contain, the free areas in between, and the definition of a suitable module. On June 22, 1950, when Scharoun was director of the Institut für Bauwesen in Berlin, he was sent the draft norm DIN 18011 "Stellflächen für Möbel im sozialen Wohungsbau" (Areas Required for Furniture in Social Housing) with a request that he comment on it without delay.[11] According to the enclosed explicatory plan, a bedroom must be large enough for a double bed measuring 2 × 100 × 200 cm with at least 60 cm clearance between the bed and the wall and at least 70 cm between the foot of the bed and the closet. As the closet is defined as 200 cm wide and 65 cm deep, the room has to be at least 3.35 m wide and 3.20 m deep, with additional free areas in which to move around. Much of the preparatory work for these specifications had been done by Siegfried Stratemann, who in his 1941 work, *Grundriss-Lehre: Mietwohnungsbau,* systematized the size of the various rooms based on their being furnished with standard furnishings.[12] Ernst Neufert had contributed to the debate of a universal measuring system for housing by proposing a new norm in his "Führer-Programm des sozialen Wohnungsbaus" published that same year. The "Oktameter System," claimed Neufert, could "determine the dimensions of the shell, the interiors, and the fittings—including the furniture—based on the same unit of measurement."[13] He tried a second time to champion his system in a 1948 essay called "Architektur und Industrialisierung des Bauwesens."[14, 15] This discussion of a new standard threw Häring's divergence from Gropius ever more sharply into relief: "My objective opposition to his work and to his whole attitude grows the more I myself turn against the technocracy that to my mind

constitutes the building industry's danger from within and one that threatens to bring all our design problems to a halt."[16] Scharoun warned against any all too hasty effort to arrive at a new norm, since the necessary floor space and wall lengths would be calculated simply by "lining up all the furniture that happens to be in use today" and then using the results to determine "room depth and from room depth balcony lengths etc. etc." The called for the type of dwelling to be taken as the starting point and for the standard dimensions to be derived from that type. Debating the relative merits of the "Oktameter System" and the "Dezimeter System" was thus a "secondary matter" that could be dispensed with altogether.[17]

What made the norm fundamentally polemical, he argued, was that it "negatively qualifies the sector of the given which does not enter into its extension while it depends on its comprehension."[18] But the debate of norms and measuring systems was not about the normativity of architecture alone; it also had to do with the normativity of West German society generally. West Germany was a modern industrial society that had to provide small apartments to accommodate its smallest standard unit, i.e. the nuclear family consisting of a married couple with or without children. Alternative dwelling forms for singles and the elderly, such as those Scharoun had proposed for the Wohnzelle Friedrichshain in Berlin and described in his lectures, were excluded from the postwar reconstruction effort as a direct result of the norms introduced for subsidized housing.

Scharoun was aware of the risky situation in Stuttgart and analyzed the possible consequences of the proposed norms in clear and unambiguous terms: "Technical necessity triumphs, not the creative idea. We see it in the way the size of the beds and the closets in the bedrooms lay claim to the space the inhabitants need to live. The remainder of what seems necessary is crammed into the living area for which no such large items of furniture are envisaged. Leading a creative life, whether in the circle of the family or in the circle of elective friendships, is impossible amid all these suites of furniture."[19]

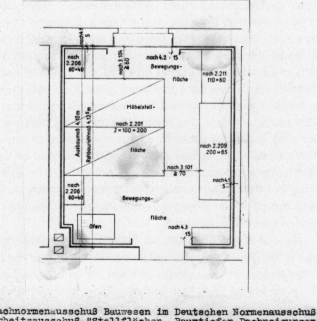

Explicatory plan on the DIN 18011 draft norm for furniture in social housing, enclosed with the letter to the IFB (1950)

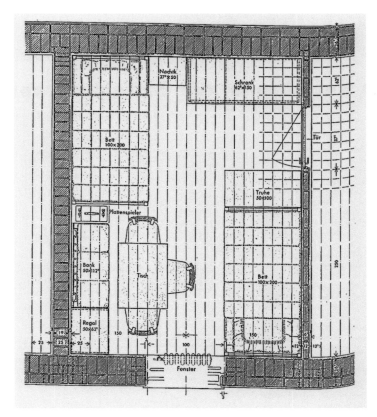

"Example of the correlation between the blocks used for the shell and the room dimensions of the finished building, as influenced by the dimensions of the windows, doors, and spaces to be occupied by furniture," Ernst Neufert, *Plan zum Oktametersystem*, 1941

Clusters, conjunctions, and turning points at which a concatenation of countless small decisions sparks something new—decisions made under very specific conditions that were nevertheless not a foregone conclusion—are a recurrent feature of the history of human dwelling research. Instead of delving deeper into the aforementioned debates on typologies and standards, however, we shall ask in what follows whether comparisons of movement and floor plans make any sense at all; we shall confront the physiological research on fatigue with the development of small apartment floor plans, and we shall analyze how the traditional relationship between floor plan and movement has been reversed in order to shed light on the consequences this reversal has had for architecture.

Many architecture critics, especially the editors of Germany's most important architectural journals of the interwar period, credited Alexander Klein with having "systematized the treatment of a problem that is fundamental to building, namely that of floor plans," in line with "those scientific methods that have long been a matter of course in most engineering disciplines." [20] Klein had attempted to open up the possibility of "gauging the utility of a floor plan even before it was executed." [21] The seventeen phases of Klein's process for ascertaining rational types of dwelling—especially the definition of need, the structural, psychological, and technical parameters, the programs, the choice of types, their selection by means of questionnaires and graphical methods, the tests conducted on models, and the serial building methods—which he proposed in a 1928 lecture to the members of the Reichsforschungsgesellschaft für Wirtschaftlichkeit im Bau- und Wohnungswesen prepared the ground for the development of uniquely new analytical criteria for the systematic evaluation of residential floor plans. They insisted on what was essentially a test run, at the core of which was Klein's "Graphical Method" for evaluating the floor plans of small apartments. In this method, Klein developed criteria for "pathways" and "lines of traffic" and allied himself with the physiological sciences and their analytical methods for ascertaining how well a

dwelling might be managed and how easy it was to use, measured purely in terms of the physical exertion required. [22] Taking a highly effective comparative approach, he contrasted a three-room apartment from the Ceciliengärten in Berlin-Schöneberg (1922–1927) by the Berlin inspector of buildings, Heinrich Lassen, with the type of the apartment without a corridor that he himself had developed and perfected. Commenting on the length of the pathways and their many intersections in Lassen's floor plan, Klein criticized the "spatial isolation and frictionless, if simultaneous, exercise of all living and dwelling functions." [23] In his own "apartment without a corridor," [24] by contrast, the traffic within the "sleeping group" was kept separate from the rest of the apartment by a special closet room with adjoining bathroom and hence formed an "isolated system." Inhabitants who worked night shifts could therefore sleep undisturbed during the day and young children put to bed at bedtime would not be kept awake by conversation and music in the living room. [25] Klein took his comparison a stage further and criticized the conventional dwelling type for its excessively long, "convoluted," and intersecting lines of traffic. These were an astounding 72.10 m long in total, whereas his own floor plan, which allowed "cooking and eating, living and relaxing, sleeping and washing" to be done simultaneously without interfering with each other, had lines of traffic that were no more than 50.50 m long in total and did not intersect at all. [26]

Klein's direct equation of movement sequences with kinetic energy drew on physiological epistemic systems. The scientific measurement of humans had its origins in the second half of the nineteenth century, when physiologists

11 DIN 18011, "Stellflächen für Möbel im sozialen Wohnungsbau," draft of February 1950, sent to the IFB Abtl. Normung-Typisierung, for comment on June 22, 1950, HSA 3996.

12 Stratemann, *Grundriss-Lehre: Mietwohnungsbau*, 1941.

13 Ernst Neufert, "Das Oktametersystem," in *Der soziale Wohnungsbau in Deutschland*, official organ of the Reichskommissar für den sozialen Wohnungsbau, Reichsorganisationsleiter Dr. Robert Ley, 1, No. 13 (1941), p. 453.

14 Ernst Neufert, "Architektur und Industrialisierung des Bauens," lecture to the first Congrèss de l'Union Internationale des Architectes Lausanne, in Walter Prigge, (ed.), *Ernst Neufert* 1999, pp. 384–385.

15 Unerring as ever, Häring emphasized precisely this technocratic continuity when responding to the charge that Modernism had prepared the ground for the industrial mass production of housing: "The Hitlerists," he opined, "prepared plans for the mass production of housing in great haste and with considerable means at their disposal. The fruits of their labors can scarcely find favor with us in terms of their intellectual quality. Faced with Neufert's machines for living in, we are appalled." (Häring, "Neues Bauen," 1947, p. 31).

16 Hugo Häring to Hans Scharoun, August 28, 1947, HSA 1055.

17 Scharoun, "Normung und Typisierung im Bauwesen, besonders im sozialen Wohnungsbau," Lecture II/21, May 16, 1950.

18 Georges Canguilhem, *The Normal and the Pathological*, trans. Carolyn R. Fawcett with Robert S. Cohen, New York 1991, p. 239.

19 Scharoun, "Zur Wohnzelle Friedrichshain," (1949) 1974, p. 187.

20 Editors' preface to "Grundrissbildung und Raumgestaltung von Kleinwohnungen und neue Auswertungsmethoden," in *Zentralblatt der Bauverwaltung* 48, No. 34 (1928), p. 541. The editors of *Die Baugilde* expressed much the same views on Klein's "Untersuchungen zur rationellen Gestaltung von Kleinwohnungsgrundrissen," in *Die Baugilde* 9, No. 22 (1927), p. 1349.

21 Klein, "Versuch eines graphischen Verfahrens zur Bewertung von Kleinwohnungsgrundrissen," 1927, p. 296.

22 Ibid.

23 Klein, "Großsiedlung für 1000 Wohnungen in Bad Dürrenberg bei Leipzig," 1930, p. 1470.

24 Klein, "Flurlose Wohnungen," 1928, pp. 454–460. This dwelling was presented as exhibit No. 18 at the *Heim und Technik* show in Munich in 1928; see Otto Orlando Kurz, *Die kleine Wohnung in der Ausstellung Heim und Technik. 21 Wohnungen in Grundrissen, Vogelschaubildern u. Erläuterungen*, Munich 1928. Klein had previously commented on the problem posed by the hall: "To summarize, I would like to stress most emphatically that in my opinion, gloomy entrance halls have no place in small apartments since the sole reason for retaining them, namely to allow the subletting of single rooms, scarcely warrants the attention of the architect concerned with the great task of creating a contemporary minimum dwelling," (Klein, "Brauchen wir Eingangsflure in Kleinstwohnungen," 1927, p. 524).

25 Klein, "Großsiedlung für 1000 Wohnungen in Bad Dürrenberg bei Leipzig," 1930, p. 1470.

26 Klein, "Flurlose Wohnungen," 1928, p. 456.

Versuch eines graphischen Verfahrens zur Bewertung von Kleinwohnungsgrundrissen

(Siehe Wasmuths Monatshefte, Heft 7, 1927.)

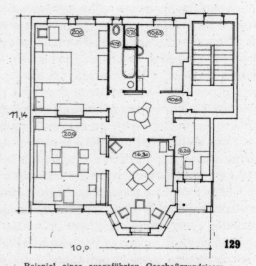

129

Beispiel eines ausgeführten Geschoßgrundrisses. Die Verteilung der Möbel ist die des Originals.

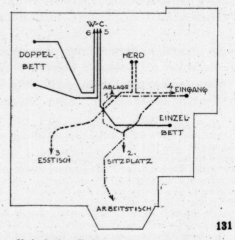

131

Verlauf der Verkehrswege und Ganglinien im angenommenen Beispiel. Alle Lebensfunktionen verlaufen auf sich kreuzenden Wegen.

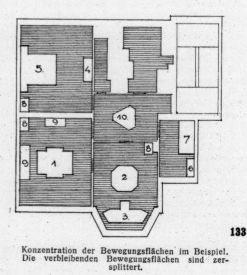

133

Konzentration der Bewegungsflächen im Beispiel. Die verbleibenden Bewegungsflächen sind zersplittert.

Nachstehendes Bewertungsbeispiel ist einer Reihe von mir vorgenommener Untersuchungen entnommen; die vorliegende Untersuchung hat keineswegs zum Ziel, den Grundriß als solchen zu kritisieren, sie will vielmehr nur veranschaulichen, inwiefern er den heute durch die wirtschaftlichen und sozialen Verhältnisse gestellten Aufgaben entspricht und die Wichtigkeit der im Vorwort zum Ausdruck gebrachten Anschauungen bekräftigen. Dieses Beispiel zeigt die Wichtigkeit klarer Trennung von Wohn- und Schlafgruppe und der Transformierung zweier Räume der Wohngruppe mit ausgesprochenen Funktionen in einen großen Wohnraum für alle Funktionen (Essen, Wohnen, Arbeiten, Ruhen), außerdem die Bedeutung richtiger Verteilung der Möbel. (Siehe hierzu Prof. Dr. E. Jobst Siedler „Der Organismus der Wohnung" im Baujahrbuch 1926 und 1927.)

Bei der bisher üblichen Beurteilung von Wohnungsgrundrissen, sei es bei Wettbewerben, bei Entwürfen oder ausgeführten Bauten, wird immer wieder eine Reihe von Begriffen und Fachausdrücken verwendet, wie Klarheit, Wirtschaftlichkeit, Raumform, Raumfolge, Verkehrswege, Flächenausnutzung, Gesamteindruck usw. Von ihnen hängt die Güte und der Wert eines Grundrisses ab. Die meisten dieser Begriffe werden aber von den einen positiv, von den andern negativ gewertet und die meisten Laien und Fachleute neigen dazu, vielen dieser Begriffe lediglich subjektive Bedeutung beizulegen. So ist eine Uebereinstimmung im Urteil auch nur zweier Fachleute oft kaum zu erzielen, da eine allgemein gültige, objektive Prüfung bisher schwierig war.

Ich habe mich daher seit kurzem eingehend mit diesen Begriffen beschäftigt und versucht, ein Mittel zur objektiven Begründung der bisher nur subjektiven Beurteilung zu finden und gelangte so zu dem hier erläuterten graphischen Verfahren, mit dem ich den nachstehenden Grundriß untersucht habe und dem ich zum objektiven Vergleich eine Studie für einen Wohnungsgrundriß von gleicher Fläche beifüge.

Diese graphischen Darstellungen (Abb. 131—146) untersuchen die wichtigsten (primären) Eigenschaften jedes Grundrisses. Raumhöhen, Farbengebung, Behandlung der Wände, völlige Möblierung, sowie künstliche Beleuchtung bleiben außer Betracht als Dinge, die den Gesamteindruck natürlich günstig oder ungünstig beeinflusen, aber doch bei aller Wichtigkeit leicht abgeändert werden können und daher nur sekundäre Bedeutung für die objektive Bewertung von Wohnungen besitzen.

1. Anordnung der Verkehrswege und Verlauf der Ganglinien

Sie kennzeichnen die Bewirtschaftungsmöglichkeit und die Einfachheit der Wohnungsnutzung in Bezug auf rein physikalischen Kraftaufwand (Abb. 131 bis 132).

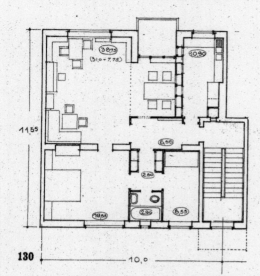

130

Studie des Verfassers zu einem Grundriß der gleichen Größe wie Abb. 129 unter Verwendung der oben angeführten Grundsätze. Treppe umgelegt, um im Erdgeschoß den Durchgang zu vermeiden und den Wohntyp durchführen zu können.

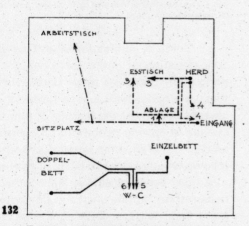

132

Verlauf der Verkehrswege und Ganglinien in der Grundriß-Studie. Die Verkehrswege kreuzen sich nicht, wodurch die ordnungsmäßige Abwicklung der Wohnvorgänge erleichtert wird.

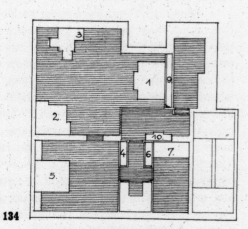

134

Konzentration der Bewegungsflächen in der Studie. Die Bewegungsflächen sind konzentriert und stehen in gutem Zusammenhang.

began to examine the human body as a machine with muscles and nerve pathways. Modern laboratory research with its exacting standards of precision, reproducibility, and controlled conditions, all of which called for rigorously standardized test series, developed hand in hand with this. The theoretical cosmos which thereupon developed rested on these physiological experimental systems and it was Hermann von Helmholtz, who in the 1850s, became the first to measure with some degree of precision the speed at which neural signals are transmitted in living organisms. Von Helmholtz conducted his experiments not just on the sensory nerves of frogs, but also on the motor nerves of humans. He thus initiated the research tradition, which through Julius Bernstein, Étienne-Jules Marey, and others gave rise to neurophysiology on the one hand and through Adolphe Hirsch, Franciscus Donders, and Wilhelm Wundt to experimental psychology on the other. The leading light in academic physiology in St. Petersburg in those days was the neurologist, neurophysiologist, and psychiatrist Vladimir Mikhailovich Bekhterev, who had formerly been an assistant of Wilhelm Wundt in Leipzig. He founded his Psychoneurological Institute for the study of reflexes in 1903, three years before Klein, together with L.A. Ilyin and A.L. Lishnevsky, built the city's largest hospital complex with 2,000 beds.[27] Just how intimately acquainted with current physiological research Klein was, and how eager he was to apply it to his study of floor plans, is evident from his demand that "the time to elapse between the appearance of the space on the retina and the formation of an impression of it in the brain" should be as short as was conceivably possible.[28] In his investigation of small apartments, Klein claimed to have pulled off precisely that feat of substitution, that according to Georges Canguilhem, is a hallmark of modern science: "Measurements substitute for appreciations, laws for habits, causality for hierarchy, and the objective for the subjective."[29]

The development of suitable tools and methods for analyzing and designing small apartment floor plans did not come about of its own accord, but was dependent on paradigmatic values and collective perceptual schemes, which we intend to visualize here, at least for the period of these debates. After the second phase of his "graphical method," in which Klein examined the location and distribution of the free areas remaining after the furniture had been installed, he devoted the third to the ratio of geometrical simplicity and the similarity of those "layout elements" that would generate nervous tension.[30] He claimed to be able to measure the physical and psychological symptoms of fatigue arising from randomly arranged layout elements. These included unnecessary differences in level, circuitous pathways, alternating areas of light and shade, and constant variations in the relative proportions of the figures' ground and area. This last point drew on Wundt's findings from the new scientific discipline of physiological psychology. Wundt had been able to prove that the lowest "apperception time" was that required by the "repetition of homologous parts [...] which within a vertical order bring forth a kind of assembled symmetry." Working in laboratories equipped with cutting-edge measuring methods, Wundt tried to do the impossible: to measure the reaction time that elapses "between the generation of an external stimulus that triggers processes inside the brain and the performance of the movement that follows on from these processes."[31] The times measured by the chronoscope developed specifically for this purpose proved that the apprehension of both vertical symmetry and repetition had the effect of significantly reducing "apperception time." What really counted was the optical impression made by the room, of crucial importance to which were the laws of binocular vision. Following Wundt, who had shown that humans "see centrally as a result of the physiological properties of the eyes," Klein called for vertical axes.[32] It was from that axis that the eyes glanced from one side to the other, taking in the outline of the object encountered so that the full visual image of it developed only gradually. It followed that understanding the successive nature of perception made it easier to describe symmetrically proportioned spaces and repetitions of the same proportional forms, and hence, ultimately, to achieve the goal of calm interiors that "spared our nerves." Klein therefore accorded "geometric similarity" the same importance as "conserving the woman's physical strength as she goes about her daily labors in the kitchen."[33]

Klein's avid interest in the laws of perception based on psychophysiological experiments also explains his fascination with the buildings of Heinrich Tessenow. Their use, almost across the board, of standing, in most cases symmetrical, openings and repetition of homologous proportions earned them a place in many of Klein's publications.[34] Thus, he was impressed by the single-family dwellings in Fischtalgrund, a Gagfah development in Berlin-Zehlendorf of 1928, which Tessenow had reduced to the bare essentials of line and area, subdividing all the openings, starting with the double-transom French windows, in a way that lent the windows both verticality and counterpoise—even if only through the double lines of the window frames.

This search for "simple and regular" geometric forms followed Wundt's laws of division, according to which "symmetrical forms become more pleasing when a large number of single parts are bound up in them. Naked symmetry without any further subdivision of form is too poor to truly stimulate us emotionally."[35] According to Tessenow himself, positioning certain parts of the picture off axis aroused an "interest in the axis and in the new parts of the picture, and as our eyes shuttle back and forth between these parts, so the whole area is suddenly set in motion and comes to life."[36] This refraction of the rigid symmetry might actually be enhanced if parts of the picture were positioned as far away from the axes as possible. Those same axes, which according to Tessenow "draw our eyes in," make us seek order and overlaps. The deliberate dissonance generated between the floor space, which is stabilized by the roof ridge, and the windows makes the symmetry seem all the better, the harder the axes are to find. Tessenow's façades with their love of symmetry and their brittleness of

27 See Werner Hegemann, "Ein russisches Krankenhaus für 2000 Betten," in Wasmuths Monatshefte für Baukunst 13, No. 8 (1929), pp. 327–330; also Karl Schlögel, Petersburg. Das Laboratorium der Moderne, 1909–1921, Frankfurt a.M. 2009, p. 74.

28 Klein, "Beiträge zur Wohnungsfrage," 1928, p. 122.

29 Georges Canguilhem, Knowledge of Life, trans. Stefanos Geroulanos and Daniela Ginsburg, New York 2008, p. 119; cf. Klein's comment: "Just recently, therefore, I began studying these concepts in some depth (room shape, room sequence, pathways, exploitation of space, overall impression) and trying to find a means of objectively justifying what have hitherto been subjective judgments, and so arrived at the graphical method explained here," Klein, "Untersuchungen zur rationellen Gestaltung von Kleinwohnungsgrundrissen," 1927, p. 1366.

30 Klein, "Versuch eines graphischen Verfahrens zur Bewertung von Kleinwohnungsgrundrissen," 1927, p. 296.

31 Wilhelm Wundt, Grundzüge der physiologischen Psychologie, Leipzig 1874, p. 698.

32 Ibid.

33 Klein, "Beiträge zur Wohnungsfrage," 1928, p. 124.

34 Ibid., pp. 121ff, 145, and idem, Das Einfamilienhaus: Südtyp, 1934, pp. 119, 125; cf. also Alexander Klein to Heinrich Tessenow, May 21, 1930: "I have just returned from viewing your bathing establishment and must tell you how much I admire it. The proportions and the composition of the colors lend your work of art a special touch." Heinrich-Tessenow-Archiv, 22.IV.37, Kunstbibliothek Berlin, Stiftung Preußischer Kulturbetrieb.

35 Wilhelm Wundt, Grundzüge der physiologischen Psychologie, Leipzig 1874, p. 696.

36 Tessenow, Hausbau und dergleichen, 1916, p. 35.

expression, for Klein embodied an ideal of modern, classical architecture that he himself would never achieve.

Klein also insisted that architects, who as draftsmen were endowed with what were literally manual skills, might produce drawings that combined geometrical analysis with spatial concepts. And as technical draftsmanship developed, it would become not just an international language, or so he hoped, but also a mode of expression and appreciation that was utterly devoid of ambiguity and misunderstandings. In his own sign-generating system, he used marks, lines, intersections, lengths, and so on, in much the same way as the psychographic tools used in the physiological experimental set-ups. The technical drawing of this physiological-psychological approach was to be part of that graphical method that had become not just representational, but also operative, as had graphical structural mechanics. Ekkehard Ramm describes this very fittingly in his analysis of Culmann's graphical statics: "Graphical statics means that mechanical variables like forces or displacements are determined with purely graphic, i.e. geometric methods, and hence serve not only as a means of visualizing analytical correlations," but also of measuring them.[37] And the application of this geometric method once again leads us straight to Von Helmholtz and his experiments. He called his method of visualizing sound frequencies a "graphical method," and believed that graphic representation of "the law of such movements" would make them much easier to understand than might any verbal description.[38] It was around the same time, moreover, that Carl Ludwig introduced graphic methods into the physiological research work being done by Wilhelm Wundt in Leipzig.

Klein's studies of fatigue were just as bound by their graphic measurability as the physiological findings. Yet the success of this analytical method in the debate of small apartment floor plans can in fact be traced back to its limitations. The systematic, geometrical rigor with which the world was to be subjected to measurable conditions was not a form of refinement achieved through artifice; it was merely the notation, that is to say, the visualization, through isolation, of the specific properties of physiological function, defined as always with the utmost rigor. It was this isolation that yielded the desired accuracy and that enabled the comparative play of functions. To be able to develop a geometric method as Klein did means learning to think like a geometrist; it means distilling a problem until it depends solely on time or the arrangement of area, the rotation of which is completely in the power of the model.

The scope of experimentation in Klein's case was monstrous—at least in the sense of his own theory. As described above, his studies brought together several different approaches that at the time were to be found only in isolation: the combinational approach of area studies in relation to floor plan depth and the number of beds and the statistical evaluation of the same as well as the methodology of physical experimentation and the didactic generalizations deduced from it. He developed, for example, what would later become a widely applied rule for evaluating small apartments, which he himself called the "beds effect." Concurring with many Modernists, most notably Ludwig Hilberseimer, Klein proposed a new, measurable unit to be generated by dividing floor area by the number of beds. These efforts to further the scientific study of small apartment floor plans trickled down into the work of the Reichsforschungsgesellschaft für die Wirtschaftlichkeit im Bau- und Wohnungswesen (RFG) appointed by the German

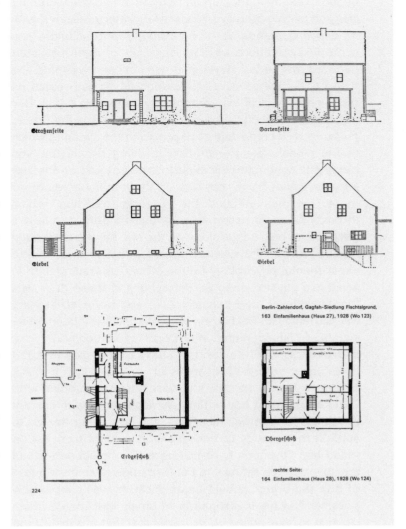

Heinrich Tessenow, design of a single-family dwelling for the Gagfah development Fischtalgrund, 1928

parliament. In a decree of December 12, 1927, the Reich Labor Minister instructed the nation's researchers to undertake a "scientific inquiry into the floor plans of minimum dwellings." And a working committee submitted an initial selection of twenty-four such floor plans as early the spring of 1928.[39] Taking these floor plans as a basis, and after consulting hygienists, another working group spent the next two years developing the four model minimum dwellings that were presented at the International Hygiene Exhibition in Dresden in 1930.[40]

As dwelling research became increasingly institutionalized, there was a risk that Klein's methods, adopted by the apparatus of the RFG, would henceforth shape the control mechanisms for apartment floor plans as well. Klein himself was an inspector of buildings and chairman of the committee for the "Formation of Floor Plans and the Spatial Design of Small Apartments and New Methods of Evaluation," and he also had a hand in the first booklet publishing the RFG's interim results on the development and "Definition of Purposeful and Optimized Dwelling Types." As one commentator noted, architects entrusted with large-scale developments could henceforth "avail themselves of the thorough and flawless programmatic work that these floor plan types represent."[41] Klein's own type of the "apartment without a corridor" was illustrated in that first booklet where it appeared as a conventionalized drawing alongside more traditional floor plans with kitchen, inside bathroom, and just one line of utilities. Owing to their optimized installations, these types did not meet Klein's demand for the strict separation of the living and sleeping areas. His own type was presented as a "new kind of floor plan that separates the living and housekeeping area from the sleeping area." The

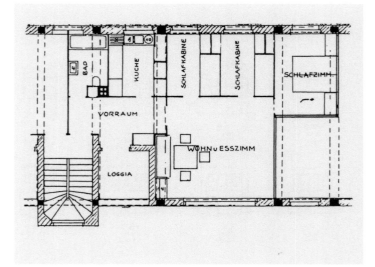

Ludwig Hilberseimer, "Kabinensystem," floor plan for a four-bed apartment, 1923

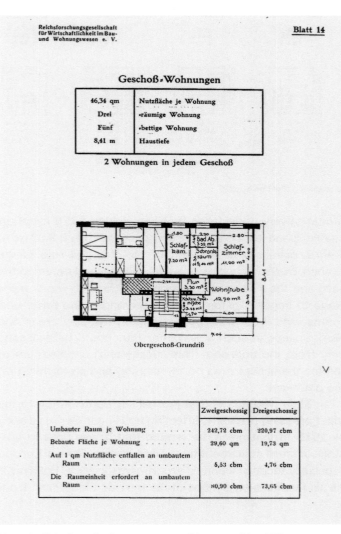

Alexander Klein, floor plan for an apartment without a corridor, 1928

latter was to have "a special room just for closets" and the bathroom was to be positioned so that it was "easily accessible from the bedrooms." He nevertheless admitted that each apartment would have to have two separate waste pipes.[42] Wilhelm Lübbert included Klein's layout in the demands he set out in his report on the activities of the Reichsforschungsgesellschaft: "Bathroom and lavatory are no longer to be situated next to the kitchen, but rather between the bedrooms."[43]

This was a major breakthrough for Klein. His method "by which the characteristics of the floor plan can be defined both clearly and objectively" would also find its way into schools of architecture, where it was used "1) for pedagogical purposes for beginners; 2) as a means for advanced students to check their own work."[44] Even before publication of the *Handwörterbuch des Wohnungswes-*

ens containing Klein's important essay on the design of floor plans for apartments and houses,[45] *Die Baugilde* published an inflationary collection of sixty-four floor plans which, being based on just four basic types (A, B, C, D), systematized the apartment types from three to six and a half beds for two apartments accessed from one landing.[46] The studies that Klein conducted after the program of the Reichsforschungsgesellschaft offer us a glimpse of how isolation and recombination gave rise to new typologies, above all the Y-type whose southeast, southwest, and east–west orientation generated greater density. This type, and the honeycomb pattern produced by combining it, was not only used by Backström & Reinius for the "star houses" of their near legendary Gröndal development (1944–1946), but as "Type 11" would also find its way into the early designs of the layout of Romeo and Julia. A more comprehensive and systematic investigation of access and floor plan types by Klein himself, which would have included three, four, or even five apartments accessed from a single landing, residential hotels, access balcony apartment blocks, and single-family dwellings, in other words a compendium of Klein's whole repertoire to be called *Wohnen und Wohnungsbau als praktische Wissenschaft,* would never be published, however. The only book devoted to his work ever to see the light of day was thus *Das Einfamilienhaus: Südtyp. Studien und Entwürfe mit grundsätzlichen Betrachtungen,* which was published as the first, and ultimately the only, volume in the series "Wohnbau und Städtebau" in 1934.[47]

The importance that Klein attached to making his floor plan analyses public is evident from the thirty articles by him and about him published in *Wasmuths Monatsheften für Baukunst* in the years 1924 to 1932. Countless other articles on his graphical method were published in all the other major architectural journals, too, and Klein's efforts to systematize the study of floor plans, which many of their editors supported, made his lines of traffic drawing one of the most widely disseminated objects in the debate of small apartment floor plans during the interwar years. Even the pugnacious chief editor of *Wasmuths Monatshefte,* Werner Hegemann, who would later author *Das steinerne Berlin. Geschichte der größten Mietskasernenstadt der Welt* (1930), wasted no time in applying Klein's graphical method to his analysis of the lines of traffic in the home of Paul Schmitthenner (1922). A new disciple in Klein's fellowship, he used the master's graphical method to measure and evaluate the lines of movement—whether they were straight or circuitous, parallel or intersecting; indeed, any factors that might make the business of living more difficult were taken into account. The individual pathways thus exposed included those from the entrance to the sitting area and workspace in the living room (III and IV)

37   Eckehard Ramm, "Vorwort," in Bertram Maurer, *Karl Culmann und die graphische Statik,* Berlin/Stuttgart 1998, XIII–XIV, here p. XIII.
38   Andreas Kahlow, "Jean Victor Poncelet und die Schwierigkeiten des visuellen Denkens in den klassischen Technikwissenschaften," in *Dresdener Beiträge zur Geschichte der Technikwissenschaften* 23/1 (1994), pp. 70–78, here p. 74.
39   Reichsforschungsgesellschaft für Wirtschaftlichkeit im Bau- und Wohnungswesen, *Kleinstwohnungsgrundrisse,* 1928.
40   *Internationale Hygiene-Ausstellung Dresden 1930,* official guide, Dresden 1930.
41   Lübbert, *2 Jahre Bauforschung,* 1930, p. 14.
42   Reichsforschungsgesellschaft für Wirtschaftlichkeit im Bau- und Wohnungswesen, *Kleinstwohnungsgrundrisse,* 1928, Sheet 14.
43   Lübbert, *2 Jahre Bauforschung,* 1930, p. 30.
44   Klein, "Beiträge zur Wohnungsfrage," 1928, p. 135.
45   Klein, "Grundrissgestaltung für Wohnung und Haus," 1930.
46   Ernst Völter, "Neue Grundriss-Studien von Alexander Klein. Engerer Wettbewerb der Reichsforschungs-Gesellschaft und Ausweitung der Wettbewerbsarbeit für die Praxis," in *Die Baugilde* 11, No. 1 (1929), pp. 596–605.
47   Klein, "Das Einfamilienhaus, Südtyp," 1934.

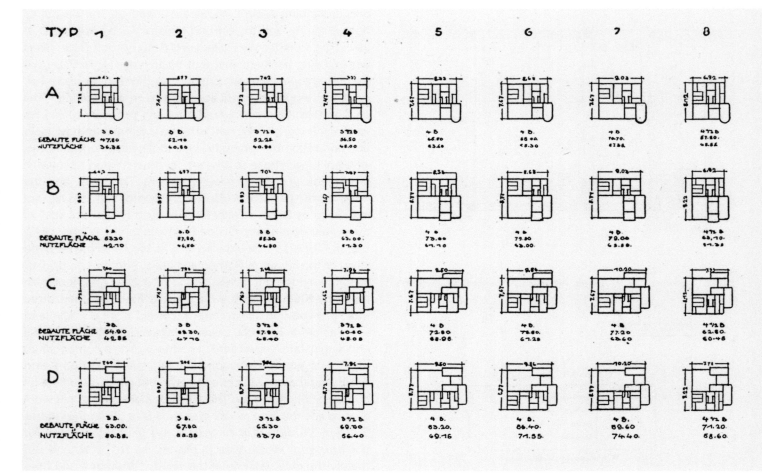

Alexander Klein, floor plan for two apartments accessed from the same landing with three to six and a half beds, 1929

and from the entrance to the children's room (V), as well as from the kitchen to the garden room (II). In an article called "Sklaven eines falsch verstandenen Klassizismus?" (Slaves of a Misunderstood Classicism?) he took pleasure in pulling apart the labyrinthine pathways leading from the bathroom to the bedrooms at the other end of the house (I), and noted how they were unnecessarily long and intersecting. He also drew attention to the position of the furniture, which as he showed, taking the table in the middle of the garden room as an example, had the effect of "barricading the main axis,"[48] as the broken lines of traffic proved. In May 1927, Hegemann and fellow editor Leo Adler curated an exhibition on the houses of J.J.P. Oud in Berlin. Adler hailed Oud as one of the "leaders of the new Dutch architecture," as it was "he who lent purest expression to the vitality and the forward-looking aspect of the much-cited new Dutch developments, and who had freed himself most effectively from mannerism, as there, too—specifically in Amsterdam—diversity comes across as repellent."[49] Hegemann took malicious pleasure in inviting confidences from architects and then telling them what they thought of each other in an attempt to needle them into taking a stand. Claiming that it "depends primarily on the matter in hand," and on the readiness and ability "to swallow a little malice without pain,"[50] he showed Klein and Oud the letters in which they had each commented on the other's work for the Weissenhof Estate of 1927. Klein then launched an attack on Oud's Weissenhof row houses and had his devastating analysis of them published as an "Attempt at a Graphical Method for the Evaluation of Small Apartment Floor Plans" in the same issue of *Wasmuths Monatshefte* as that in which Oud's own article appeared.[51]

The graphical method and the tactic of making a counterproposal exposed the potency of this methodological epistemic process. The comparison of living areas de-

monstratively undertaken by Klein yielded 23.20 m² of unusable space in Oud's house compared with just 8.00 m² in Klein's, primarily as a result of the changed role of the kitchen. Oud's kitchen, which was sandwiched between the yard and the living room, was both a through room and a place to linger. Upstairs, Klein rearranged the three bedrooms with a corridor by positioning the play areas and work spaces in such a way that they could be accessed only from the bedroom. This sneaky shift enabled him to reduce the access area on the landing and so to minimize the pathways.

Klein penned his first journalistic contribution to the most pressing problems affecting housing in Berlin as early as 1926. In that piece, he argued that it was time to take stock of small apartment floor plans all over Central Europe, especially those of Vienna's experiments in social housing. [52] He also ventured a critique of the famous "Taut Plan" from

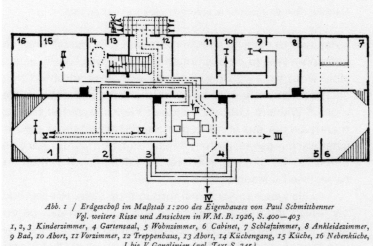

Abb. 1 / Erdgeschoß im Maßstab 1:200 des Eigenhauses von Paul Schmitthenner
Vgl. weitere Risse und Ansichten in W. M. B. 1926, S. 400—403
1, 2, 3 Kinderzimmer, 4 Gartensaal, 5 Wohnzimmer, 6 Cabinet, 7 Schlafzimmer, 8 Ankleidezimmer, 9 Bad, 10 Abort, 11 Vorzimmer, 12 Treppenhaus, 13 Abort, 14 Küchengang, 15 Küche, 16 Nebenküche, I bis V Ganglinien (vgl. Text S. 345)

Werner Hegemann, floor plan of Paul Schmitthenner's house of 1922 with the lines of traffic drawn in, 1928

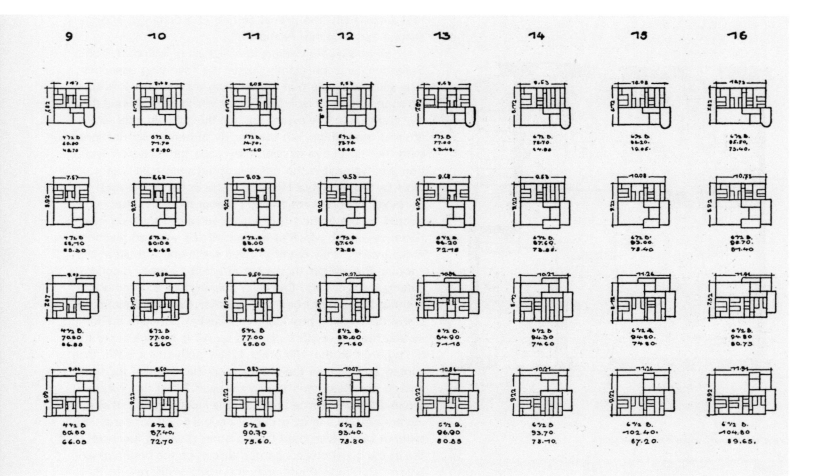

BrunoTaut's book *Die neue Wohnung. Die Frau als Schöpferin* of 1924.[53] Kitchen layouts were dependent on the location of the stove and drain, which frequently gave rise to an awkward arrangement of cabinet, table, and shelves, and hence to randomly crisscrossing lines of traffic. Taut borrowed a "Diagram of badly arranged equipment" by American home economist Christine Frederick, whose studies on the subject had featured in the *Ladies' Home Journal* as early as 1912 and were presented in much greater detail in her book *The New Housekeeping: Efficiency Studies in Home Management* of 1918.[54] Applying Taylorist principles of efficiency to the work of the housewife, Frederick broke down her household chores into a series of actions and calculated the amount of time needed to perform each of them. Interest in rationalizing the work of the housewife alongTaylorist lines developed early on in the United States, where the human organism was to be adapted to the function of the machine even in private households. The aim was to eliminate redundant movements for the sole purpose of maximizing efficiency. The implementation of the modern fetish for speed in the development of housing, like the efforts to maximize productivity in the factories, promoted the reduction of all activities to a monotonous sequence of movements and hence brought with it the danger of making dwelling itself an all too repetitive process. But the refusal of both producers and inhabitants alike to be mechanized proves just how misguided these theoretical concepts that rested on the breakdown of complex movements into crude mechanical reflexes actually were.

As the sciences increasingly turned their attention to intellectual and perceptual work, their focus shifted from the physiology of the working muscles to the physiology of the working brain. Fatigue, a sensation induced by both physical and mental exertion alike, seemed to be the key factor underpinning this concept creep. A psychophysiology of labor and hence, by extension, of dwelling, such as

that proposed by Klein, came about not in opposition to the physiology of labor, but rather as a continuation of the same and hence constituted one of the breakthroughs in how the design process that produced small apartment floor plans was to be steered.

After this lengthy digression on the history and reception of Alexander Klein's graphical method, let us now return to Hans Scharoun's fascination with Klein's experimental setup. The graphical method is premised on stable and homogeneous preconditions; this allows the variables to be isolated from all forms of disturbance and to be given a constant form, which in its turn can be subjected to systematic variations. To understand the epistemological breach of Scharoun's floor plans, we first have to supplement factual history with a history of values and how they evolved over time. The recalibration effected by Scharoun cannot be properly appreciated without first acknowledging the exchange of values that he posited as an alternative to Klein's scientific-physiological way of thinking. Scharoun adopted a sociological research method, whose hypotheses and guiding principles had been developed within the narrower field of floor plan design. At the same time, as we shall see, he mistrusted those principles, perspectives, and attitudes that came from other sciences—even fields that

48   Werner Hegemann, "Sklaven eines falsch verstandenen Klassizismus?" in *Wasmuths Monatshefte für Baukunst* 11, No. 8 (1928), pp. 345–348, here p. 346.
49   Werner Hegemann, "Vorwort zu 'Ja- und Nein-Bekenntnisse eines Architekten,'" in *Wasmuths Monatshefte für Baukunst* 9, No. 4 (1925), pp. 140–146, here p. 140.
50   Caroline Flick, *Werner Hegemann (1881–1936)—Stadtplanung, Architektur, Politik. Ein Arbeitsleben in Europa und den USA*, Munich 2005, p. 679.
51   Klein, "Versuch eines graphischen Verfahrens zur Bewertung von Kleinwohnungsgrundrissen," 1927.
52   Alexander Klein, "Tagesfragen der Berliner Wohnungswirtschaft," in *Städtebau. Monatshefte für Stadtbaukunst, Städtisches Verkehrs-, Park- und Siedlungswesen* 23, No. 6 (1926), pp. 90–104.
53   Taut, *Die neue Wohnung* 1924.
54   Christine Frederick, "The New Housekeeping: How it Helps the Woman Who Does Her Own Work," in *Ladies' Home Journal*, No. 13, September 1912, pp. 70–71.

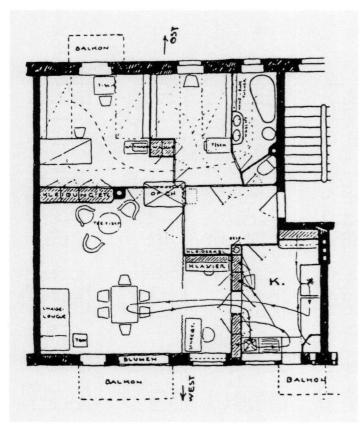

Bruno Taut, work processes in the home, 1924

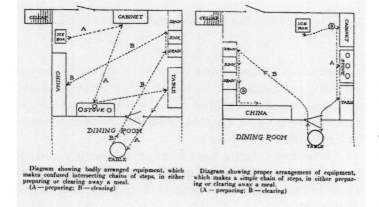

Diagram showing badly arranged equipment, which makes confused intersecting chains of steps, in either preparing or clearing away a meal. (A — preparing; B — clearing)

Diagram showing proper arrangement of equipment, which makes a simple chain of steps, in either preparing or clearing away a meal. (A — preparing; B — clearing)

Christine Frederick, a comparison of badly and properly arranged equipment, 1912

were so highly regarded as to be indispensable, as ergonomics and the study of fatigue were to the physiologists of the early twentieth century.

The field of experimentation's shift to other values manifested itself in the studies of dwelling types that Scharoun and his students conducted at the Institut für Bauwesen (IFB), in which the inner movements were analyzed according to the dialogical principle of "isolation" and "connection."[55] The philosopher of religion, Martin Buber, had written extensively on this principle both in *Daniel. Gespräche von der Verwirklichung* of 1913 and in *Ich und Du*[56] of 1923, and his thoughts on the subject resonated all the more powerfully in the aftermath of the Second World War[57] Buber's hypothesis of the close connection between anarchy, messianism, and utopia had already captured the imagination of Expressionist writers, all the more so since with his admirably felicitous choice of words, he effectively lent his voice to a mystical, subliminally Sephardic spirituality. The theory of the dialogical principle was again the subject of his essay "Urdistanz und Beziehung" (Distance and Relation) of 1951, in which he described the principle of human life as twofold, "being built up in a twofold movement which is of such kind that the one movement is the presupposition of the other. I propose to call the

first movement 'the primal setting at a distance' and the second 'entering into relation.'"[58]

Several years earlier, in a lecture of March 3, 1950, Scharoun had confidently made the following assertion: "The societal problem of the dwelling rests on the concepts of 'connection and isolation,'" after which he explained that by "connection," he meant not just the cultivation of family life and friendships, but the totality of human connections with the "collective mission they pose for society."[59] Isolation was to enable the uninterrupted accomplishment of work by the individual followed by his or her withdrawal for purposes of recuperation and regeneration. The study conducted by the Institut für Bauwesen raised thirteen questions, seven of which were concerned with connection: "Does every family member have somewhere to sit in the 'room in the middle' that is not affected by other functions (eating and working)? Can he or she work or do handicrafts without being disturbed by the other dwelling functions? Does the dwelling provide an optical link between the family and the housewife's place of work? Is there a separate dining area so that the other family activities are not disrupted by it? Does the child's room have space for both shared entertainment and school work? Can the 'room in the middle' be enlarged through the incorporation of sleeping areas? Can a large group of people enjoy conversation without being disrupted by the other dwelling functions?" Six of the questions concerned turned on the notion of isolation: "Can individual family members withdraw to their bedrooms in order to write or sew? Can the sleeping areas be partitioned off from the 'room in the middle'? Can the housewife's place of work be properly partitioned off? Can the spaces for work or handicrafts be visually kept apart from the 'room in the middle'? Can the dining room be visually kept apart from the 'room in the middle'? Can the 'room in the middle' be accessed from the outside without disrupting the other dwelling functions?"[60]

Only some of the demands made by the IFB's participating architects, Theodor Effenberger, Otto Haesler, Hoffmann, Karl Müller-Rehm, Siegmann, and Tepez were fulfilled in this "Study of Dwelling Types with Regard to their Suitability for Good Neighborly Relations."[61] But Scharoun had already demonstrated one possible solution to these "problems of connection and isolation" in two of the floor plan types that he developed during his work on the Wohnzelle Friedrichshain in 1949, specifically the one called "Silo" for small apartments and the one for a single-family dwelling (fig. p. 148), which he regarded as a realization of the idea

55 Scharoun, Lecture IX/16, February 27, 1956.
56 Buber, *Daniel* 1913; *Ich und Du*, 1923.
57 The reference to Martin Buber's dialogical principle was also noted by Kirschenmann and Syring, *Hans Scharoun*, 1993, p. 225, and by Pfankuch, *Hans Scharoun*, 1974, p. 228, albeit without any further comments on how Scharoun applied it to his floor plans. Scharoun himself acknowledged his conceptual indebtedness to Buber in a 1957 essay called "Struktur in Raum und Zeit": "These twin concepts, which Martin Buber originally applied to relationships between people, concern us, too, and are of service to us, for example, when contemplating the structure of old and new towns," Scharoun, "Struktur in Raum und Zeit," 1957, p. 17. Cf. also the pointers provided by Simone von Hain: "'Ex oriente lux' Deutschland und der Osten," in Lampugnani, V.M.; Schneider, R: *Moderne Architektur in Deutschland 1900 bis 1950. Expressionismus und Neue Sachlichkeit*, Stuttgart 1994, pp. 133–157.
58 *Martin Buber on Psychology and Psychotherapy, Essays, Letters and Dialogue*, edited by Judith Buber Agassi, Syracuse NY 1999, p. 4.
59 Scharoun, Lecture II/7, March 3, 1950.
60 Scharoun and the Institut für Bauforschung, "Untersuchung von Wohntypen auf ihre Eignung zur Bildung wirksamer Nachbarschaft," n.d.
61 The floor plans were commented on and rated with a points system. Hoffmann's description of a five-bed duplex, for example, read as follows: "The 'room in the middle' can only be described as inadequate in terms of its dimensions. Hence its inadequate fulfillment of the societal demands made of it. The separation of the sexes must be rated positively." (Floor plan unavailable, HSA 4010 and HSA IFB I/17).

Abb. 113—116 zeigen einen Vorschlag zur Aufschließung und Bebauung von Wohnvierteln. Dieses System enthält Ersparnisse an Bau- und Aufschließungskosten und bietet verbesserte Wohnbedingungen. Das Wohnviertel liegt zwischen zwei Nord-Süd-Verkehrsstraßen. Diese erhalten hohe Randbebauung mit öffentlichen Gebäuden, hochliegende Schnellbahn und Autoschnellverkehrsstraße. Der Verkehr aus dem Wohnviertel wird durch hinter der Randbebauung, der Verkehrsstraße parallel verlaufende Sammelstraßen aufgefangen, die nur jede 1—1,5 km eine Verbindung mit der Verkehrsstraße haben. Die Haltestellen der Hochbahn sind durch Brücken mit den Bürgersteigen verbunden. Zwischen zwei Verkehrsstraßen liegen nur zwei mittlere

113

Wohnstraßen; die Zufahrten zu den meisten Treppenhäusern sind in Form von schmalen, privaten Einbahnsackwegen gedacht. In 30 v. H. der wabenförmigen Höfe von je 1300 qm Fläche liegen solche Zufahrten; die übrigen 70 v. H. sind ruhige abgeschlossene Gartenhöfe. Auf Kosten der ersparten Wohnstraßen können außerdem noch weiträumige öffentliche Grünanlagen geschaffen werden für Erholung, Sport und Spiel. Hier könnten auch Schulen Platz finden. Die einstöckigen Bautrakte an diesen Grünflächen sind als Kindergärten, Sporthallen, Leseräume usw. gedacht, die an den Wohnstraßen als Läden für Lebensmittel. Die Zahlenwerte dieses Systems im Vergleich mit einer der üblichen, der Bauordnung entsprechenden Bebauung sind folgende:

Gesamtbild der Wabenbebauung.

Grundriß des Erdgeschosses. Treppenhaus von zwei Seiten zugänglich. Im Halbgeschoß Garagen für Autos und Motorräder.

114

Totalfläche 265 000 qm; davon Bauland mit Grünstreifen 89 v. H. (77 v. H.), Straßenland 11 v. H. (23 v. H.); Bebauungsziffer 28,4 v. H. (27,8 v. H.); bebaute Fläche 66 393 qm (54 500); Anzahl der Wohnungen 2006 (1680); Anzahl der Treppen 252 (280); auf eine Treppe 8,2 Wohnungen (6); Straßenlänge pro Wohnung 1,2 m (2,28); desgl. Straßenland 22,2 qm (44,8); Geländeanteil pro Wohnung 117 qm (121); durchschnittliche Hofbreite 43,3 m (26); durch die Schrägstellung erhalten die meisten Wohnungen auch Südbelichtung, die übrigen sind entweder Ost-West oder reine Südwohnungen.

Grundriß der oberen Geschosse. Drei Wohnungen an einem Treppenpodest. In der oberen Wohnung beiderseitige Belichtung des Wohnraums; diese Wohnung ist um ein halbes Geschoß gegenüber den schrägstehenden versetzt. Die Lauben verschatten die Wohnräume nicht und belichten die Diele.

115

S—N

S—N

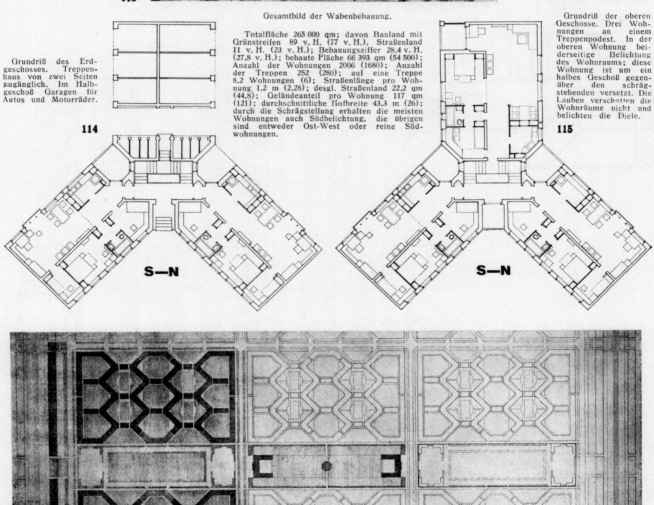

116 Lageplan eines Wohnviertels im Wabensystem

Fortsetzung der Untersuchungen auf Seite 1365

Alexander Klein, "Floor plan types for the honeycomb system", 1927

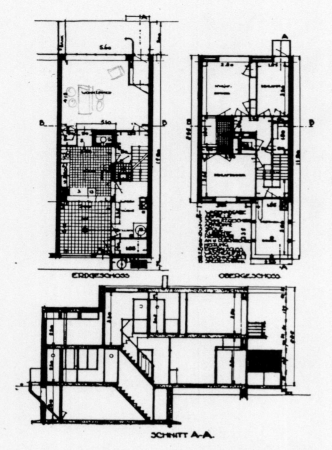

Bei Fortfall der sägeförmigen Anordnung werden Bad und Treppe wie bei Oud nicht mehr unmittelbar belüftet.

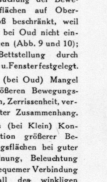

Abb. 9 bis 11 | Reihenhäuser für die Ausstellung „Die Wohnung" in Stuttgart
Architekt: J. J. P. Oud, Rotterdam

Abb. 12 bis 14 | Studie zu Reihenhäusern gleicher Größe wie in Abb. 9 bis 10
Architekt: Alexander Klein, Berlin

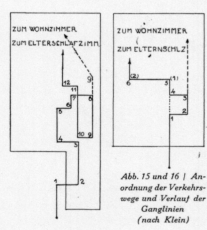

*Abb. 15 und 16 | An-
ordnung der Verkehrs-
wege und Verlauf der
Ganglinien
(nach Klein)*

Die Ganglinien links zeigen (bei Oud) vom Hof ins Wohnzimmer 9, vom Hof ins Schlafzimmer 12 Windungen. Der Hofeingang ist gewählt, weil er laut Lageplan (Abb. 30) zugleich Straßeneingang ist; der zweite Eingang ist nur durch den Garten erreichbar.

Die Ganglinien rechts (bei Klein) haben nur 2 und 6 Windungen; da die Wendelung der Treppe (Abb. 12) fortfallen kann, ist weitere Vereinfachung (schwach gestrichelt) möglich.

Vgl. Text Seite 296 und 298

Untersuchung der Bewegungsflächen auf Obergeschoß beschränkt, weil Möbel bei Oud nicht eingetragen (Abb. 9 und 10); die Bettstellung durch Türen u. Fenster festgelegt.

Links (bei Oud) Mangel an größeren Bewegungsflächen, Zerrissenheit, verwickelter Zusammenhang.

Rechts (bei Klein) Konzentration größerer Bewegungsflächen bei guter Anordnung, Beleuchtung und bequemer Verbindung (Fortfall des winkligen Flures).

Vgl. Text Seite 296 und 298

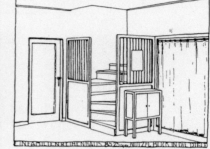

*Abb. 17 und 18 | Konzentration der Bewegungsflächen
in den Obergeschossen
(nach Klein)*

Abb. 19 bis 22 | Geometrische Ähnlichkeit und Zusammenhang der Grundrißelemente (nach Klein)

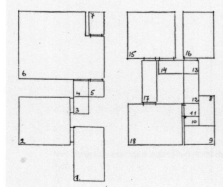

Links (bei Oud) im Erd- und Obergeschoß 18 Elemente verschiedener Rechteckform und Größe, immer wieder andere Längsrichtungen.

Rechts (bei Klein) im Erd- und Obergeschoß nur 11 Elemente, deren Form, Größe und Richtung untereinander ähnlich oder gleich sind (z. B. 2 und 4, 10 und 11, 7 und 9). Die Darstellungen für Klein sind spiegelverkehrt gezeichnet.

Vgl. Text Seite 296 und 298

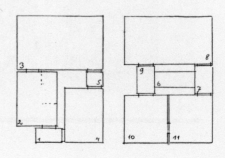

297

Alexander Klein, study of the lines of traffic and circulation areas in the row houses of J.J.P. Oud (1927) and his own single-family dwellings (1927), 1927

IV   The Physiology of Movement

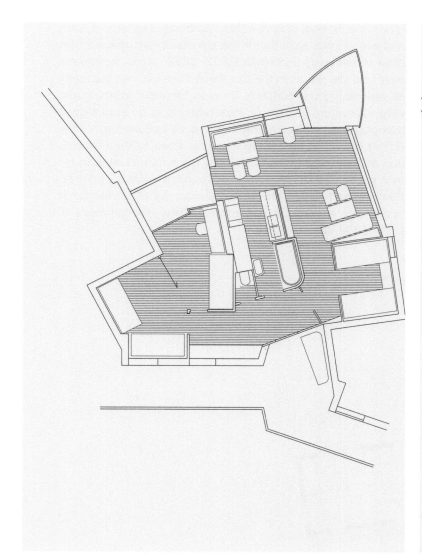

Julia, floor plan type 1 showing the free areas, September 1

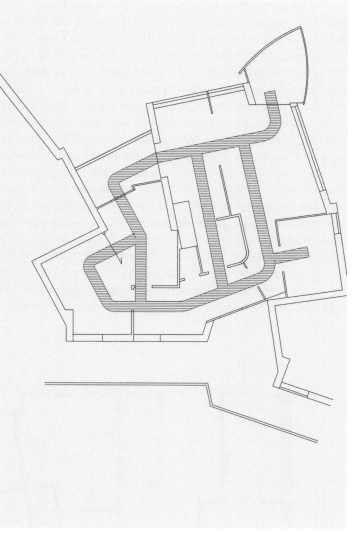

Julia, floor plan type 1 showing lines of traffic, September 1

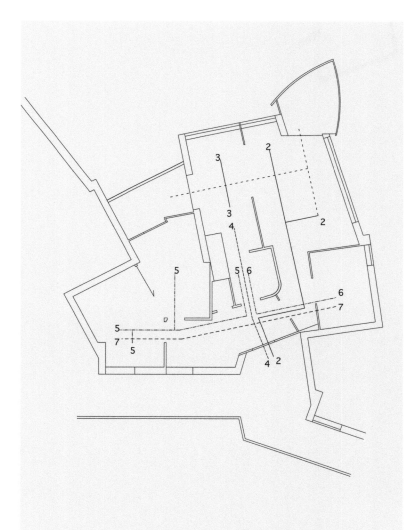

of the "room in the middle." One solution to the discrepancy between the "abundance of tasks and economic limitations"[62] lay in assigning the same spaces two different functions: a daytime and a nighttime function, which inevitably entailed either removing furniture or using multipurpose furniture.

The floor plan design that Scharoun presented in his lecture of July 1, 1957, and that clearly references the first types 1 and 2 of Julia, even if that project was never actually mentioned by name, can be read as his answer to the demands for connection and isolation[63]. The floor plans were premised on the necessity of separating dwelling and housekeeping, he explained. Apart from the—where possible, separate—children's bedrooms, which in addition to the bed niches were to have a small space for playing and working, the division of the apartment into a housekeeping area, a living area, and a sleeping area was intended to permit several different combinations with maximum accessibility. Such a layout, Scharoun continued, would allow the dining area to belong either to the living area or to the kitchen, ensuring that the "various dispositions of the biological or social family have various places in the dwelling at their disposal."[64] If the bathroom and kitchen were combined and lavatory kept separate, the bathroom could be a through room and the kitchen could have an adjoining dining area. Being conscious of the advantage of such an inside unit, Scharoun emphasized that in areas of high housing density, every meter of façade was costly and hence should be reserved for more important purposes.

62 Scharoun, Lecture II/9, February 24, 1950.
63 Scharoun, Lecture IX/16, February 27, 1956.
64 Ibid.

The conceptual significance of the outside walls to a four-bed, access-balcony apartment of just 61 and 64 m² in size is evident from the way he stretched Julia's south-facing façade to the limit, making it more than twice as long as the access-balcony side of the apartment. Also striking are the many different types of partition used within the apartment: the countless doors, double doors, room-high sliding doors, a folding partition combined with two single doors, and the curtain closing off the bed niche in the parents' bedroom make for constantly spatial relations and hence for the desired range of options for isolation and connection. Scharoun's assertion that even technically superfluous movements are nevertheless a necessary function of dwelling constituted a radical departure from the exclusively physiological adherence to movement studies that had previously prevailed in the study of floor plans. Venturing beyond Klein's systematic investigation of the psychotechnical or even psychological conditions, he conceived of the dwelling process as part of the process by which society comes into being.

made magisterial use of in his Landhaus Baensch of 1935 and even earlier than that in the parallelogram-shaped footprint of his Haus Schminke (1932–1933), while movement over two stories, as in the Landhaus Baensch, has the effect of connecting the house to its own terraces, loggias, and verandas and of hence of integrating it in its stupendous topographical situation. The importance to Scharoun of the circuit type that ultimately was sacrificed to the introduction of fixed standards is evident from its inclusion in his own repertoire of floor plans and in his the slightly later application and realization of that same type of cross-corner apartment in the Charlottenburg-Nord development of 1955–1960. ●●

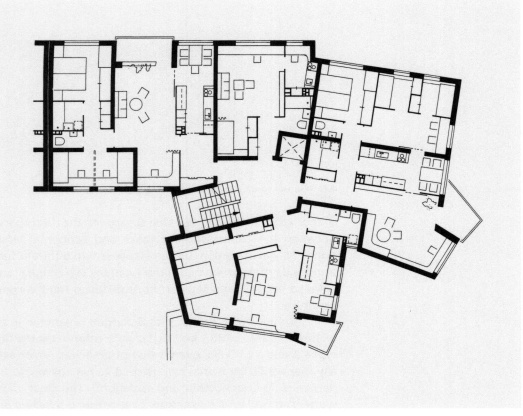

Apartment type 4 BC, east–south, Charlottenburg-Nord development, 1955–1960

The utopian notion of working and dwelling underlying Scharoun's "*Gesamtarbeiter*" was posited as an alternative to the concerted efforts of kinetic engineers and Taylorist psychotechnicians to break down all human activity into homogeneous, elementary gestures. Scharoun's fundamentally different definition of the dwelling process rendered Klein's distribution criteria null and void. Subjecting the Julia floor plan types to the self-checks that Klein demanded of all advanced students bears this out: the lines of movement to which the relationships between connection and isolation give rise change fundamentally. Not only do they undermine the strict separation of living and sleeping, but they also generate a series of circuits in which two smaller units are overlaid by a larger one; no longer are movement sequences closely tied to reproduction, as they are in Klein. Using the outside space of the children's balcony to facilitate connection was a principle that Scharoun

V Historical Pictures

Model of Block A and Block B with view from the west

Model of Block A and Block B with view from the northeast

Model of Block A and Block B with view from the west

Model of Block A and Block B with view from the southeast (top) and south (bottom)

Model with light from the south

Presentation model of Julia

Presentation model of Julia and Romeo

117

Julia under construction

Julia, courtyard side under construction

Julia, west façade under construction

View of the stairwell on the south façade of Julia

Julia and Romeo, view from the southeast

Bird's-eye view of Romeo and Julia with the sun in the south

Bird's eye view of Julia with the sun in the south

Rooftop studio, Romeo

Rooftop studio apartment by Hans Scharoun in Romeo

133

Julia, view from the east

Balconies on the southwest façade of Romeo

Balcony and loggia of the duplex apartment in Romeo

Julia, view from the southeast
Completion, 1959

141

Julia, view from the east

Romeo, view from the east

VI   The Sawtooth Type

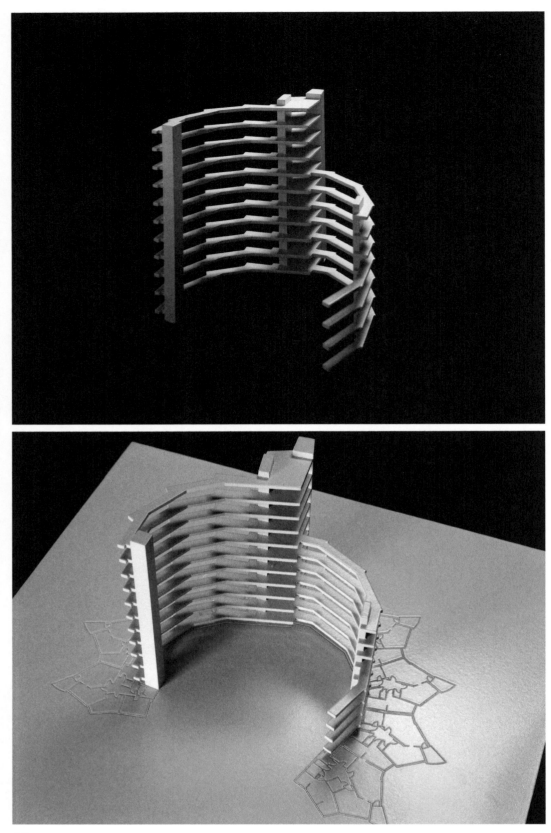

Julia, access system

"A period of crisis [...] is also one of theoretical research."

Karl Marx to Ferdinand Lassalle, January 23, 1855[1]

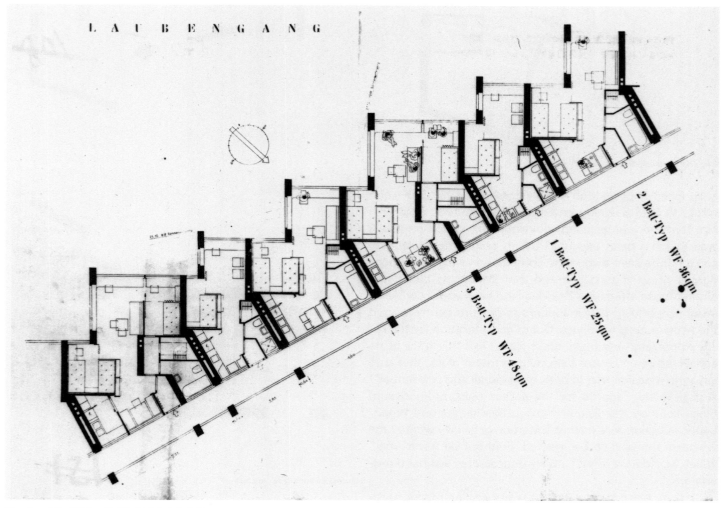

Site plan of the "Wohnzelle Friedrichshain," 1949

Hans Scharoun's list of the "post-1945" photographs that he intended to use for a lecture on February 20, 1950 includes "All the Friedrichshain types."[2] These were housing studies that he had begun working on at the Institut für Bauwesen on November 1, 1947 and that influenced the project for the reconstruction and remodeling of Friedrichshain in Berlin.[3] The plans show the results of his wide-ranging studies of access systems and of various combinations of heterogeneous housing types; also reflected in them is a striving for spatial complexity. Most important of all, they reopened the debate of interwar years of the optimum light orientation, and over and above this laid the foundations of a new type of small apartment with access balcony: the sawtooth type.

Scharoun explained that with this new access balcony type he had succeeded in "generating spaciousness [...] despite limited living space."[4] But the introduction of the sawtooth type also raised another aspect of floor plan design that the literature had hitherto by and large disregarded: the principle of sunlight exposure. After the "Wohnzelle Friedrichshain" project on the Frankfurter Allee of 1949–1950 came to nothing, the sawtooth type, which in fact comprised six different layouts lined up in a row, was carefully filed away in Scharoun's floor plan collection. But he would find a use for it on numerous occasions later in his career, including for the initial plans for Romeo and Julia in Stuttgart.

Such floor plan collections tend to amount to more than just a catalogue or list. For most architects they are more like a guiding principle for their daily work. As we shall attempt to show, this epistemological metaphor served Scharoun as a means of setting his own projects apart from an excessively narrow dogmatism on the one hand and from directionless, largely arbitrary developments on the other. Joachim Zimmermann, Scharoun's coworker from 1953 to 1963, recalls revisiting this repertoire for the appraisal of the Berlin-Charlottenburg-Nord development of 1954–1961. Among them were what could only be described as "montages, simply pieced together [...] which is understandable enough, since you can't have everything there right from the start."[5] The question of where to draw the line between consolidated objectivity, typological generalization, and their degeneration into purely speculative positions has to be renegotiated with each new use, given that it can never be decided once and for all. Most proposals made advances that went beyond the familiar and tried not to resist fixation per se. The sawtooth type was ultimately realized as part of the Charlotten-

1   *Marx & Engels Collected Works*, Vol. 39 Letters 1852–55, London 2010, p. 511.
2   Scharoun, "Zur Wohnung," Lecture II/4, February 20, 1950.
3   Type catalogue for the Wohnzelle Friedrichshain, HSA WV 170, 1340, 1193.
4   Hans Scharoun, "Zur Wohnzelle Friedrichshain," manuscript dated November 7, 1949, in Peter Pfankuch, (ed.), *Hans Scharoun. Bauten, Entwürfe, Texte*, Schriftenreihe der Akademie der Künste Berlin, Vol. 10, Berlin 1974.
5   Conversation with Joachim Zimmermann, Stefan Heise, and Friedrich Mebes about the residential high-rises Romeo and Julia; Markus Peter and Ulrike Tillmann, recorded September 18, 2006 in Berlin-Gatow.

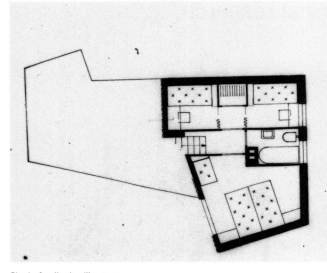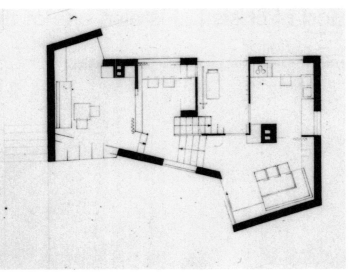

Single-family dwelling type

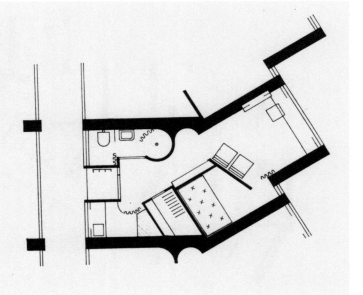

Access balcony type, one bed

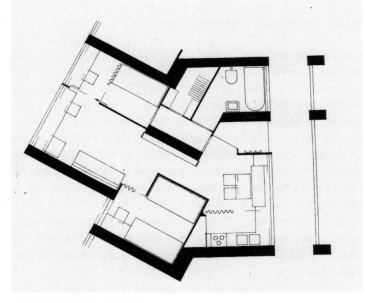

Access balcony type, two beds

burg-Nord II project on Goebelstrasse of 1957. Scharoun wrote to Otto Bartning on September 24, 1955 to inform him that the Siemensstadt development, which originally was to have been executed by an architects' collective, could not be seen through to completion owing to the conditions prevailing on site and that Bartning's block was among those affected: "The idea is to have your row curve away properly so that it appears to gesture gently toward the twelve-story residence. Out of consideration for the really important new buildings, I would like this tract to be conceived as an access balcony apartment block, that is to say with a design that is both transitional and referential."[6] A note in the records for the access balcony apartment block kept by the Gemeinnützige Siedlungs- und Wohnbaugesellschaft tells us that Scharoun originally wanted the western stairwell to be erected "without an outer wall," which would have left it "utterly unprotected against the elements."[7]

If we were to return to the history of floor plans to reassess both its values and limitations, we might want to draw on a text that fits this genuinely Modernist terrain very well: Hans Scharoun's "Besonnung, 'Neuzil',"[8] in which he discusses Walter Neuzil's ground-breaking work on the systematic quantification of the caloric value of indoor sunlight: *Messungen der Besonnung von Bauwerken*.[9] Neuzil had opened the debate with an article called "Die Besonnungstechnik. Eine neue Wissenschaft" back in the 1930s, and its development since then had seen the kind of deconcretization of fundamental concepts that is symptomatic of all emergent sciences. Neuzil proposed a new unit of measurement for sunlight intensity to be called a "Sol." He defined one Sol as "100 kilocalories of thermal energy per hour falling at a right angle onto an area of 1 square meter."[10] The correction factor that he went on to develop—to take account of oblique incident light, the refractive effect of the atmosphere, the share of diffuse light reflected back by the walls of a building, and, not least, the degree of cloud cover—allowed the relationships underlying the concept now robbed of its empirical value to be concretized. This parameter spawned new tables and data, since "no amount of practice can supply a theory with theoretically usable and valid data as long as the theory itself has not already invented and defined the validation conditions according to which the data are to be appropriated."[11] Solar radiation had not split into a scientific object of study and a phenomenon of its own accord; rather, the science of physics was able to address it as an object of study only after finding a method with which to build a theory out of concurring propositions—a theory controlled by the efforts being made to develop its capacity for intervention and methods.

Among the eleven criteria drafted by the Reichsforschungsgesellschaft for the adjudication of the competition entries for the research development Spandau-Haselhorst in 1928–1929 is the one described as "scientific investigation and graphic representation of the dwellings' exposure to sunlight at different times of year, allowing for variations in building height and spacing."[12] Enclosed blocks were ruled out in favor of building in rows to "ensure the same

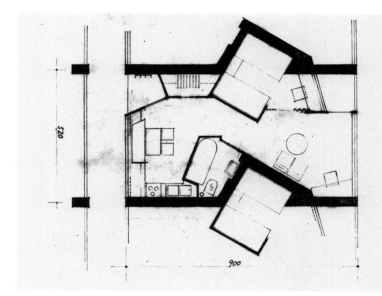

Access balcony type, two beds

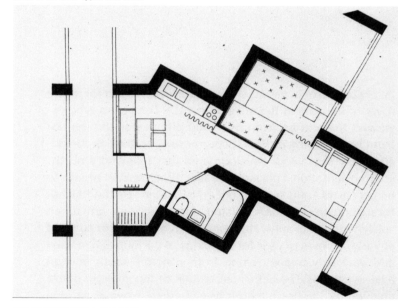

Central corridor type, two beds

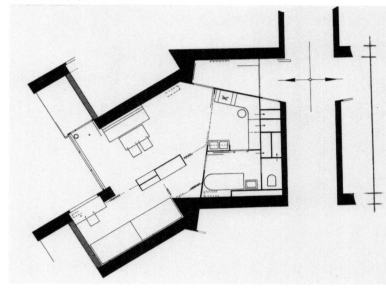

Access balcony type, two beds

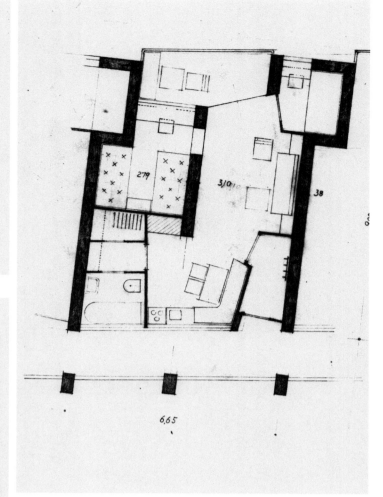

Access balcony type, two beds

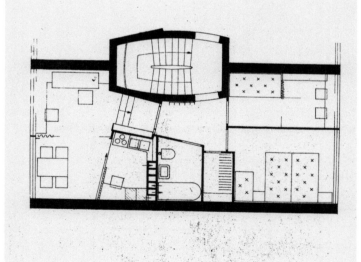

Shared landing type, three beds

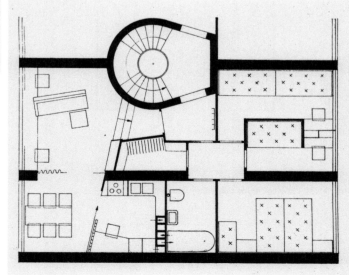

Shared landing type, five beds

6   Hans Scharoun to Otto Bartning, September 24, 1955, in Geist and
    Kürvers, *Das Berliner Mietshaus* 1989, p. 412.
7   Bauakte Goebelstr. 1–9, Berlin, Charlottenburg-Nord II, Bauakten-
    archiv Charlottenburg-Wilmersdorf, Berlin, July 9, 1957, p. 11.
8   Hans Scharoun, "Notizen," Lecture XI/4, n.d.
9   Walter Neuzil, *Messungen der Besonnung von Bauwerken. Ein
    neues Messverfahren und seine Anwendung auf die Bebauung*,
    Berlin 1942.
10 Walter Neuzil, "Die Besonnungstechnik. Eine neue Wissenschaft,"
    in *Die Baugilde* 13, No. 5 (1931), here p. 403.
11 Georges Canguilhem, "Zur Geschichte der Wissenschaften vom
    Leben seit Darwin," in idem, *Wissenschaftsgeschichte und
    Epistemologie. Gesammelte Aufsätze*, edited by Wolf Lepenies,
    Frankfurt a.M. 1979, pp. 134–153, here p. 141.

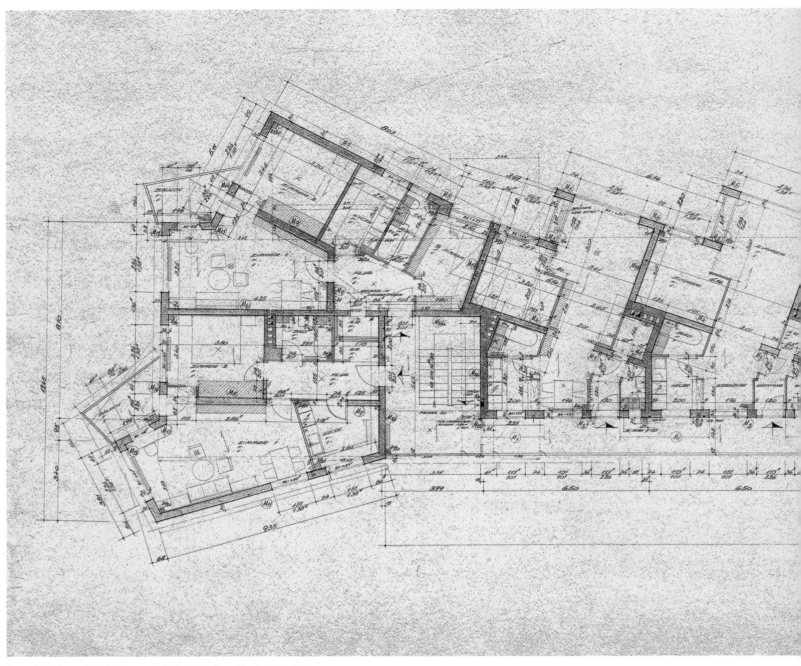

1st and 2nd floor of Goebelstrasse 1–9, Charlottenburg-Nord, 1955–1960

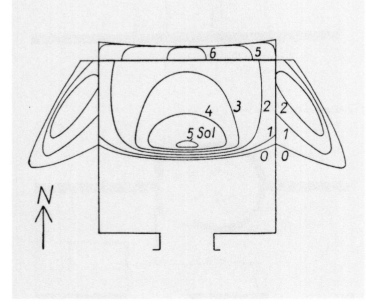

Walter Neuzil, drawing for the Sol unit of measurement, 1942

favorable fall of sunlight with optimum ventilation for all the rows of housing in the development."[13] The jurors who reviewed the entries from over 600 architects—though not from Hugo Häring or Hans Scharoun—nevertheless considered only those row developments that followed a north-south orientation. This was the last experimental object to be prepared—and realized only much later—by the Reichsforschungsgesellschaft. Walter Gropius was entrusted solely with the graphic representation of the fall of sunlight at various times of year for buildings of various dimensions and variously spaced along both a north–south and an east–west axis. The actual calculation of the sunlight hours enjoyed by the north–south or east–west rows at various times of year was the responsibility of the senior inspector of buildings, Johannes Grobler. While Grobler would not prevail—as the winner of the debate of north–south linear buildings, Gropius managed to shift the debate from the question of orientation to that of low-rise versus high-rise[14]—he did formulate a fundamental critique of the consideration of sunlight on which the winning solution was premised. He began by recapitulating the line of argument used by the protagonists of such row developments: "Both sides of the building receive the same amount of sunlight. Living rooms can therefore be located on both sides of the building, safe in the knowledge that these rooms, no matter which side of the building they are on, will receive some

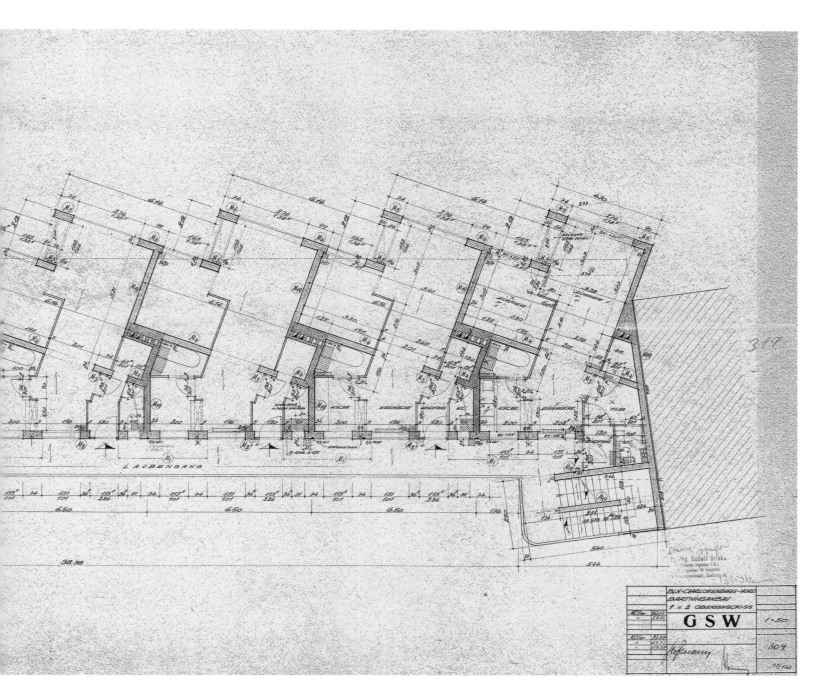

sunshine. The sun shines on both façades throughout the year […] The distance between the blocks can be kept relatively small as the sun will still shine on the façades, no matter how small the distance between them."[15] Only then did he begin to undermine the advantages of freestanding north–south row developments, which despite ostensibly having two equally sunny fronts, were no more than briefly touched by the sun in the months of November, December, and January since, "in this direction especially, it takes a relatively long time for the sun to get beyond the window reveal. Assuming a 38-cm-thick wall and a normal-sized window, the sun can be expected to take ¾ hour in summer, 1¼ hours in spring and fall, and 1½ hours in winter to overcome the angle between the outside and inside of the window reveal." [16] The research being done on lighting, which rested on the application of existing measuring methods, first had to be conceptualized so that it could steer the practice rather than merely following it.

Alexander Klein paid special attention to "the exploitation of the sun as a source of light and warmth" when planning his Aufbauhaus in 1931. He also produced diagrams for measuring light conditions[17] and used these to analyze the results of "Wachsende Haus" competition,[18] organized by Martin Wagner as Berlin's inspector of buildings for the Berlin trade fair of 1932. Klein railed against the results with a reversal of the Modernists' rallying cry: "No light! No air! No sun! And no house for all!"[19] and fought for

what was still lacking, namely a method of implementing daylight calculations in floor plans. Klein was not the first to remove sunlight from the hygienists' remit so as to make it a subject of relevance to architectural floor plans worthy of research in its own right; but he was certainly the most radical. In his own unique way he formulated those rules for the combination of attributes that would undermine the doctrine of east–west orientation, though without bringing it down altogether. Klein first tried to appropriate sunlight calculations in his diagrams of the light conditions in the Aufbauhaus. His aim was to subject these, too, to a graphical method at floor plan level. The plan combines south-facing main rooms, which are again staggered much as they were in his row house plans of 1927, with wide connecting doors based on the same layout principle as that developed for the access balcony apartment in Bad Dürrenberg. Tak-

12   Lübbert, *2 Jahre Bauforschung*, 1930, p. 28.
13   "Der Wettbewerb der Reichsbauforschung. Aufteilung und Bebauung des Geländes der Forschungssiedlung in Spandau-Haselhorst.," in *Bauwelt* 7, 1929, pp. 137–142, here p. 137.
14   Cf. Winfried Nerdinger, *Walter Gropius*, Berlin 1996, p. 116.
15   Johannes Grobler, "Der heutige Stand der Untersuchungen über die Besonnung," in *Die Baugilde* 15, No. 9 (1933), pp. 315–317, here p. 315.
16   Johannes Grobler, "Beim Zeilenbau ist die Nordsüdrichtung die schlechteste," in *Die Bauzeitung* 66, No. 16 (1932), pp. 315–317, here p. 315.
17   Klein, "Das Aufbauhaus," 1931, p. 1812.
18   Martin Wagner, *Das Wachsende Haus. Ein Beitrag zur Lösung der städtischen Wohnungsfrage*, Berlin/Leipzig 1932.
19   Klein: "Um die Frage 'Das wachsende Haus,'" 1932, p. 305.

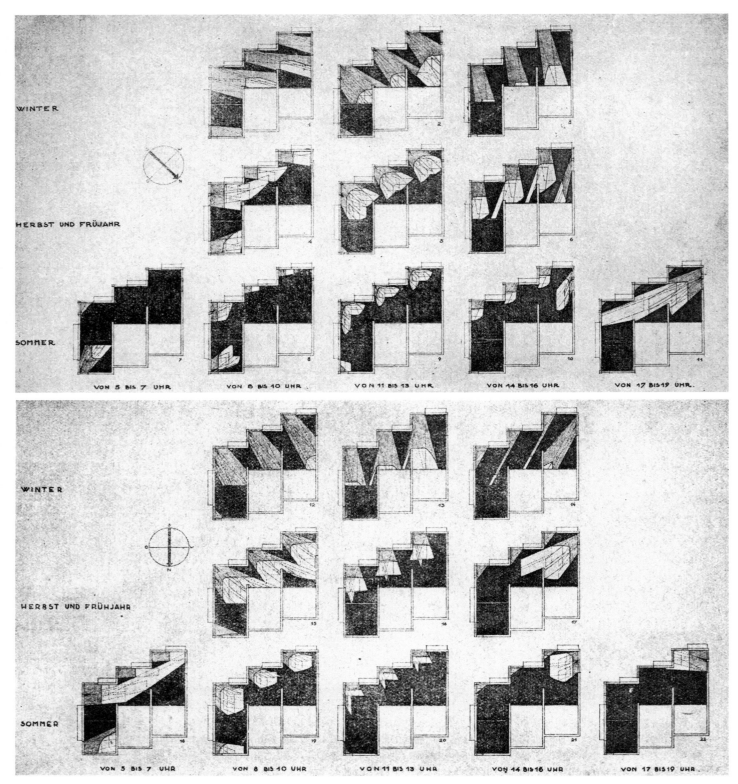

Alexander Klein, drawings I and II of the light conditions in the *Aufbauhaus*, 1931

ing the approach of a laboratory scientist, Klein proceeded to use his plan as an experimental set-up with which, using his graphical method, he was able to measure the effect of a change of orientation and a different arrangement of windows, both of which were factors in the fall of sunlight in the interior. In this way, he was able to ascertain which of the measured parameters yielded the best results. As one of a new breed of "solar scientists," Klein wrote an accompanying text in which he acknowledged the limitations of his experimental set-up and alerted his readers to the difficulties afflicting statistical and graphical analyses of sunlight based on just four days' worth of data collected at a rate of just once an hour. Rather less scientific, however, was the third point that Klein was obliged to concede: namely that he had not been able to take account of "variations in sunlight intensity throughout the year and the distribution of sunlight hours over any given day."[20] Klein, the

"biological master-builder with a scientific mask," as Martin Wagner sneeringly described him in an attack on "Das wachsende Haus,"[21] preferred "a staggered floor plan with diagonals running in a north–south direction."[22] Such a design also demonstrated the advantages of the corner window for maximizing the sunlight hours. This produced a layout with a southeast–southwest orientation, as we can see applied to both the sawtooth type and the access balcony apartment.

One argument in favor of the apartment block typology that surfaced in the demonstration of the 36 and 45 m² floor plan types with two and a half and three and a half beds for buildings with an access balcony, developed by Klein as part of the Reichsforschungsgesellschaft's program of extras and the emergency housing act, was the possibility of putting all the living rooms and bedrooms on the sunny side.[23] In Bad Dürrenberg, for example, Klein created just such an access balcony type rental apartment with just 41.72 m² of floor space (1928–1930). The apartments actually built, now a largely forgotten contribution to the history of architecture, are the most interesting object Klein ever realized. Their large sliding doors—notwithstanding their low lintel—have the effect of aligning the interior with the south-facing façade, which is also the axis along which the living room and bedrooms are arranged. This access balcony type was the first to break Klein's own rules for lines of traffic, according to which an apartment should have no through rooms and be basically divisible into two clearly defined groups. Realizing that sleeping and living functions would have to intersect, Klein shrewdly decided not to visualize the lines of traffic at all. As much as he tried to base his floor plans on scientific data, he had to learn the hard way that new elements soon ruin such findings, the most ruinous element of all, as epistemologists are always eager to stress, being the ephemeral nature of scientific data themselves.[24] When open, the sliding doors allow diagonal lines of sight and spatial relations that Klein would build on in other projects. In his 1934 book, *Das Einfamilienhaus: Südtyp,* he even made a point of seeking the "diagonal tendency of the floor plan composition"[25] that defined the relationship between house and garden and was

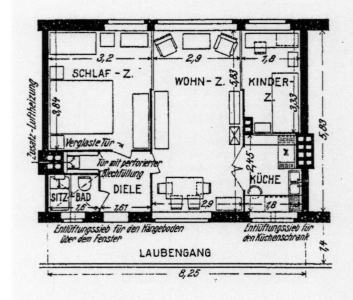

Alexander Klein, "Grundrissstudie im Rahmen des Zusatzprogramms 1930"
three and a half-bed access balcony rental apartment with 45 m² space

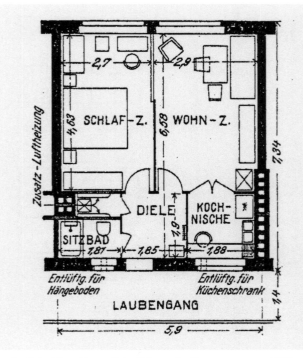

Alexander Klein, "Grundrissstudie im Rahmen des Zusatzprogramms 1930"
two and a half-bed access balcony rental apartment with 35.95 m² space

reflected in the distribution of windows, doors, and furniture. But what mattered most, he wrote, was "to achieve as much spaciousness as possible; that is to say, to prevent any sense of confinement by means of views from one room into another" and, "to connect the apartment to the world outside by means of wide sliding doors and windows arranged accordingly," the idea being "to make the surroundings seem closer while affording views of the same."[26]

Not until over a decade later, during the postwar period, would Karl Böttcher embark on a systematic analysis of the sunlight and furnishing options for apartment floor plans with perpendicular and diagonal walls. This he did by means of diagrams, taking as his benchmark the floor area exposed to sunlight at the winter solstice on December 21. Böttcher assiduously shows the maximum extent of the incident sunlight on the inside walls.[27] This new method, based on Neuzil's projections, redefined the object of study. The question was no longer how the sun traveled, but rather: "Do I have sunlight on this window, on this wall? When? For how long and how much?"[28] In his report, Böttcher, who headed the department of building materials and construction at the Institut für Bauwesen, listed its current and future research projects: "3. Special field: Interior climate studies. a) Theoretical study of the dispersal of direct sunlight indoors as a contribution to the question of adequate exposure to daylight. [...] c) Is there such a thing as meteotropic or solar affectivity? And if so, can it be proven and what does it mean for human habitations?"[29] In his "Studie zu schrägen Innenwänden"[30] of 1949, he studied how the fall of sunlight in rooms with diagonal walls differed from that in perpendicular rooms and produced analytical diagrams of his floor plan III showing the floor and wall area exposed to sunlight on December 21, March 20, June 21, and September 23. One crucial factor influencing incident sunlight, according to Neuzil, was "the size and shape of the window," and its location in the room. He also noted that the "paramount precondition is that the outside wall be exposed to the sun."[31]

Neuzil drew up eight basic rules,[32] of which Scharoun cited the east-west floor plans, which benefited from sunlight on both sides at different times of day, at least as long as they had window fronts facing both east and west—although deviations of up to 22 degrees were admissible—and the east–southeast, south and west–southwest floor plans, which had a sunlit front and permanent shade at the rear.[33] In his third rule, Neuzil developed a paradigm that was to prove decisive for postwar housing, according to which the

20 Klein, "Das Aufbauhaus," in *Die Baugilde* 24, No. 13 (1931), pp. 1807–1813, here p. 1812.
21 Martin Wagner, *Das Wachsende Haus*, Berlin/Leipzig, 1932, p. 29. Following Nietzsche, Wagner characterizes Klein as a conceptual engine of the late nineteenth century "with a souterrain of knowledge-truth-cunning." (Friedrich Nietzsche, *Nachlass 1887–1889,* KSA 13, Munich 1999, p. 303).
22 Klein, "Das Aufbauhaus," 1931, p. 1812.
23 Alexander Klein, "Neue Entwürfe und Studien," in *Die Baugilde* 13, No. 10 (1931), p. 811.
24 Cf. e.g. Gaston Bachelard, "Die Aktualität der Geschichte der Naturwissenschaften," in Hyondok Choe and Gaston Bachelard, *Epistemologie. Bibliographie, Philosophie und Geschichte der Wissenschaften,* Vol., 27, Frankfurt a.M./Bern 1994, pp. 223–228.
25 Klein, "Das Einfamilienhaus: Südtyp," 1934, p. 30.
26 Klein, "Die Kleinwohnung als wirtschaftliches, wohntechnisches und raumgestalterisches Problem," 1931, p. 215.
27 Geist and Kürvers (eds.), *Karl Böttcher,* 1990, p. 70.
28 Walter Neuzil, *Messungen der Besonnung von Bauwerken. Ein neues Messverfahren und seine Anwendung auf die Bebauung,* Berlin 1942, p. 17.
29 Geist and Kürvers (eds.), *Karl Böttcher,* 1990, p. 28.
30 Karl Böttcher, "Studie zu schrägen Innenwänden," TU Berlin, Architekturmuseum, Inv. No. 34398.
31 Walter Neuzil, *Messungen der Besonnung von Bauwerken. Ein neues Messverfahren und seine Anwendung auf die Bebauung,* Berlin 1942, p. 21.
32 Ibid., p. 41.
33 Scharoun, "Notizen," Lecture XI/4, n.d.

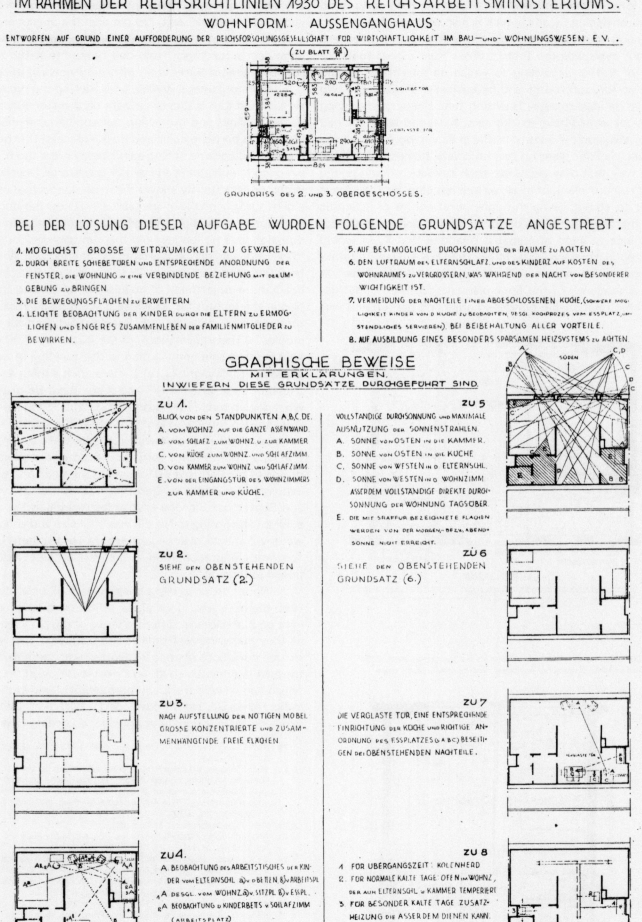

Alexander Klein, graphical analysis of the access balcony floor plan, 45 m²

View through the sliding door of a balcony apartment, Bad Dürrenberg by Alexander Klein

best "incident angle and distance between rows" was achieved by "rows of housing with windows facing either southeast or southwest."[34] Otto Völcker's publication *Neuzeitliche Miethausgrundrisse* features "small apartments in a staggered, asymmetrical arrangement that can be used for both a north–south and an east–west orientation."[35] These were the work of Otto Jäger and were singled out for mention on grounds of their sunny living rooms and the privacy of their balconies. The projects had originated in a competition in the autumn of 1947, the purpose of which was to obtain proposals for future housing projects and the building of experimental housing developments. The competition was organized by the Forschungsgemeinschaft Bauen und Wohnen presided over by Richard Döcker.[36] The advantages of the sawtooth floor plans were cited by Chen-kuan Lee, an

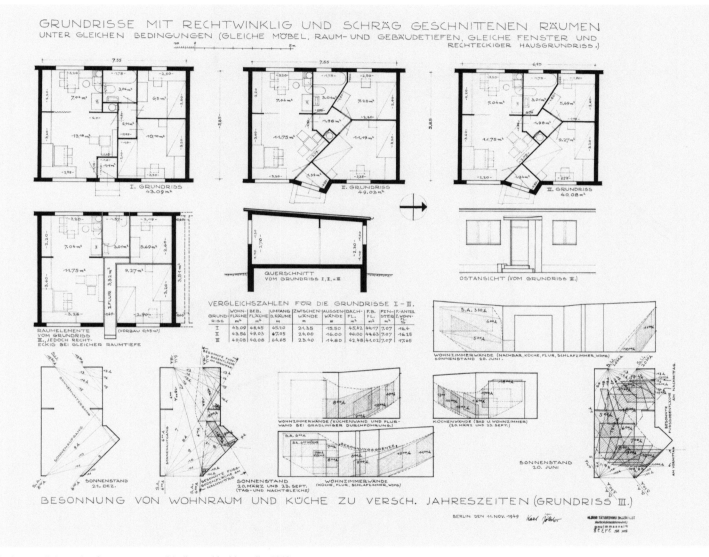
Karl Böttcher, sunlight study of an apartment with diagonal inside walls, 1949

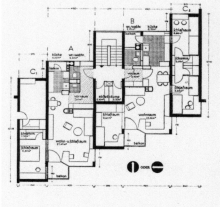

employee in Scharoun's office from 1937 to 1943 and from 1947 to 1953, in support of his argument for the "Akademie" type apartment. "The kink in the apartment," wrote Lee, "allows the available sunlight to be exploited to the full as the east–southwest window fronts, which we know from experience are the best, are facing the sun."[37] The seasoned

34 Walter Neuzil, *Messungen der Besonnung von Bauwerken. Ein neues Messverfahren und seine Anwendung auf die Bebauung,* Berlin 1942, p. 21.
35 Otto Völckers, *Neuzeitliche Miethausgrundrisse,* Veröffentlichung der Forschungsgemeinschaft Bauen und Wohnen (FBW), No. 1. Stuttgart 1947, p. 34.
36 The Forschungsgemeinschaft Bauen und Wohnen (Research Council for Building and Housing), came into being as a charitable foundation of the Land Württemberg-Baden in 1947. It was mandated to study problems of all kinds "to alleviate the shortage of living space and to put building on a modern footing," (Landesarchiv Baden-Württemberg, EL 80).
37 Chen-kuan Lee, "Wie die Wohnungen des Laubenganghauses 'Typ Akademie' funktionieren sollen," in Geist and Kürvers, *Das Berliner Mietshaus* 1989, pp. 420–529, here p. 466.

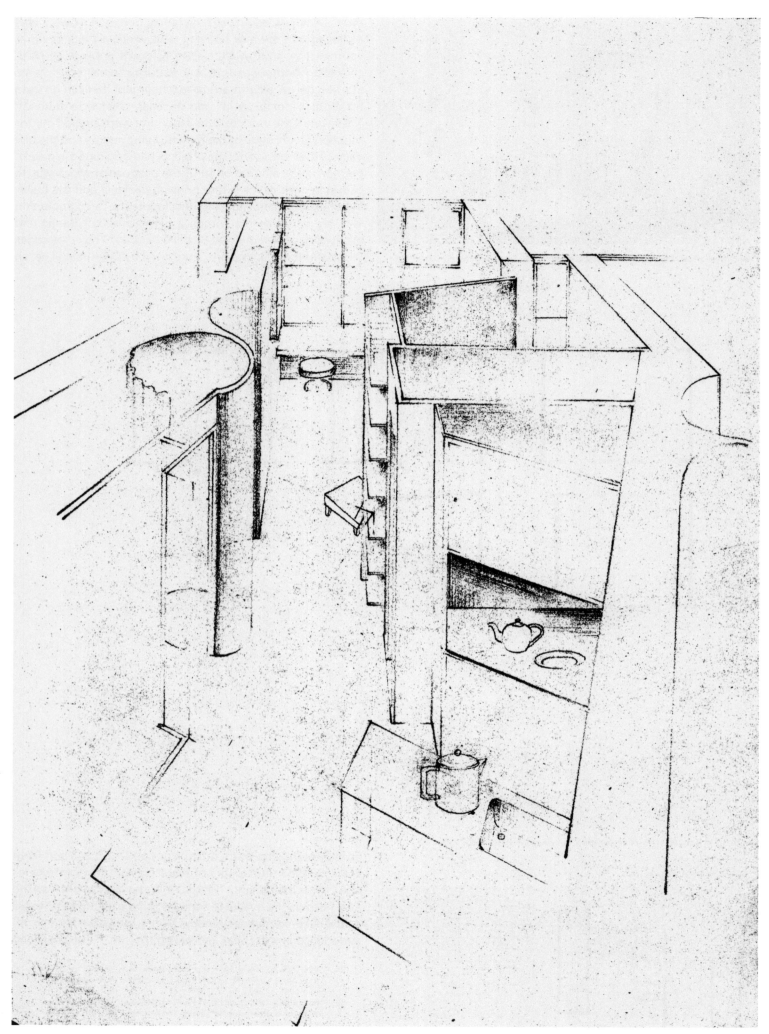

Perspective view of a one-bed access balcony apartment in Friedrichshain, 1949

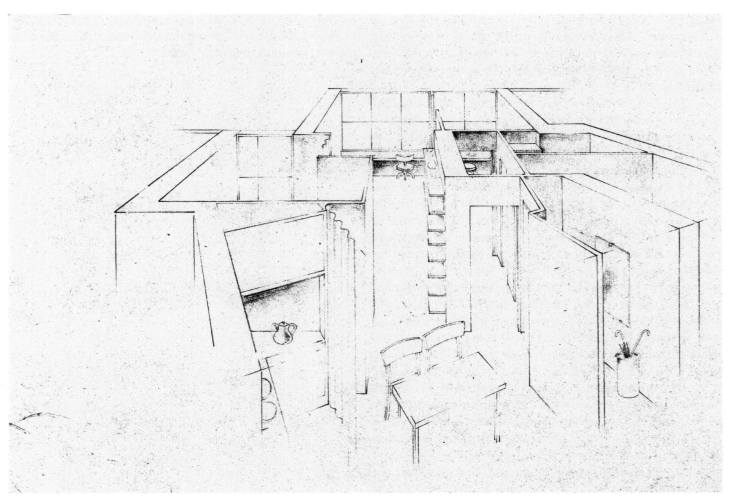

Perspective view of a 3-bed access balcony apartment in Friedrichshain, 1949

designer instantly spotted the diagonal tendency informing this layout: "The kink also allows the relatively small living space to be experienced as larger than it actually is and so expands the interior, which with appropriately proportioned rooms can then be divided up according to function."[38]

In his manuscript on the Berlin-Friedrichshain development of 1949, Scharoun called for "differentiated housing," to be achieved through an "intermingling of low-rise and high-rise types, apartment blocks and single-family dwellings" as a precondition for "spreading the same residential attractions over the whole city." The repertoire he envisaged to this end included some well-known typologies: "[…] larger residential units in multistory blocks, preferably built on a north–south axis, smaller residential units in blocks with access balconies on an east–west axis."[39]

The demand for "clarity in cell formation in the city"[40] led Scharoun to once again revisit his housing studies as part of his endeavor to reactivate the notion of society as growing out of a village-like way of life. The access balconies and galleries of old courtyards or the medieval *Kanzelhäuser* (Dom galeriowy) in Gdansk for him constituted this "cellular" principle. The gallery which, by providing access to the upper story, allowed the layout of the ground-floor apartments to be repeated, was regarded by architectural historians as "such an ancient Germanic motif that one is inclined to regard these *Kanzelhäuser* as older than the houses with inside staircases."[41] In his lectures, Scharoun also referenced southern Germany's courtyard galleries that provided access to rented or owner-occupied apartments. "We know of some spatially pleasing solutions of this kind from the Renaissance and the Baroque."[42] Yet the access balcony or gallery, being exposed to the elements, failed to meet any of the textbook requirements to be made of residential high-rises. According to Hassenplug and Peters, for example, "These forms of access are problematic in our climatic zone as unless the apartment entrances are

treated like the entrance to a house, the access balconies, or at least those in exposed locations, have to be protected at great expense against rain, wind, and snow."[43] But as if his application of access balconies to a residential high-rise were not provocation enough, Scharoun followed it with a whole series of apartments which at either end demonstratively turned away from the optimum sunlight exposure.[44] Yet the access principle was the key to the relationship of the part to the whole. The advantage of the access balcony lay in the comparatively easy connection and direct relationship it permitted between the individual apartment and the building as a whole.

This doubtless explains Scharoun's interest in the horseshoe-shaped collective access system, even if by folding the outer façade to make it almost twice as long as the inner façade facing the access balcony he took the logic underlying the one-sided apartment type to an extreme. In the end, the collective space that is freely accessible only from one side as it stands in Stuttgart-Zuffenhausen provokes a conflict with the much lower, single-story entrance from Haldenrainstrasse to the south, which was intended to be the main entrance to the complex.[45] Not everything is done in the collective space and the access balconies sur-

38 Ibid.
39 Hans Scharoun, "Zur Wohnzelle 'Friedrichshain,'" HSA 2944.
40 Scharoun, "Von der Wohnung zur Gliederung der Stadt," Lecture II/12, May 30, 1950, June 5 & June 8, 1950.
41 Felix Gentzen, *Die Kanzelhäuser und* ähnliche *Miethäuser Alt-Danzigs*, Königsberg 1909, p. 41.
42 Scharoun, Lecture VI/9, July 7, 1952.
43 Gustav Hassenplug, Paulhans Peters, *Scheibe Punkt und Hügel. Neue Wohnhochhäuser*, Munich 1966, p. 25.
44 "You can see this with the Romeo building, which doesn't have that much sun […] but then you can't have everything. One side has more sunshine and the other more shade. […] and back there I have an apartment [in Julia] where sundown is at 11 in the morning, although for that they're surrounded by greenery," conversation with Joachim Zimmermann, Stefan Heise, and Friedrich Mebes about the residential high-rises Romeo and Julia; Markus Peter and Ulrike Tillmann, recorded September 18, 2006 in Berlin-Gatow.
45 Information provided by Peter Faller in the seminar on Romeo und Julia by Ulrike Tillmann and Markus Peter, ETH Zurich 2006.

rounding it form an armature onto which the apartments are mounted. The recesses have the effect of rendering these visible as distinct units just as they assert their individuality in the other direction by facing south, southwest, or southeast.

The history of small apartment floor plans in larger residential developments shows that the relationship between the principles of sunlight exposure and access is defined by the calculation informing the whole. It follows that if all efforts are concentrated on building apartments that face southeast on the one side and southwest on the other, then, logically speaking, the staggering of the apartments along the axis of orientation is inevitable. Such vector-like monsters, with "for the most part axially symmetrical, north–south axes arranged around an access core at the northern end of the building,"[46] are an elegant way of minimizing the costs incurred for the installation of elevators, staircases, waste chutes, and the prescribed fire exits, and at the same time enforce a symmetrical layout. There is a latent symmetry in the compositional rules underlying the design for Julia, in particular, which take as their starting point the dominant stairwell. The affinity to the organic rules of composition that is hinted at here has to do with the laws of symmetry, which according to the popular theories of the philosopher-biologist Ernst Haeckel are inherent in almost all organic forms. This promorphological system permits the appropriation of many symmetrical figures and rotational corpuses, which ingeniously are classified according to the geometric center.[47] On the other hand, one of the distinguishing features of organic forms is that they are based on the repetition of elementary units. It was out of this that Scharoun developed the specific individuality of each apartment that he sought, even if in the case of Romeo and Julia, this was not so much an end in itself as one element in a relationship. Scharoun apprehended society as more than just a random grouping of atomized individuals, since the individual's exercise of autonomy always takes place in relation to others and is enabled by "cooperative institutions of the community."[48]

Here we see how the problem of individuality resurfaces and how the aspect of the whole that originally resisted all forms of division can gain the upper hand over the aspect of fragmentation as the putative end point of division. In an address given on receiving an honorary doctorate from the University of Rome, Scharoun mentioned two of his works: the Berlin Philharmonic (1960–1963) and Julia. What had concerned him in the latter, he explained, was "the 'dwelling process' on which the configuration rests."[49]

As Buber might have said, there could be no development of individuality there without its counterpart: the "'development of genuine sociality.'"[50] ●●

Sketch of the first site plan drafts for Stuttgart, 1954

46 Faller, *Der Wohngrundriss*, 2002, p. 93.
47 Cf. Ernst Haeckel, *Die Lebenswunder. Gemeinverständliche Studien* über *Biologische Philosophie*, Stuttgart 1905, pp. 198–215.
48 Scharoun, Lecture II/8, May 8, 1950.
49 Hans Scharoun, Address on Receiving an Honorary Doctorate in Rome on June 21, 1965, HSA 2907.
50 Scharoun, Lecture II/8, May 8, 1950.

VII Polygonal Apparatus

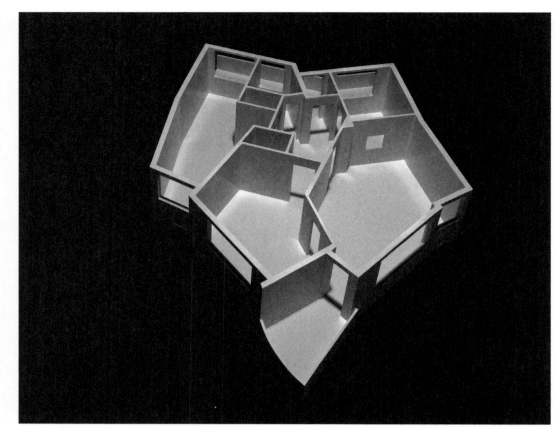

Julia, apartment type 1

"The true is never probable."

Friedrich Nietzsche, *Nachgelassene Fragmente,* 1887–1889[1]

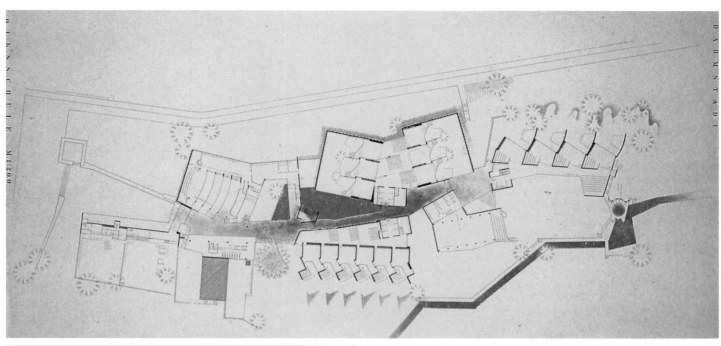

Elementary school, Darmstadt, 1951

Model, 1951

That Hugo Häring left his stamp on Scharoun's thinking as did no other is apparent even in a correction he made to his preliminary remarks on his lectures. There, Scharoun replaced the concept of the "milieu" with Häring's theory of "workspaces."[2] For Scharoun, social milieu forged a link between socioeconomic circumstances and the relative autonomy of domestic cultures; it was what made housing, in the sense of the "dwelling process,"[3] palpable as an "active element" and "indivisible whole, whose design and whose wholeness cease to be the moment any one of the components serving the functions of health, action, and contemplation is suppressed."[4] In a text on his widely discussed design of an elementary school for the exhibition organized as a tie-in with the Darmstädter Gespräche *Mensch und Raum* (literally, "Man and Space") of 1951, Scharoun used the workspace concept in the context of what he called the "schoolscape." His demand that each classroom be articulated as a distinct unit tailored to the developmental stage of the children who were to occupy it, so that their surroundings, "presented as a workspace," might directly influence their burgeoning "emotional, creative, and intellectual powers,"[5] shows him applying Häring's concept without actually shedding light on its specifics.

Yet Häring himself had in fact been very specific, as in his letter to Scharoun on the design research being done at the Institut für Bauwesen (IFB) in Berlin: "I divine more of what you want than I might ever glean from your program. But the goal is cultural morphology in the Spenglerian sense, not the problem of design, which is where the focus should be as far as building is concerned. Design in all its intellectual and technical aspects, the secret of planning and modeling, the function of geometry in construction, the higher function of organic principles as another stage of building, with what come out of the workspaces of certain designs as laws, the authority and the design imperative of these laws etc.—All of this is indeed a field that might supply the institute with content, which by taking the place of the deadly boring and sterile history of art and architecture might shed some light on what the creation of design actually is."[6] After retiring to his attic apartment in Biberach and knowing of their shared interest in this line of inquiry, Häring had written to his friend Scharoun as follows: "Now I have to inspect the Greek and Roman workspace."[7]

Whereas Scharoun's notion of the workspace would remain forever vague, Häring's *"Leistungsform"* (literally, "performance form") offered scope for a more exact un-

1   Friedrich Nietzsche, *Nachgelassene Fragmente 1884–1885,* KSA 11, Munich 1999, p. 30.
2   Scharoun, "Vorbemerkung," Lecture I/1, n.d.
3   Häring recommends developing "a floor plan from the dwelling process," and apprehending the dwelling "as a dwelling body" since "ostentatious furnishings can have no purchase in such a dwelling. What counts is solely the use of the furniture and its design, not its style," (Häring, Hugo, Letter to the West German Housing Minister concerning the problems of modern housing, March 17, 1952, HHA 318). Scharoun took note of this a few months later: "Hugo Häring's demand that we proceed from the dwelling process provides pointers for modern housing," (Lecture VI/7, June 23, 1952).
4   Scharoun, Lecture VII/2, May 18, 1953.
5   Scharoun, "Volksschule," 1951, p. 189.
6   Hugo Häring to Hans Scharoun, February 9, 1948, HSA 431. Häring adds a critical remark to his commentary: "That is a life's work, something that monopolizes all one's powers. You don't have the time for this, or, if I may say so, your restless brain simply does not have the staying power for it—quite apart from the fact that work in this field is not your thing at all."
7   Hugo Häring to Hans Scharoun, ca. 1943, HSA 431.

161

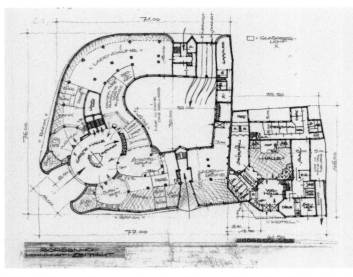

"Börsenhof" competition entry: floor plan of the ground floor of an office building in Königsberg, East Prussia, 1922

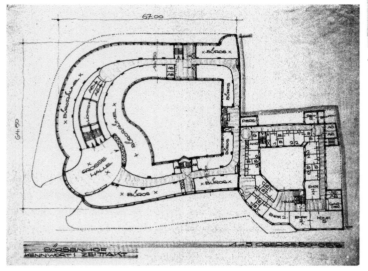

"Börsenhof" competition entry: floor plan of floors 1–5 of an office building in Königsberg, East Prussia, 1922

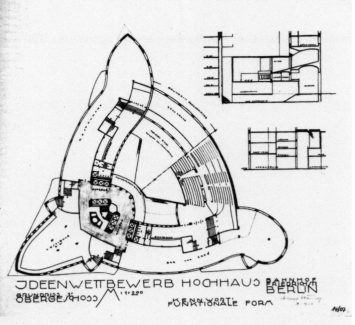

"Hochhaus Bahnhof Friedrichstraße" competition entry: ground floor, 1922

derstanding of the design impetus. This second terminological borrowing from Häring's theoretical frame of reference, Scharoun argued, provided a term with which "our achievements in the field of new building" might be not just summarized but also categorized. It was "currently the only way," he continued, "of arriving at a design that follows its own immanent laws."[8] In one of his first postwar lectures, delivered in both Ulm and Stuttgart, Häring diagnosed the "structural problems of building" as follows: "The concept of *Leistungsform* has uncircumscribed validity in contemporary engineering and has supplanted the concept of *Stilform*."[9] To Häring, aircraft and other such feats of engineering represented the triumph of the organic over the "geometric forces" to which engineering had long been in thrall. The design of all objects of use, all tools, and even the "objects" of civil engineers, were increasingly eluding the clutches of geometry, he said, since their performance forms were "defined by use."[10] The organic-geometric polarity would pervade Häring's thinking right to the end.

The discursive revival of "*Leistungserfüllung*" ("performance fulfillment"),[11] a concept he had coined back in the 1920s, is identical with Adolf Behne's famous definition of functionalism as unconditional adaptation to technical and economic performance, which, if taken to its logical conclusion, would ultimately nullify the concept of form altogether. Yet the use of Behne's "modern purpose-built building"[12] in much the same way as a treatise is used—in other words for paraphrasing or summarizing the commentary—had by then become standard practice in the

teaching of architecture.[13] Häring lent additional weight to Behne's position by repeating his formula of "purpose fulfillment—performance fulfillment—design comes into being,"[14] and in 1948 he revised the paper in which he first set out the "concept of *Leistungsform*."[15] Yet not one of those who referenced this key text on modern architecture saw fit to offer a selection of genuinely heuristic examples of experimentation that might have attested to the importance and impact of Häring's methodological theorizing. Not one of them took the trouble to position the text in the history of architecture, nor did anyone bother to relate Häring's language to his actual practice, which invariably entailed a search for the constants of a given function or use, or at the very least an attempt to translate those problems into geometric space. What should be of interest to us in the history of floor plans is not so much the results of such work, which after all are to be found in all the relevant textbooks on the subject, as the way in which problems are solved, or if not solved, at least formulated. In this study, therefore, the emergence of hypotheses such as those that Häring pondered in his unpublished texts immediately after the war[16] will take precedence over any attempt to take stock of the plans actually drawn.

In the early years of the twentieth century, the debate of the architectural concept of functionalism was shaped largely by the adoption of biological organisms as a model. For biologists like Hans Driesch and Jakob von Uexküll, organisms formed the elementary units of life. As essential processes such as reproduction, regulation, and metabolism were recognized as properties of the organic, so organisms took pride of place alongside cells in the nascent science of biology. Driesch's *Die organischen Regulationen. Vorbereitungen zu einer Theorie des Lebens* was published in Leipzig in 1901 and launched animal biology as a specific object of scientific study in its own right. The author was an embryologist famed for his recourse to the vocabulary of the Aristotelian concepts of ontology and teleology as a means of making philosophical sense of his experimental findings. At Wilhelm Roux's suggestion, the "theory of causes, factors in the differentiation of living beings"[17] was called "developmental mechanics." It is the latter source we have to thank for Behne's famous definition of organic life as knowing neither right angles nor straight lines, and of the same straight lines as actually thwarting the final stage of adaptation to functional mobility and fluidity.[18] Roux's underlying idea supplemented the descendent principle of the struggle for existence, also known as the individual survival strategy, with physiological maxims, according to which the tissue, cells, and cell parts within a given organism were likewise engaged in a constant battle for maximum nourishment. What was new for Roux was the impact of these functions "on the inner organization, on the structure of the organs."[19] The study of natural selection exposed the struggle for existence as the same principle as that governing the organs' adaptation to specific functions and types of performance. Not until relatively late did Roux realize that "self-regulation in the exercise of their performance" in fact constituted "the characteristic of living beings that had hitherto been missing."[20] Behne, who transferred the principle to architecture, proved the point by citing means of access as an example. "When Häring and Scharoun visualize the corridors in their office block floor plans for Berlin and Königsberg not as conduits whose shape remains the same over their entire length irrespective of the volume of traffic they carry, but as paths that must be wider there, where they are used by many, and narrower there, where only a few must pass to reach the last remaining doors, then they are thinking functionally, almost in the sense of Roux's 'developmental mechanics of animal organisms'."[21]

But surely this inquiry into the emergence or discovery of functionalism—and its simultaneous stigmatization by Behne himself, who saw the inevitable consequence of functionalism in "its overdrawn and excessively individualistic corpuses"[22]—had by then already gone awry? Would not corridors modeled on arteries so that they became ever narrower—in other words, corridors adapted to a "unique space and time and personality, but not to an open-ended future, change, and diversity,"[23] as Behne never tired of pointing out—prove hopelessly antifunctional every time there was a change in the preconditions? Or was it not necessary rather to admit that any one organ in an organism can have several functions at once? Can we not agree that there is rather less finality and rather more potentiality in the organism? We might even say that the machine is actually more fit for purpose than the organism, since its finality is set and unambiguous. In the organism, by contrast, we observe what Georges Canguilhem called "a vicariousness of functions, a polyvalence of organs. Doubtless this vicariousness of functions and polyvalence of organs are not absolute, but they are so much greater than in the machine that there can really be no comparison."[24] And so the meaning and the value that are intrinsic to every experiment with organic architecture, no matter how audacious or how doomed to failure it is, are changed—inevitably, and profoundly. But the gap between theory and practice is wide, and in architecture in particular, it is not easy to prove that the results obtained really do derive from the theories cited in support of the floor plan method applied, especially when it is the theory that elucidates and defines the practice, as is the case with Häring's architecture.

The hypothesis of the polyvalence of spaces and "vicariousness of functions" first trickled down into Häring's theoretical writings in 1952, when he declared that "genetically speaking," the minimum dwelling was best developed by growing a "one-room apartment" rather than by cutting a much larger apartment down to size. After all, with the exception of the kitchen, the spaces in such an apartment were not tied to any one function, but could be "used for all manner of things, not just one prescribed purpose."[25] The specifics of performance fulfillment are not bound by the specifics of a given space in floor plan design. As far as the polyvalence of spaces is concerned, it should be pointed out that only rarely do we inquire which other functions might be fulfilled by those rooms that we traditionally associate with one specific function. This was a position rejected by Alexander Klein, who, as Scharoun noted, adopted Gustav Wolf's "staggered floor plan" concept[26] and insisted that the rooms of "every one of today's floor plans should be viewed not as 'variable,' that is to say, arbitrary, but rather as usable for one predefined purpose [...] The tenant of an apartment frequently uses the rooms at his disposal for purposes very different from those envisaged in the plans, and frequently without impairing domestic culture in any way."[27]

It was on this last undogmatic redefinition of the polyvalence of residential floor plans that Häring began working immediately after the war. As surprising as his use of the rhetorical technique of catachresis in a piece on floor plan epistemology may be, the rather bald heading "Floor Plan Potato 2" blazoned on the first page of his manuscript of "grundrisse und ihre probleme"[28] was to be followed by "Potatoes 3 and 4." One of the said "potatoes" is the now legendary drawing known as the "Home of H.H.," which Behne discussed, along with countless other historical examples, in his didactic pamphlet *Eine Stunde Architektur* of 1928. Its purpose there was to demonstrate the "complete adaptation to life"[29] as the ultimate objective of all building. According to Behne, there could be no talk of dwelling unless "the house is no longer apprehended as a

8   Scharoun, "Landesplanung," Lecture I/21, n.d.
9   Häring, "strukturprobleme des bauens," 1946.
10 Häring, "über das geheimnis der gestalt," 1954.
11 Häring, "Wege zur Form," 1925, pp. 3–5.
12 Behne, *Der moderne Zweckbau,* (1923) 1964.
13 Its persistence is borne out by Adrian Forty, who for the definition of "Function" in his "Vocabulary of Modern Architecture" borrows Behne's hyperbolic critique of functionalism as an "excess of individuality" almost word for word (Forty, *Words and Buildings* 2000, p. 183). The charge of insufficient flexibility with regard to future changes of purpose has likewise remained caught in a discursive loop. One exceptionally dogmatic example is Heinz Hirdina, according to whom, the "more exactly the functionalist meets the needs of the individual, all the more certain it is that he will fail to meet the needs of society." Functionalism, for him, stands with the organic curve as an individual and isolated form, as opposed to the mechanical forms of rationalism, whose right angles enable "the coming together of forms and hence typologized or standardized forms," (Heinz Hirdina, "Funktionalismus," in Karlheinz Barck, et al. [eds.], *Ästhetische Grundbegriffe. Historisches Wörterbuch in sieben Bänden, Vol. 2: Dekadent–Grotesk.* Stuttgart/Weimar 2001, pp. 588–608, here p. 600).
14 Häring, "Wege zur Form," 1925, pp. 3–5.
15 Häring, "Die Idee der Leistungsform," n.d.
16 Häring, "grundrisse und ihre probleme," 1946, and Häring, "grundrisse," 1946.
17 Wilhelm Roux (ed.), *Terminologie der Entwicklungsmechanik der Tiere und Pflanzen. Eine Ergänzung zu den Wörterbüchern der Biologie, Zoologie und Medizin sowie zu den Lehr- und Handbüchern der Entwicklungsgeschichte, allgemeine Biologie und Physiologie,* with Carl Correns, Alfred Fischel, and Ernst Küster, Leipzig 1912, p. 128.
18 Behne, *Der moderne Zweckbau,* (1923) 1964.
19 Wilhelm Roux, *Der Kampf der Teile im Organismus. Ein Beitrag zur Vervollständigung der mechanischen Zweckmäßigkeitslehre,* Leipzig 1881, p. 27.
20 Wilhelm Roux, "Die Selbstregulation, ein charakteristisches und nicht notwendig vitalistisches Vermögen aller Lebewesen," in *Nova Acta Leopoldine,* Vol. 100, No. 2 (1914), pp. 4–89, here p. 12.
21 Behne, *Der moderne Zweckbau,* (1923) 1964, p. 43.
22 Ibid., p. 47.
23 Ibid., p. 52.
24 Georges Canguilhem, *Knowledge of Life,* trans. Stefanos Geroulanos and Daneila Ginsburg, New York 2008, p. 89. Häring, however, does not distinguish between machines and organs. Rather, in his conceptual model, the machine comes ever closer to nature, "which in many ways it already resembles [...] and to which it will one day be inferior only to the extent that it is not self-renewing in the way that nature is," (Häring, *Kunst- und Strukturprobleme des Bauens,* 1931, pp. 429–432).
25 Hugo Häring, Letter to the West German Housing Minister concerning the problems of modern housing, March 17, 1952, HHA 318.
26 Wolf, *Die Grundriss-Staffel,* 1931, p. 15.
27 Hans Scharoun, "Die Bezeichnung von Wohngebäuden und Wohnungen," Lecture, n.d., HSA 4455.
28 Häring, "grundrisse und ihre probleme," 1946.
29 Behne, *Eine Stunde Architektur,* 1928, p. 7.

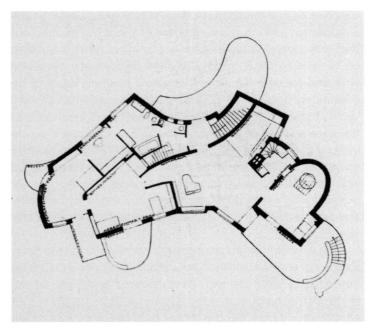

Floor plan of the upstairs of the home of H.H., 1924

monument subject to a canon of forms, but rather as an instrument that molds itself most malleably to the will to live and the human way of life."[30] As Bruno Reichlin so presciently emphasized, what stood out in this concept of 1923 was "the idea of spatial continuity, in which every room or every space extends into the next, in which a curved wall suggests a threshold etc. Just look at the living area available: Where does the music corner end and the fireplace niche begin? What does the recessed corner of the living area tell us? And what are we to make of a living room that tapers off into the boudoir, and that by doing so cuts off the library niche from the desk standing at the window?"[31] To grasp the complexity of Häring's plans, it is no longer enough to follow Franco Borsi and Giovanni Klaus Koenig, who claimed they could be understood only by bearing in mind the function assigned to each room.[32] Häring's notes "Zur Wohnung" talk of what he calls "interchangeable space" and of the "need for space and its usability" to be derived from the various life functions, specifically recreation, the pursuit of knowledge and study, the service of friendship, the service of social functions."[33]

The 45.2 m² apartment that Häring designed for the exhibition *Wie Wohnen* ("How to Live"), held in the immediate aftermath of the "Competition for the Promotion of Modern Furniture-Making" in Stuttgart in 1949, had two projecting bays in the façade, four normal doors, four sliding doors to the kitchen and living area, and two curtains partitioning off the sleeping areas. Flexible partitioning was crucial to Häring's concept of the small apartment "dwelling process," which was premised on the inhabitants being able to "isolate themselves, whether to work or to rest."[34] The second projecting bay with inside alcove contained a workspace built into the angled façade, generating an atmosphere that recalled Häring's own description of his attic apartment in Biberach as "a friendly place to sit and drink tea with a chaise longue for naps."[35] The zoning of an apartment in terms of depth harks back to Häring's studies of medium-sized and small apartments of 1924, which were organized so that the vestibule, bathroom, and dressing room formed the first layer, and the kitchen, entrance, and bed niche the second, which opened straight onto the living room and bedroom. With an inside length of 8.80 m, the façade was unusually long and during the day remained open or could be partitioned off according to function. That first formulation of the decoupling of a window's many different functions—as a source of ventilation, light, and a view—and the development of a bedroom deep inside the apartment with no more than a skylight and a "closet column" for ventilation would resurface, twenty-five years later, in the visible refusal of a window in the sleeping area along the façade; hence the need for closet ventilation. Häring's positioning of the beds along a north-south axis, moreover, hints at the increasingly esoteric conceptual world that had manifested itself in the studies of Chinese housing that he and Scharoun, Chen-kuan Lee, and John Scott had conducted in Berlin during the war.[36] The demand that the bedrooms be usable as living space and/or workspace during the day changed the specifications to be made of the furniture: "The bed should be made so that it can be used as seating during the day or even converted into a desk."[37] Furniture, for Häring, was no less essential to the transformation of the "dwelling process." That all his projects, from his early historicist Römer House and his coun-

Model apartment at the *Wie Wohnen* exhibition, 1949

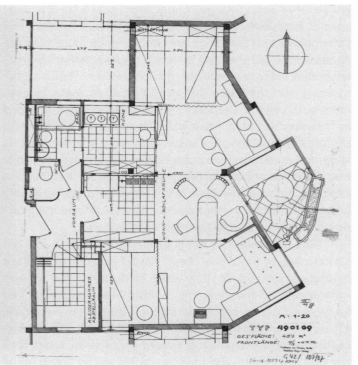

Floor plan of a 45.2 m² apartment developed to showcase furniture at the *Wie Wohnen* exhibition in Stuttgart, 1949

try house to his demonstration of a three-room apartment with central corridor at the *Wie Wohnen* exhibition in Stuttgart in 1949, were furnished at the planning stage is thus not surprising.

Returning to the specific difficulties that arose as a result of Häring's claim that organic building has nothing to do with "the imitation of organic works in the world of nature,"[38] it makes sense to examine, on the basis of a concrete example, exactly which methodological precautions the organic architect must build into his experimental approach, given the specificity of the technical purposes being answered. Behne's surest pole star, that of "purely objective, necessary, extra-aesthetic design,"[39] meant making the building an utterly subordinate tool.[40] And there can be no doubt that to his mind, the chair from Schloss Friedrichsdorf or the armchair by Heinz and Bodo Rasch that he also included in his *Eine Stunde Architektur* pamphlet, were likewise tools. Häring's reflections on modern housing and on modern furniture-making included the following: "Every home should have a small room for storing all those things that are not actually in use, such as items of clothing, linens, boxes, suitcases etc., without any special cupboards being required to this end."[41] This "room in a room" concept spelled the end of the interior shaped by furniture, as Josef Frank had predicted it would back in 1923, when he noted that the movable tables and chairs that remained once everything else had been stowed away could exert "no influence at all, since they are put in the room as if by chance and have no fixed place there. Each of these items therefore has to be independent of the others."[42] True to the spirit of this radical rejection of the "suite," that is to say, of the set of items of furniture which, although different in type, are nevertheless matched so that they belong together, Häring dutifully argued that "furniture in its totality" should rather "form a community of pleasingly shaped single pieces."[43] Just how attentive Häring was to developments in Vienna is evident from his remarks on the Werkbund's exhibition in Vienna-Lainz, and the furniture designs of Frank, Wlach, and Strand on show there, which to his mind showed "no tendency at all toward a formal, architectural style of interior design." Vienna, in other words, had accomplished "what has long been demanded but not yet accomplished in Germany."[44]

It was not just the burning topicality of the small apartment in the immediate aftermath of the war that induced Häring to publish a whole raft of studies on it; he was also driven by his determination to see his three-decades-long project through to completion in the form of an enduring contribution to the advancement of small apartment floor plans. Even if building contractors were still "a long way away from building such houses," he wrote, "these studies still look ahead to where the design problems of the future will lie."[45] In a design project of August 1945, Häring stacked eight duplex apartments to create a slightly set-back residential block. The apartments are lined up along an inside corridor, which points south and has a two-story office block at its northern end. But his first real central-corridor-type building with apartments lined up along the north–south axis of a linear corpus was the one he designed for a residential project in Friedrichshafen in 1949.[46] This study envisaged twenty residential units with communal spaces at the northern end of the complex. The apartments facing either southeast or southwest might be one of two types, both of which were 9 m long and either 5.5 m or 5 m deep. The *rue intérieure,* kitchens, and bed niches were to be illuminated by symmetrical atriums. According to the plans of January 10, 1949, these atriums were to provide

access to the three-story building, too, although this idea was dropped in favor of a central entrance the very next day. The atriums limited the application of this floor plan type to buildings of a certain height only, but at the same time drew attention to the problem of how the inside space of three or four-bed apartments with only one façade might be used. Häring thus rekindled the dormant debate of the "southern type," i.e. the south-facing dwelling, and in the draft of his text "grundrisse und ihre probleme" concluded that building styles had never really addressed the problem of sunlight: "Yet the value of sunlight to living spaces is still not accorded the importance it deserves either in floor plan design or in construction."[47] Improved exposure to sunlight could be achieved by opening up two 30-degree "flaps" in the façade and inserting a balcony into the corner thus created. The critics of the east–west orientation of linear buildings favored in the 1920s had either fallen silent during the economic crisis of the early 1930s and the period of fascist tyranny that followed, or, like Alexander Klein, had emigrated to Israel.

Scharoun studied Häring's design in great detail and immediately spotted the potential of this floor plan type, which promised to be far more than just an alternative to the *rue intérieure* proposed by Häring's lifelong rival, Le Corbusier, and which with its southwest–southeast layout softened the monolithic impression made by the closed corpus. Residential units in multistory linear buildings accessed via an inside corridor generally have only one window front and hence have to cope with the problem of no cross-ventilation—which at least in Modernist terminology constitute a major disadvantage; the same problem also afflicts blocks in which four apartments are accessed from a single landing. Inside corridors permit residential units on both sides, making this access principle unbeatable in terms of both the efficient use of space and ease of access—at least for very small residential units and above all for rooms and apartments in hotels and residential homes. Examples of such buildings from the United States, Sweden, and the Soviet Union from the early days of Neues Bauen were included in the collection of floor plans that supplemented the

30 Adolf Behne, "Luxus oder Komfort?" in *Das Neue Frankfurt* 3, No. 1 (1928), pp. 6–7.
31 Bruno Reichlin, "Mies' Raumgestaltung: Vermutungen zu einer Genealogie und Inspirationsquellen," in Reichlin and Stiller, *Das Haus Tugendhat*, 1999, pp. 53–64, here p. 55.
32 Borsi and Koenig, *Architettura dell'espressionismo*, 1967, p. XX.
33 Hugo Häring, "Zur Wohnung," HHA 1005.
34 Häring, "Wettbewerb zur Förderung des neuzeitlichen Möbelbaus" in which he explains the thinking behind a competition for the promotion of modern furniture-making.
35 Hugo Häring to Hans Scharoun, ca. 1943, HSA 431.
36 Hugo Häring, Hans Scharoun, Chen-kuan Lee, John Scott, minutes of a meeting held on November 14, 1941, HHA 996. Chen-kuan Lee founded the Chinese Werkbund with the support of both Häring and Scharoun in 1941. In one of his lectures, Scharoun made the following remark: "Hugo Häring positions the beds on a north–south axis and elevates this position of the beds to yet another fundamental for the structure of the dwelling. Apprehended as a process and as rhythm and recreation, this has to do with the activities most essential to living space in the West." (Lecture IX/16, February 27, 1956)
37 Häring, "Disposition für ein arbeitsprogramm des fachausschusses nr. IX der forschungsgemeinschaft bauen u. wohnen."
38 Häring, "geometrie und organik," 1951, p. 12.
39 Behne, *Der moderne Zweckbau*, (1923) 1964, p. 41.
40 "The pole which building approximates is the perfection of the instrument," (Behne, *Eine Stunde Architektur*, 1928, p. 7).
41 Häring, Erläuterungstext "Wettbewerb zur förderung des neuzeitlichen möbelbaus."
42 Josef Frank, "Einzelmöbel und Kunsthandwerk," in *Innendekoration* 34 (1923), pp. 241–243 and pp. 336–343, here p. 337.
43 Hugo Häring, "Bemerkungen zum grundriss- und möbelproblem," IX 1949, HHA 1005.
44 Häring, "Bemerkungen zur Werkbundausstellung Wien-Lainz," p. 205.
45 Häring, "grundrisse und ihre probleme," 1946.
46 "A natural order will ensue in which the striving to position oneself in relation to the sun will have such an impact that the house will radiate southward and from east to west, while turning its back on the north. It will behave like a plant that turns its organs to face the sun," (Häring, "arbeit am grundriss," 1952, p. 22).
47 Häring, "grundrisse und ihre probleme," 1946.

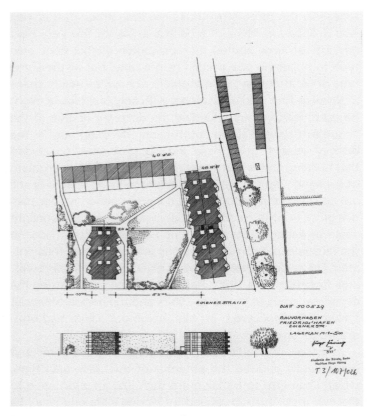

Hugo Häring, site plan of the Friedrichshafen project, 1950

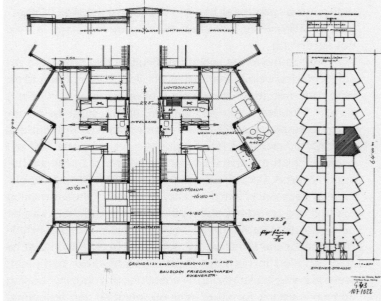

Hugo Häring, floor plan of the residential story of the Friedrichshafen project, 1950

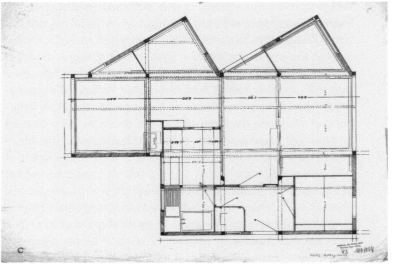

Floor plan of a central corridor-type, four-bed apartment with 50.9 m²

report on the second CIAM conference on "The Minimum Dwelling."[48] One of the most spectacular and most lucid examples, however, was undoubtedly the project for small urban dwellings that was developed by Hans Scharoun in late 1929 for Heidelberger Platz in Berlin, but was never actually built. The complex comprising 138 one- and two-room apartments, without kitchen facilities but with a restaurant, a store, a hairdresser, and a communal hall on the ground floor, undoubtedly belongs in the aforementioned lineage of those urban dwelling types that come closest to a hotel. The plans show two-room apartments organized along a central corridor that for the first time in Scharoun's oeuvre have an angled façade and are zoned in terms of depth. This combination of techniques enabled Scharoun to break with the conventional dimensions of this type of dwelling, while the elongated façade had the effect of flooding the south- or at least southwest- or southeast-facing living area with daylight. The small trapezoid space created by Scharoun's axial rotation of the apartments in the Heidelberger Platz project was partitioned off by means of a curtain and declared a workspace. The discerning reader will discover in this apartment, which is barely 40 m² in size, a circulation principle that returns the inside movement to the living area via the loggia.

That Scharoun's Romeo and Julia marked his emancipation from Häring's guiding principles is especially apparent in his adoption of steel-frame construction and the application of the grid as organizing principle. Let us first recount the development of Häring himself, who like many other Modernists followed the broad technical consensus in his Berlin-Wedding housing project of 1929 by blithely switching to steel-frame construction with little heed for the difficulties thus entailed. With teleological hyperbole, he even went so far as to equate the shift "from solid to skeleton construction" with that "from the crystalline structure to the vertebral structure."[49] The 45.2 m² apartment type that he designed for the Friedrichshafen project twenty years later still rested on a skeleton-type building with a grid of 4.5 m long and 2.75 m or 2.25 m wide. Here, he sup-

plemented the façade support in the inside corner of the angled façade with a round post on the same axis and used these two uprights as the endpoints of a sliding partition. Häring's plans show him cushioning geometry's "formative imperative" in favor of rational building methods in a strikingly unspectacular way: the insertion of an angled support as a load-bearing structure for the angled façade. Even if organic building ran up against its own limitations in what Häring called the "space of mass,"[50] the perpendicularity that he associated with steel-frame construction was to be respected solely as a technical principle that left "ample scope for the demands of dwelling itself to shape the interior design."[51]

Here he was in agreement with Mies van der Rohe, who in his famous emblematic text on the Werkbund exhibition *Die Wohnung* of 1927 identified the steel skeleton as a realization of the relationship between the individual and the type, since its standardized steel sections made it the only construction method that allowed both rational manufacture and complete freedom with regard to the organization of the interior space.[52] By inviting twenty-nine interior designers, among them thirteen members of the Schweizer Werkbund headed by Max Ernst Haefeli, to furnish six apartments in section A1 of the Stuttgart development, Mies elevated steel-frame construction from an abstract principle to a high-profile demonstration of difference. In the apartment that he himself furnished, he demonstrated a system of stud walls made of plywood that allowed the space to be partitioned independent of the system of steel supports. But since he did not come anywhere close to the minimum number of beds required (and delivered by the other participants), his interiors shaped by movable plywood partitions came to be associated with the luxury of a fluid spatial continuum.

Several years later, Jobst Siedler, a member of the Reichsforschungsgesellschaft and author of its bulletin no. 10, "Verwendung des Eisens zum Wohnungsbau" ("The Use of Iron to Build Housing") as well as various other profound articles on steel-frame construction, blamed its failure not on the engineering itself, but on organizational issues. Since it entailed "coordinating two separate work processes, first the assembly of the steel skeleton and then its infill with ceiling and wall panels inserted between the horizontal and vertical rods and beams,"[53] the method was prone to complications. His rhetorical question, "What are the general advantages of steel-frame construction?" was intended to show that one of its key advantages—that it allowed inside walls to be defined by function and to be made of a wide range of materials, each of which might be limited in itself, but was still infinitely superior to the homogeneous materials of conventional construction—could quickly become its greatest disadvantage. For contrary to Mies's cryptic dictum that "architecture starts when you carefully put two bricks together"—which had perhaps led an entire generation astray—the difficulties afflicting modern engineering arose out of its joining together of radically different materials. The walls of Häring's residential development

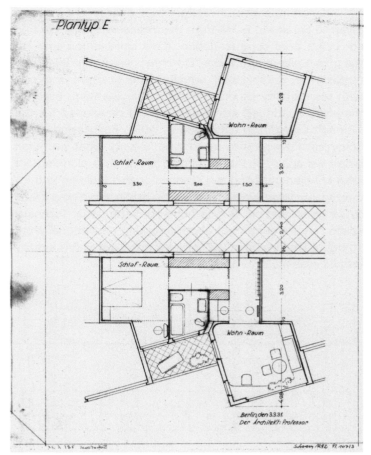

Design of a small apartment for a building with a central corridor, 1931

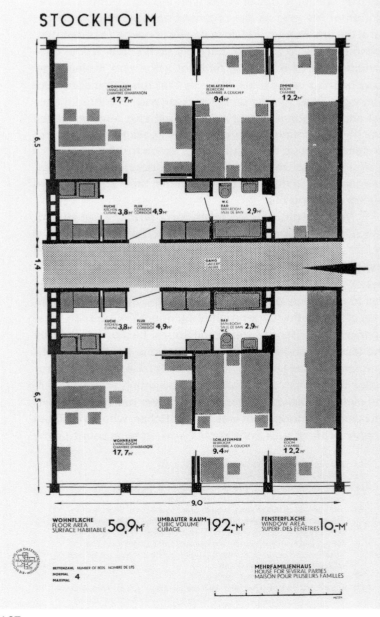

Floor plan of a central corridor-type, four-bed apartment of 50.9 m²

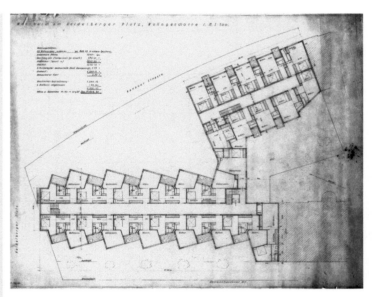

Design for a residence on Heidelberger Platz, 1929

in Berlin were essentially made up of several layers: an "outer skin of no more than a few centimeters thick broken down into various layers fulfilling various functions," as he himself described it.[54] This composite wall was the work of Karl Böttcher, who, starting on the inside with 5-cm-thick pumice board, first added a layer of peat insulation that would also sheathe the steel frame and only then an outer shell made of bricks paired together horizontally and vertically in a basket-weave pattern.

48 Internationale Kongresse für Neues Bauen and Städtisches Hochbauamt Frankfurt a.M. (eds.), *Die Wohnung für das Existenzminimum*, 1930.

49 Häring, "Kunst-und Strukturprobleme des Bauens," 1931, p. 430.

50 Häring, "Kunst- und Strukturprobleme des Bauens," 1931, pp. 429–432.

51 Hugo Häring, "grundrisse," November 16, 1946, HHA 1005/6.

52 Ludwig Mies van der Rohe, "Zu meinem Block," in Behrens and Deutscher Werkbund (eds.), *Bau und Wohnung* 1927, pp. 77–83.

53 Eduard Jobst Siedler, "Der Stahlskelettwohnungsbau," in *Die Baugilde* 12, No. 4 (1930), pp. 317–325, here p. 318.

54 Häring, "Versuch einer Orientierung," 1932, p. 219. Karl Böttcher explains the technical background to wall construction in Geist and Kürvers (eds.), *Karl Böttcher*, 1990, pp. 24f.

If, continuing our investigation, we follow the mention given to Scharoun in Häring's theoretical writings, we find not just a brief commendation of his competition entry to the urban planning project "Durchbrüche durch die Ministergärten in Berlin 1926," which was concerned primarily with the mobility aspects of traffic management, but also the aforementioned elementary school developed for the *Mensch und Raum* exhibition of 1951. For Häring, what Scharoun's design expressed was "exactly what we mean when we speak of the 'organic' [...] The first planning act here entailed studying the essence of this building and inquiring into what would be going on inside it and how it was to serve education. It was not about the usual technical space requirements, but about adopting educational work as a goal. The design of the complex grew out of this inquiry into its essence."[55]

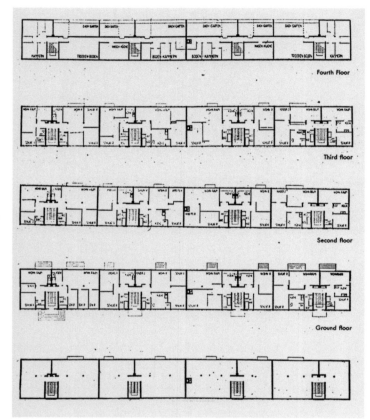

Ludwig Mies van der Rohe, variant floor plans for the residential block at the Weissenhof Estate, Stuttgart, 1927

Notwithstanding their many points in common, however, the focus of our attention in what follows will not be the like-mindedness of Hans Scharoun and Hugo Häring postulated by Blundell Jones, among others.[56] Rather, we shall take a closer look at how Scharoun's proposals for small apartment floor plans became an ever more creative law unto themselves. Scharoun's urban planning studies for the Tor Siemensstadt development of 1952 show him revisiting aspects of Häring's plans for the Friedrichshafen project. Not only was the façade again angled out—this time by sixty degrees—to the southeast and southwest, but Scharoun rotated the whole apartment with it, and not just the projecting bays in the façade. This geometric, spatial tensioning of an orthogonal layout and the rotation on which it is premised took the sawtooth type of the Berlin-Friedrichshain development a stage further. The apartment floor plans convey very vividly the refraction thus effected, which is visible both in the acute angles of the apartment walls next to the bed niche and in the more subtle shifts in the walls defining the entrance, bathroom, and kitchen.

As he refined his plans for the residential high-rise Tor Siemensstadt, Scharoun elected not to subject it to the principles of linear expandability and the overlapping of orthogonal and trapezoidal layouts that had characterized the first draft. The distance between premonition and anticipation matches exactly the distance separating Häring from Hans Scharoun. Scharoun's plans seem increasingly to follow the third decree of Lord Bad Taste in Carlo Emilio Gadda's allegorical tale, *Plan of Milan: Dignity of Palaces,* in which the said sovereign and his consort Lady Tedium impose all sorts of prohibitions on the architects of the new city they are planning: study trips to Rome are outlawed, as is the viewing of any buildings by Palladio and the creation of square or round piazzas. Also banned are "the sixty-degree angle, the ninety-degree angle, and the halving of the same, as well as all rows and straight lines."[57]

Increasingly apparent in Scharoun's experiments is that what was behind his ever more emphatic, categorical rejection of all things geometrical was his growing realization that the capacity of engineering to adapt to its surroundings is essentially heteropoietic and that only after overcoming a long succession of obstacles and acknowledging their own errors can humans succeed in transferring biology's autopoietic[58] genetic processes to the processes by which human exo-organs are created. The forms through which a purpose is fulfilled do not come about "naturally and as it were anonymously," as Häring had hoped they would in his *Wege zur Form.*[59] Concealed behind Scharoun's oft invoked rejection of the right angle is his true epistemological break with the past, namely his rejection of the grid as the organizational mode of architectural design. Romeo and Julia were supposed to prove that, when it came to housing, not only could steel-frame construction be to a large extent set aside and replaced by load-bearing wall panels, but also that this same construction logic, in an almost unspectacular way, admitted diagonal and polygonal spatial systems without any resistance worthy of mention. The architectural space that Scharoun's sketches open up turns out to be a space for the creation of oblique-angled objects, which trickle down into the engineering plans in the form of intersected, tapered, and kinked reinforced concrete.

What might now be taken for a strategy, given how successful this approach to housing would later become, is in fact no more than the retrospective illusion of a targeted line of inquiry. Scharoun's design experiments are actually better described as "a 'blind tactic' [...] that to find its way has to rely solely on the resonance of the available possibilities of generating experimental signifiers."[60] One such "resonance" is evident in the architectural battles sparked by the technical and economic specifications for the competition for a senior citizens' home in Berlin-Tiergarten, the revision of which in 1953 had the participating architects falling over themselves to come up with ever more experimental designs. Among them was Karl Böttcher, who formulated a whole raft of wall constructions to "take account of the

55 Häring, "geometrie und organik," 1951, p. 18.
56 Blundell Jones, *Hans Scharoun,* 1980.
57 Carlo Emilio Gadda, "Pianta di Milano. Decoro dei Palazzi," first published in *L'Ambrosiano* on January 7, 1936.
58 The concept of autopoiesis, which refers to a system capable of reproducing and maintaining itself, was first coined by the neurobiologists Humbert R. Maturana and Francisco Valera. (Humbert R. Maturana and Francisco Varela, *Autopoiesis and Cognition: The Realization of the Living,* Boston Studies in the Philosophy and History of Science, Vol. 42, Boston 1980).
59 Häring, "Wege zur Form," 1925, p. 3.
60 Hans-Jörg Rheinberger and Michael Hagner, "Experimentalsysteme," in idem (eds.), *Experimentalisierung des Lebens. Experimentsysteme in den biologischen Wissenschaften 1850/1950,* Berlin 1993, p. 16.

Steel-frame construction of Hugo Häring's residential block in Berlin-Wedding, November 1930

Façade of the residential block

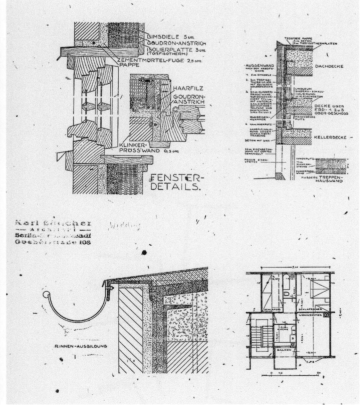

Karl Böttcher, details of Hugo Häring's residential block in Berlin-Wedding, 1930

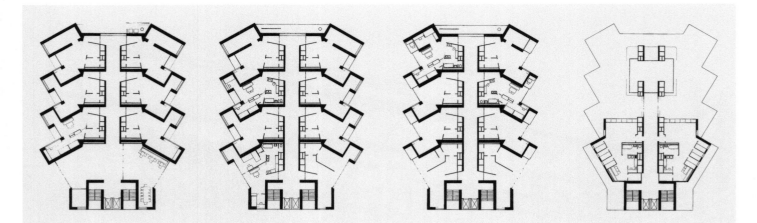

Design of the "Tor Siemensstadt" high-rise, 1950

Perspective view of the "Tor Siemensstadt" high-rise, 1950

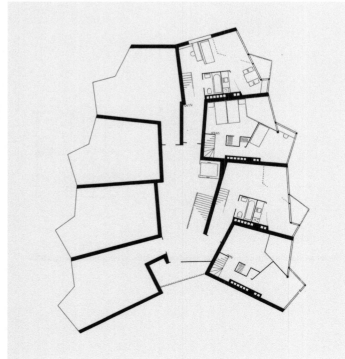

Design II of the "Tor Siemensstadt" high-rise, 1950

most diverse functional requirements such as sound-proof-ing, thermal insulation, thermal radiation, fire safety [...] heat storage, and much more besides,"[61] albeit without be-ing able to prevent yet another project by Scharoun from being shelved. Steel-frame construction could no longer bear comparison with privileged solid-wall structures whose inside or outside insulation preferably took the form of lightweight, wood-wool panels, which when rendered formed a coherent system.

For Scharoun's next building, in other words for Ro-meo and Julia, this knowledge would form the crucial pre-condition within an extremely risky floor plan operation. It was Wolfgang Triebel who undertook the scientific system-atization of solid-wall structures and who from 1957 to 1959 published a series of booklets on the subject for the Federal Housing Ministry.[62] Cast concrete, as the second of the methods listed, had been widely used even in the 1920s, despite the high costs incurred for erecting and dismantling the necessary formwork. As spokesman for the advisory board of the Reichsforschungsgesellschaft, Max Taut told of a comparison of hollow pumice concrete blocks and poured and stamped concrete with an iron frame implemented at an experimental development in Munich.[63] During construc-

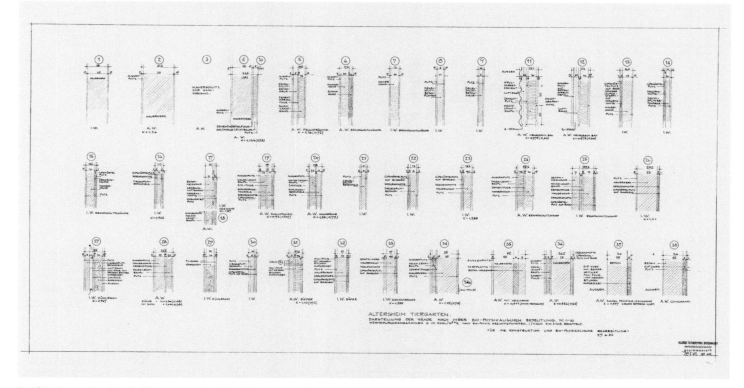

Karl Böttcher, wall options for Tiergarten senior citizens' home according to their biophysical properties, 1953

tion of Alexander Klein's Gagfah housing development in Bad Dürrenberg near Merseberg, detailed records were kept not only of which types of machinery were needed and for how long, but also of the additional man-hours required for the delivery of the cast concrete, whether it was by wheelbarrow, conveyor belt, casting tower with arms, or "ship." The introduction of more rational formwork and the more widespread deployment of machinery in the early 1950s greatly enhanced the productivity of building with cast concrete.[64]

Of crucial importance to the high-rises Romeo and Julia were the 1:10 scale pencil drawings of the wall and ceiling structures that Böttcher published as "Hochhaus, Stuttgart (1954)."[65] The solid concrete slabs executed in Stuttgart permitted a level of horizontal sound-proofing that could be further enhanced by formwork facing made of pliable, mineral-fiber matting and a 2-cm-thick layer of render. The outer walls were made of 15-cm-thick stamped concrete, which using the lost formwork method was clad in 6-cm-thick pumice concrete panels on the outside and in 2.5-cm-thick Heraclite panels on the inside. The publication "Bauen in die Zukunft" by Universum Treubau-Wohnungs-GmbH, not only points proudly to this "hitherto virtually unknown sheathing method,"[66] but it also describes in great

detail the other crucial advantages of building load-bearing walls. Despite the loads that increase significantly from top to bottom of the nineteen-story-high Romeo, the adoption of this method of construction meant that the load-bearing walls could be made of normal concrete no more than 12- to 20-cm thick, with no more than light reinforcing at the joints and at the ends of all the outer walls. This in turn resulted in what, at least in those days, was an amazingly low ratio of wall area to total surface area. The engineers' plans show the new geometry in all its clarity and precision, notwithstanding the many non-load-bearing inside walls made of pumice concrete panels. According to Friedrich Mebes, Scharoun had always supported the idea, though perhaps not explicitly, that apartments should be adaptable, i.e. that they should have as few load-bearing walls as possible. "The original floor plans that he—and others—planned for the Siemensstadt development of 1930 were premised on post and beam construction, which in those days, of course, was too expensive. So then it went across the Wupper along with all the others, where it was in fact built, as was one of Häring's types with masonry piers instead of posts. When you look at the apartments it's like looking at a warship; there's this huge block in the middle, whereas everything else is just 5 cm thick and ready to fall over at the first puff of wind. The posts of the frame have become panels, but the idea behind them is the same."[67] To be able to advance into new fields, it was first necessary to destabilize the grid system. Stabilization and destabilization are mutually dependent, however—hence the design aggregate operating

61 Geist and Kürvers (eds.), *Karl Böttcher*, 1990, p. 92.
62 Wolfgang Triebel, "Auswertung vorliegender Arbeiten über die Wirtschaftlichkeit von Wandbauarten I," 1957; "Die Entwicklung wirtschaftlicher Wandbauarten," 1957; "Die Entwicklung wirtschaftlicher Wandbauarten II," 1959; special issues of *Wirtschaftlich bauen* edited by the Institut für Bauforschung Hannover, Wiesbaden/Berlin.
63 Reichsforschungsgesellschaft für Wirtschaftlichkeit im Bau- und Wohnungswesen e.V. (ed.), *Bericht über die Versuchssiedlung in München*, special issue No. 5, April 1929.
64 Wolfgang Triebel, "Wandbauarten im Wohnungsbau," in Amtlicher Katalog der Constructa-Bauausstellung. Hannover 1951, pp. 222–227.
65 Karl Böttcher, "Hochhaus Stuttgart" (1954), drawing, TU Berlin, Architekturmuseum, Inv. No. 34714.
66 Willi Oppenländer, *Bauen in die Zukunft. Lebendiges Bauen in Stuttgart*, Stuttgart 1962, p. 31.
67 Conversation with Joachim Zimmermann, Stefan Heise, and Friedrich Mebes about the residential high-rises Romeo and Julia; Markus Peter and Ulrike Tillmann, recorded September 18, 2006 in Berlin-Gatow.

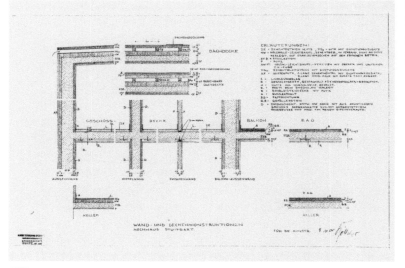

Karl Böttcher, wall and ceiling construction for the high-rise in Stuttgart, 1954

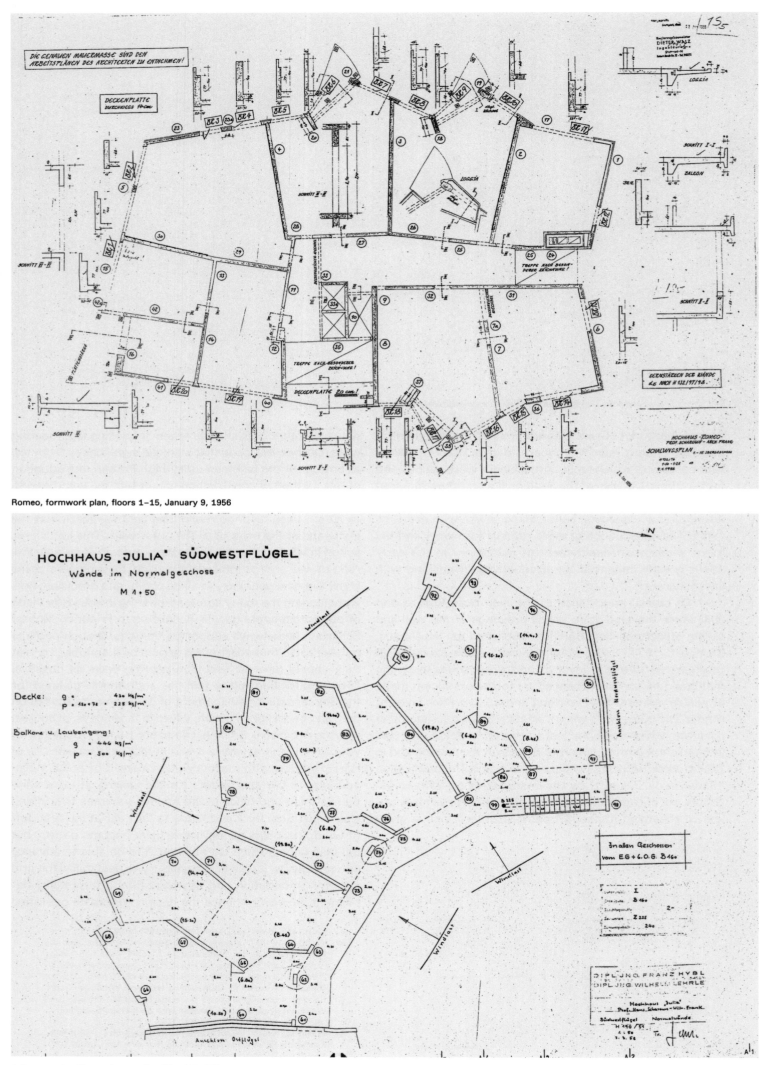

Romeo, formwork plan, floors 1–15, January 9, 1956

Julia, normal walls, southwest wing, March 7, 1958

Julia under construction, 1959

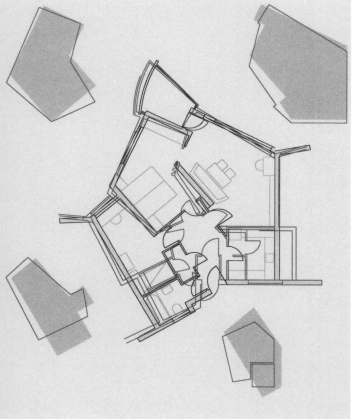

Julia, floor plan overlaps, 1954 (gray) and 1957 (red)

on the brink of collapse. The floor plan variants were to retain the same overall form on the outside, but were to be utterly transformed on the inside.

What emerged from this process was a pentagonal living room conjoined with a hexagonal bedroom, both of which are connected to the corridor by the circulation within the unit. These planimetric figures, which define the delimited area of a given level by means of a closed polygonal chain [P1 P2 ... Pn], are polygons. They have at least three corners and the sum of the inside angles on a figure that is not self-intersecting = (n-2) × 180 degrees so that the average sum of the angles increases in proportion to the number of corners. Multicornered polygons thus tend to be obtuse-angled for the most part. The high sum of the inside angles led to the discovery of simple connecting principles for polygons, the design processes for which concentrated on the declination of the said inside angles. This strategy of avoiding acute and preferring obtuse angles wherever pos-

sible would be brought to bear on many later designs, too. The inside angles of the convex pentagon, for example, add up to 540 degrees, meaning that for the most part they are obtuse. In his greatly altered living area, Scharoun therefore has not just one right-angled and three obtuse-angled corners, but also one acute-angled corner, which play out the directional thrust of the tapered room shape and defines the transition to the balcony—i.e. opens out onto it. The bedroom thus becomes an autonomous space that can be stretched until the floor space needed for the furniture and the necessary clearances has been obtained. The accreted figure of the bedroom causes two shared walls to meet at an even more obtuse angle, although not even this is enough to force the even greater sum of the hexagon's inside angles into another acute angle. In Julia's mirrored apartment types 1 and 2, the polygon is consolidated by the many different ways in which it belongs to the different levels; or, to put it another way, the essence of a geometrical model can be gauged by the deformation possibilities that would augment the said model's area of application.

The competition for the Geschwister Scholl Gymnasium, a new girls' high school in Lünen (1956–1962) held just a short time later shows how the polygonal apparatus had developed in the meantime. Here we find heptagons, octagons, and even nonagons. The main rooms are defined by the obtuse angles of their geometry, while the polygons at the same time accrete anterooms with lower ceilings. But the real center of each unit is the patio, which in the angle by which it points either inward or outward takes account of the developmental level of the pupils who are to use it. It is of course in the nature of organic forms that they are based on the repetition of one elementary unit. The forms are rhythmic. The ground floor in Lünen is like a chain, for example, but is a lot less rigorous than the armor plating of an armadillo, even if it resembles the same inasmuch as its form is generated by a series of interlocking elements. The technique of the polygonal apparatus, in other words, rests on recurrence and repetition, a theory that will be examined in more detail in the next chapter, "Multiplication."

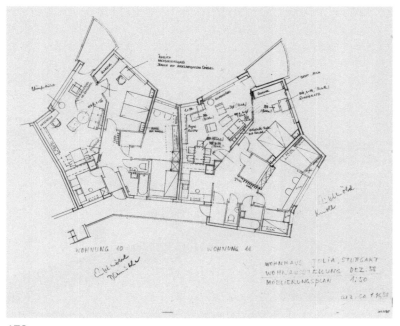

Geschwister-Scholl-Gymnasium, Lünen, 1955–1962

Outside view

VII Polygonal Apparatus

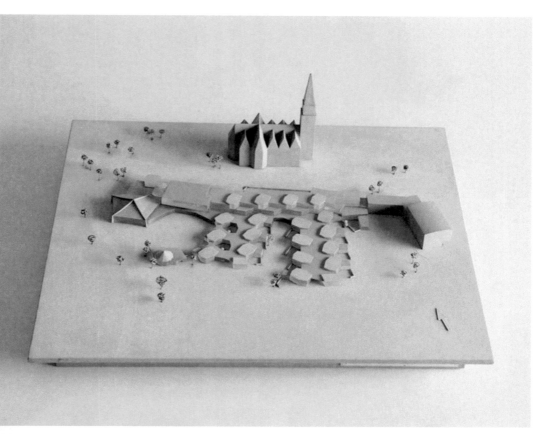

Model

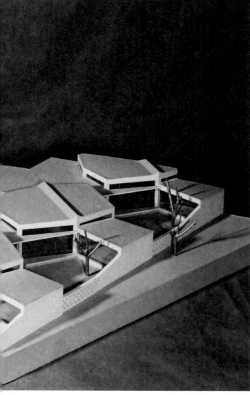

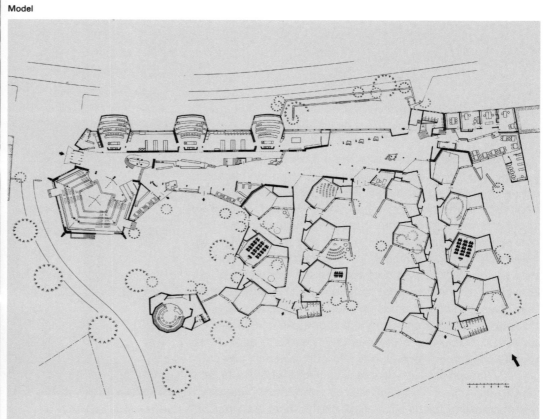

Classroom floor plans for the junior and intermediate grades

Model of the junior and intermediate grades

Outside view of the intermediate (below) and senior grades (above)

One of the key themes of twentieth-century building culture, mastery of geometry and design through the application of grids and modules, found a new technique in the geometry of the polygonal apparatus.[68] What is important about this technique is that it is both a design tool—a modus operandi—and a way of seeing and drawing. The organic as a guiding principle in Scharoun's design work is thus no longer merely a concept, but for him was fast becoming an operative design technique that he would use for the active creation of small apartment floor plans. It exists through the objects and drawings that make it intelligible to us. And it makes the phenomenon it claims to explain not merely phenomenological, but also phenomenographical.

Scharoun's design processes achieve what Paul Valéry captured in one of his most inspired aphorisms: "Geometry is the science of forms such as we create them and not such as they are given to us. As for the givens of geometry, they are not forms, but, rather, operations."[69] ●●

Classroom of the junior grade

68 In the course of the eighteenth century, the concept of "apparatus" was broadened to refer to the totality of humans and equipment needed to fulfill specific tasks. In the course of time, however, its semantic scope was steadily reduced until it essentially signified "equipment" alone. This gave rise to the ever more pronounced tendency to use it simply as a synonym for "machine." The active, and hence most fascinating, dimensions of the Latin concept of *apparatus* have by and large been lost, even as its implication of processuality has gained in importance—at least with regard to architecture.

69 Paul Valéry, *Cahiers/Notebooks* 4, edited by Brian Stimpson and translated by Norma Rinsler, Brian Stimpson, Rima Joseph, and Paul Ryan, Frankfurt/M. 2010, p. 183.

VIII   Multiplication

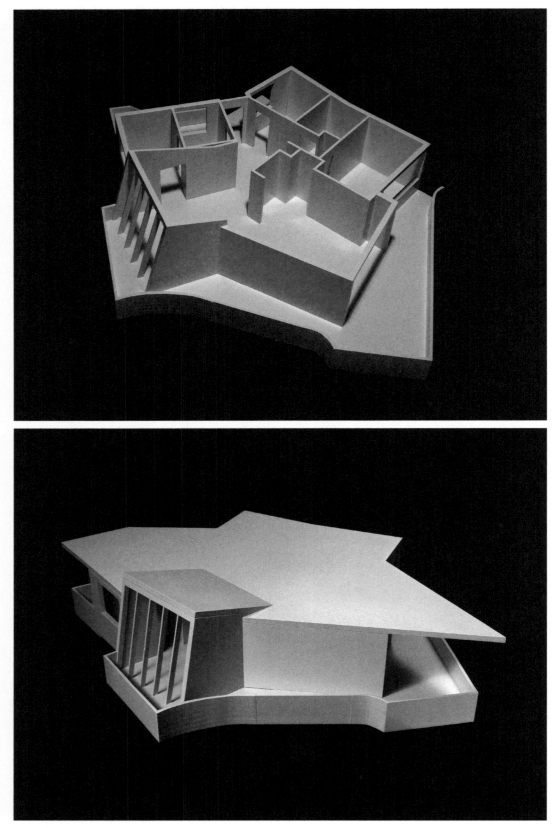

Julia, rooftop studio

"It is, however, in the difference itself—in divergence—that hope is concentrated."

Theodor W. Adorno, "Culture and Administration," 1960[1]

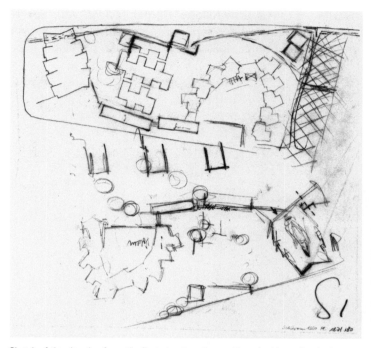

Sketch of the site plan from the first planning phase with and without the single-family dwellings, 1954

The observation that the polygonal apparatus eludes the rule of geometry and design through the application of grids and modules is not confined to small apartment floor plans; Hugo Häring and Hans Scharoun in fact viewed whole cities, indeed the whole universe, as an organism. This vitalistic faith in the laws of organic construction is apparent in Scharoun's refusal—a refusal that in Häring's case was coupled with revulsion—to countenance a society based on the repetitive addition of dwelling types joined together in homogeneous blocks or subdivisions. Häring postulated that the ordering principle inside the organism is "higher than that in the crowd. It vouchsafes variety, not uniformity; it demands the individuation of what is to be designed." Polyphony and multiplicity arise, he argued, when "we tip the balance of crowd and individual in favor of the individuation of the crowd."[2] Adolf Behne objected to this vision on the grounds that "only in the singular, in the individual" can the form of performance fulfillment come anywhere close to being realized, and following the same logic accused Häring of wanting to "forfeit the city which after all is bound to resist the radically individual."[3] Somewhat disquietingly, the really crucial passage that lent weight to Behne's doubts is to be found in Häring's "attempt at orientation," in which he argued that "The organic design of a contemporary residential building [...] can develop only in the countryside, as ties to the city and its building lots will always inhibit it."[4]

The surprising findings of the research on Chinese street maps and urban layouts that Häring, Scharoun, Chen-kuan Lee, and John Scott conducted during the war,[5] and that Scharoun referenced in his very first lectures after the war, reveal a rather more nuanced take on the geometrical organization of the city. According to the said findings, the city is a "cellular formulation of the sociological and spiritual structure of the demographic corpus—a living organism with scope for mutation, whose structure follows natural growth."[6] In his detailed notes on the "Gliederung der Stadt" ("Organization of the City") that were penned at a later date, Scharoun used the widely circulated term "residential cell" or "dwelling place." It was these, he argued, that "as a single element or clustered together in neighborhoods, larger groups, districts, or towns"[7] constituted the true "urban structure."[8] In a lecture to a conference of the Reichsforschungsgesellschaft called "Städtebau und Wohnungsbau" ("Urban Planning and Housing"), Fritz Block used the concept of the residential cell to define one of the functions of the city as the "fulfillment of residential and communal life";[9] Ernst May, moreover, explained the subdivision as "the sum of these residential cells," which were to be incorporated into the urban fabric in such a way "that equally favorable conditions are created for each individual residential element."[10]

Ernst Haeckel in Germany had used the concept of the cell as a sociological metaphor long before that, in 1899, when he described cells as "the real, self-active citizens which, in combinations of millions, constitute the 'cellular state,' our body."[11] The notion of the city as an organism made up of cells was seized upon by almost all architects of the postwar period.[12] It was on this well-trodden ground that Scharoun developed his "Wohnzelle Friedrichshain," a project that attempted to concentrate "the powers that are to be active" and make them "recognizably organ-like." This led to a "clearly visible boundary to the outside" and to the "development of various points of live action inside the cell:

1 Theodor W. Adorno, "Culture and Administration," in idem, *The Culture Industry,* edited by J.M. Bernstein, New York 1991 (1960) p. 131.
2 Häring, *Neues Bauen,* 1947, p. 35.
3 Adolf Behne, "Formel—Form—Gestalt," in *Zentralblatt der Bauverwaltung* 52, No. 52 (1932), p. 561. Behne was replying to Hugo Häring, *Kunst- und Strukturprobleme des Bauens,* 1931.
4 Häring, *Versuch einer Orientierung,* 1932, p. 223.
5 Wang, *Chen-kuan Lee,* 2010, Chapter II, "Ansatzpunkte der Gedanken Lees: Chinesischer Werkbund," pp. 67–208.
6 Scharoun, "Chinesischer Städtebau," Lecture I/7, January 11, 1945.
7 Scharoun, Lecture I/16, n.d.
8 Scharoun, Lecture II/13, June 12, 1950.
9 Reichsforschungsgesellschaft für Wirtschaftlichkeit im Bau- und Wohnungswesen e.V. (ed.), *Technische Tagung in Berlin vom 15.– 17. April 1929. Gruppe 4: Städtebau und Straßenbau.* Vol. 4, Berlin 1929, p. 1.
10 Ernst May in Internationale Kongresse für Neues Bauen and Städtisches Hochbauamt Frankfurt a.M. (eds.), *Die Wohnung für das Existenzminimum* 1930, p. 14.
11 Ernst Haeckel, "Die Welträtsel. Gemeinverständliche Studien über monistische Philosophie" (1899) (here quoted from http://www.gutenberg.org/files/42968/42968-h/42968-h.htm#CHAPTER_II, accessed: July 4, 2019).
12 The Nazis had initially embraced the concept of cell formation and had incorporated it into their ideologically driven urbanist tracts, in which big cities were demonized and life in the small town idealized. "This urban organism will be made up of a series of cells, which will then form clusters within the various subcenters grouped around the city center. Often, several of these subcenters will join together to form a cellular alliance of a higher order, after which various cellular alliances of a higher order may join together to form a whole organism with amenities to serve the whole community," (Gottfried Feder, *Die neue Stadt. Versuch der Begründung einer neuen Stadtplanungskunst aus der sozialen Struktur der Bevölkerung.* Berlin 1939, p. 19). Cf. Durth, *Deutsche Architekten* 1992, pp. 126–136.

When planning Romeo and Julia, Scharoun at first retained this heterogeneity. As already mentioned, the floor plan repertoire in the first four site plans drafted for this project was spread over two high-rises, various linear buildings, and both bungalow-style single-family dwellings as well as two-story row houses. The number of apartments is recorded in many of the site plan sketches for Stuttgart-Zuffenhausen-Rot so that the drawing of the twin towers, for example, contains the notation $67-9-80-8=164$. The total is essentially a control instrument that is always noted down and checked as a gauge of the required density. Scharoun's sketch of the definitive site plan distributes the units as follows: Romeo "$63+4$" attic apartments, low-rise in between with nine and at the western end with eight units, Julia $80=164$. The site plan later sub-

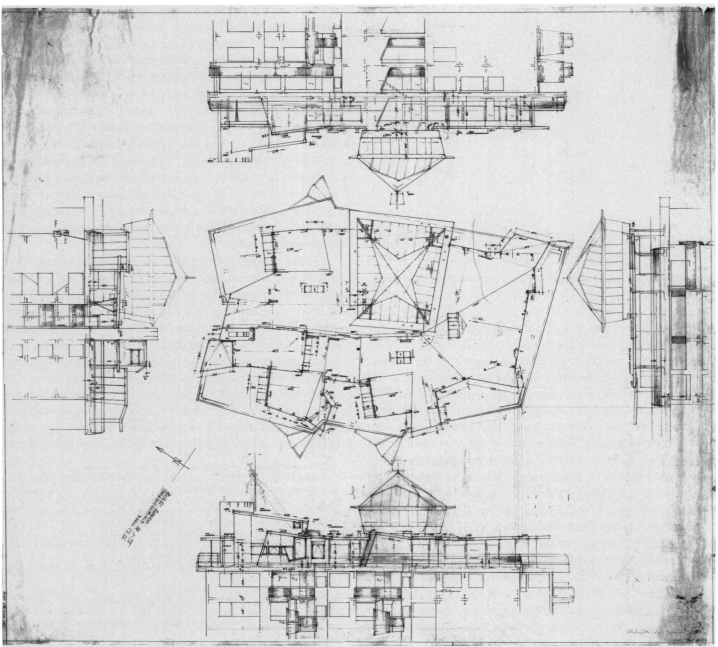

Sketch of the site plan from the first planning phase

Floor plan and elevation of the studio apartments on Romeo, planning phase, July 5, 1956

a market, a place of social interaction, a cultural center, a cluster of craft shops with artisans working at productive tasks [...] The figure is 'nest-like,' i.e. the idea is that every cell should be self-contained and have its own spiritual existence."[13] In Scharoun's vision of the "neighborhood" or the "urban cell," the units consist of up to 200 households in both low-rise and multistory buildings, punctuated by the occasional high-rise.[14]

mitted reduces the various low-rise types to be interspersed between the high-rises to eight. In the end, the official site plan of January 26, 1955 featured a garage with twenty-three ground-floor parking spaces adjoining Schwabbacher Strasse and a green space with children's play area between Romeo and Julia. This insistence on a combination of high-rise and low-rise is also demonstrated by the three—originally five—single-family dwellings that Scharoun planned for a low-rise group at the 1957 Interbau housing development in Berlin's Hansaviertel, which, like the Z-shaped patio types in Stuttgart, exemplified the kind of urban low-rise type that he favored but never actually realized.

In the operative process of urban planning, Scharoun immediately radicalized the loss of the low-rise buildings by lending the single rooftop studio an even more idiosyncratic formulation. This remodeling of the design injected a new dynamism into the communal property, as Scharoun himself noted in a letter to Wilhelm Frank: "I intervened rather more generously in 'my' rooftop apartment—including by widening and thickening the chimney block. I think that can be tolerated."[15] The studio apartments were especially important to Scharoun as they were what really demonstrated the multiplication of floor plans and delivered proof—assuming the "owner-occupied apartment in a residential high-rise is thought through to its logical conclusion"—of an "economically viable, 'flexible' dwelling."[16]

Scharoun, together with Frank, would revisit and broaden the scope of this promise of flexibility that was put to the test in Romeo and Julia in another high-rise project in Dortmund (1959) and later in the Salute high-rise (1961–1965)[17] in Stuttgart-Fasanenhof. For Dortmund, a project that was never actually built, Scharoun not only wanted dwelling types with a high degree of flexibility, but he also demanded that "the procedure be handled in such a way that wishes regarding the apartments and the location of the apartments might be submitted in good time so that further details (the bricking up of one or more windows, for example) might be taken into account."[18] Yet not even Scharoun himself succeeded in defining these features "in good time," since not until extremely late, by which time the shell of Julia was already standing, did he write to Frank on March 5, 1959 to request that "the roofs over the studios' outdoor areas be moved in relation to the original plan [...] so that they do not become too high as a result of the rising studio roofs."[19]

The German magazine *Film und Frau,* which in 1957 had begun publishing two special editions a year devoted to architecture and sophisticated living, in 1959 ran a report on Scharoun's studios erected on the rooftop of Romeo. Among the photographs is one of a roofed-over shower niche with a hot and cold shower and another of the north-facing studio room with its large, slanting window and wide window ledge for plants at the bottom of it. The text "Zwischen Himmel und Erde" ("Between Heaven and Earth") written by Scharoun himself[20] was subtitled "Ferienhaus auf dem Dach" ("Holiday Home on the Roof").[21] Thus the interiors and interior furnishings were implicitly put on a par with themes such as "Beachwear," "Leisurewear," "Bathing Costumes," and "The New Make-up,"[22] merging seamlessly with the world of fashion. The large-format magazine (26.5 × 36 cm) was aimed at an upper middle-class readership, which thanks to Germany's postwar "economic miracle" was now in a position to take an interest in the fashions and glamour hitherto known to it only from the movies. The text mentions the built-in shutter that allows the serving hatch connecting the living area to the kitchenette to be partitioned off or to be used as a bar "from time to time." The Elysian choice of materials—a shelf made of ash, a workspace with poplar desktop and simple, built-in drawers, and a bed niche clad in unpainted spruce—was further enhanced by the walls and ceilings, which were painted in colors ranging from "sand and white to pink and Pompeian red to ochre and shades of umber."[23] All in all, the studio was a paean to unpretentiousness, further enhanced by the simple curtain separating the living area from the bed niche—supposedly a nod to the bohemian lifestyle cul-

tivated by artists. In this model of the interaction of two spaces, in this case the socioeconomic concerns of the apartment owners and the lifestyle of the studio occupants, taste functions as the homology between the hierarchy of lifestyles and the economically driven social hierarchy of the owners. When designing his studio apartments, therefore, Scharoun availed himself as did no other of the capacity of West Germany's domestic, leisure, and consumer culture of the late 1950s for appropriation and adaptation.

Following Häring's interpretation of the notion of wholeness in organic architecture and in opposition to Behne's dictum of repetition, Scharoun now tried to show that what makes a city organic is not the sum of all its many individual reactions to a performance that is divisible into functional units, but rather that it reacts as a whole to objects in their wholeness. This stance of irreducibility in the interplay of elements sets in motion a different perspective, or *"Gestaltsehen"*[24] (literally, "figure seeing") to use Nietzsche's term. For Scharoun, there were no architectural reasons for arresting the formative power of individuality at the boundaries of the cell, and the concept of "dwelling places as manageable cells of urban coexistence" multiplied accordingly.[25] The individuality of the dwellings unfolded in what one commentator described as "the staggering, organizing, and faceting of the twin buildings," which constituted "a shared domestic world right up to the rooftop, where the studio apartments conceived as a penthouse add the finishing touch."[26] These had effectively transported Scharoun's ideas for the individual low-rise to the world of the rooftops. To Klaus-Jakob Thiele, one of the most ardent acolytes in the Scharoun fellowship, the residential high-rises Romeo and Julia, and especially the rooftop studios that projected the "image of diversity that Scharoun constantly speaks of [as] an expression of the individuality of each apartment,"[27] seemed a good deal more varied than the Berlin-Charlottenburg-Nord development of 1956–1961 that was built in a great hurry and with a limited budget.

In Romeo, Scharoun created a prismatic corpus—at least when compared to the zigzagging arc of Julia, then still in planning—which with its sloping and cantilevered roofs, the slanting glass fronts of its studios, and gondola-like balconies seems to dissolve all solid outlines. It is defined by two congruent, fifteen-cornered polygons, whose parallel levels form the ceiling of the ground floor and the floor of the attic story. The top of the building is articulated by a raised band of concrete, which in a twelve-cornered polygon spans the folds below it by eliminating what are es-

13 Scharoun, "Zur Wohnzelle 'Friedrichshain'" (1949) 1974, p. 185.
14 Scharoun, "Von der Wohnung zur Gliederung der Stadt," Lecture II/12, May 30, 1950, June 5 & 8, 1950.
15 Hans Scharoun to Wilhelm Frank, May 12, 1955, HSA WV 187, I, Correspondence 1955.
16 Scharoun, "Zum Begriff der Eigentumswohnung," 1960.
17 Dortmund-Vosskuhle high-rise project, HSA N73; Salute high-rise project, Stuttgart, HSA WV 217.
18 Hans Scharoun to Wilhelm Frank, August 6, 1959, HSA WV 187, I, Correspondence 1959.
19 Hans Scharoun to Wilhelm Frank, March 5, 1959, HSA WV 187, I, Correspondence 1959.
20 Hans Scharoun, HSA WV 187.
21 "Zwischen Himmel und Erde. Das Ferienhaus auf dem Dach," in *Film und Frau* 11, No. 6 special edition on architecture (1959), pp. 216–217.
22 *Film und Frau* 12, No. 10 (1960), pp. 64f.
23 "Zwischen Himmel und Erde. Das Ferienhaus auf dem Dach," in *Film und Frau* 11, No. 6 special edition on architecture (1959), pp. 216–217.
24 Friedrich Nietzsche, *Nachgelassene Fragmente 1869–1874,* KSA 7, Munich 1999, p. 487.
25 Scharoun, "Vortrag anlässlich der 31. Referendartagung" 1961.
26 Margit Staber, "Hans Scharoun. Ein Beitrag zum Organischen Bauen," in *Zodiac* 10 (1962), pp. 52–93, here p. 71.
27 Thiele, Über *Hans Scharoun,* 1986, p. 25.

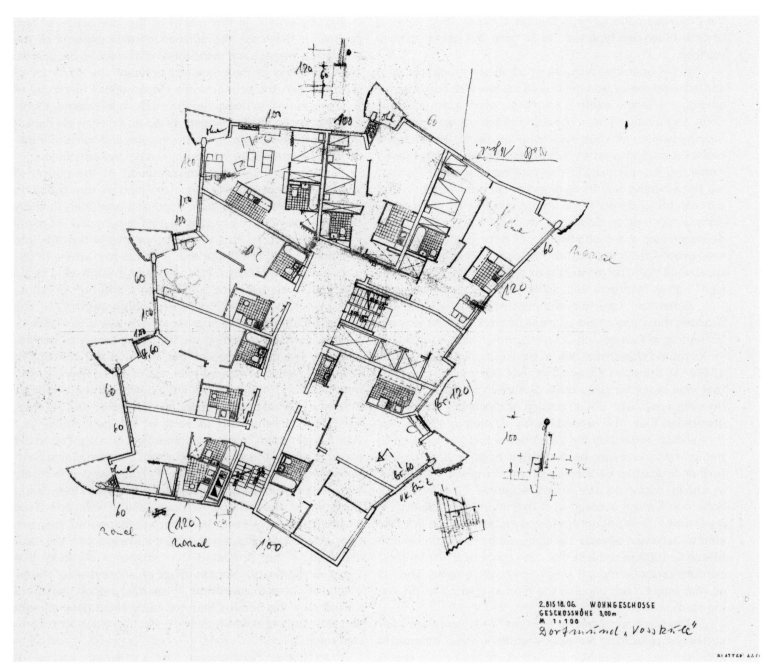

High-rise project for Dortmund Vosskuhle, floors 2–18, 1959

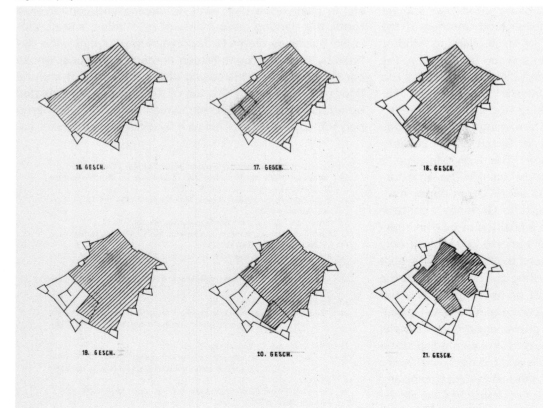

Plans, floors 16–21, 1959

VIII Multiplication

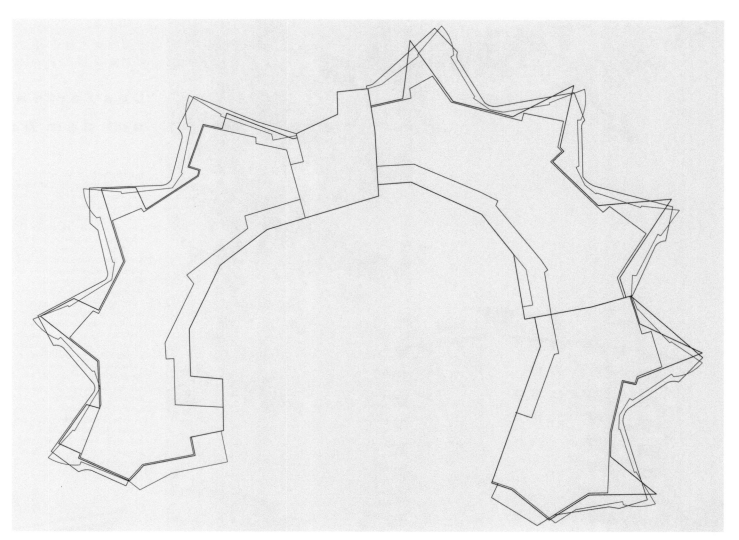

Julia, footprint, drawing ETH 2007

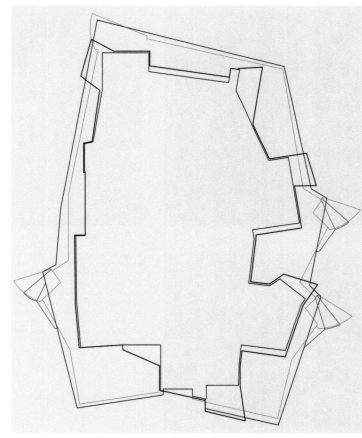

Romeo, footprint, drawing ETH 2007

sentially just kinks in the façade. This also lends additional dynamism to the view from below of the façades meeting at an angle. The idea was to generate movement in the work and to make it convey a sense of oscillation, rotation, revolution, and gravitation.

"Expressionism can claim kinship with a pure kinetics," Gilles Deleuze tells us. "It is a violent movement which respects neither the organic contour nor the mechanical determinations of the horizontal and the vertical; its course is that of a perpetually broken line, where each change of direction simultaneously marks the force of an obstacle and the power of a new impulse."[28] The diagonal lines have a hidden meaning and the perception of form cannot elude these manipulations of perspective. The oblique, the hasty, the chopped-off, the abruptly rising or falling—they all evoke very different sensations than does architecture with rich transitions.

In a letter to Frank about the design of the studios built on the rooftop of Julia dated March 5, 1959, Scharoun was explicit to a degree that is unusual for him: "What interests me when drawing up the plans is not so much the floor plan as such as rather the aesthetic appearance of the whole, in other words, 1) the rhythmic succession of the outside view already mentioned, and 2) the variously set back outer walls of the studios as opposed to the outer walls of the high-rise." The experience of both Romeo and the studios already surmounting Julia, he continued, had shown how important it was to heed this, and "how sensitive the preferred parallelism of the outer walls and the universal exploitation of the 'slab' available are."[29] A passerby looking up might identify the jerky rhythm, the obsessive repetition, and the exaggerated verticality of the architectural vision of these expressionistic projects alone from the sloping profile of the façades—the little huts that appear to be dancing on the rooftop or the slant of their little roofs.

Despite the loss of causality between dwelling type and built corpus resulting from the elimination of the duplex apartments in the Romeo high-rise, the accumulation

28 Gilles Deleuze, The Movement Image, trans. Hugh Tomlinson and Barbara Habberjam, New York 1986, p. 51.
29 Hans Scharoun to Wilhelm Frank, March 5, 1959, HSA WV 187, I, Correspondence 1959.

Das Ferienhaus
auf dem Dach

Am Rande Stuttgarts und im Mittelpunkt des neuen Wohnbezirks Zuffenhausen-Roth stehen zwei Hochhäuser – in ihrem Wesen und in ihrer Form aufeinander bezogen und dennoch differenziert wie ihre Namen: „Romeo" und „Julia". Der 19stöckige „Romeo", dessen Höhe durch vertikal angeordnete Farben der gefalteten Fassaden noch hervorgehoben wird, wirkt dabei kräftig und stämmig. Auf seiner Dachplatte trägt er, locker gruppiert, einige Atelierwohnungen.

Der hier abgebildete Typ ist eine Architektenwohnung – gleich gut geeignet zum Arbeiten wie als Ferienhäuschen. Hier wird der Sinn des Wohnens auf dem Hochhaus besonders deutlich, das einen von mancherlei Belastung befreit, die das erdgebundene Wohnen verursacht. Man ist dem Himmel und den elementaren Kräften aufs neue nahe. Sonne, Mond, Gewitter und Sturm werden ebenso intensiv erlebt wie die überraschende Helligkeit, das Licht, dessen sich der Großstädter schon fast entwöhnt hat. Dieses einmalige, beinahe eruptive Herausgehobensein aus der Masse der Häuser verbindet den Bewohner auf eine neue Art mit dem umfassenden Schauspiel dessen, was Manfred Hausmann die Himmelschaft nennt ...

Form und Farben des Hochhauses „Romeo" verbinden sich in ihrer Struktur der Landschaft und den Bäumen. Zusammen mit dem noch im Bau befindlichen Hochhaus „Julia" entstehen hier fast 200 Eigentumswohnungen. „Romeo" wurde vor einem Jahr, „Julia" wird in einigen Monaten bezogen. Charakteristisch für die Grundrisse beider Häuser ist, daß alle Wohnungen durch ihre Form ausgiebig Licht einfangen!

Diese beiden Aufnahmen (Bilder links und oben) geben einen Eindruck von der Terrasse, welche die Atelierwohnung umgibt. Links sieht man den Raum vor dem schrägen Atelierfenster, von dem aus man die hier noch im Bau befindliche kapriziösere „Julia" überblickt. Das Geborgene und Wohnliche des Freiraums stehen im spannungsvollen Kontrast zur Weite der großzügigen Landschaft. Bild oben zeigt den überdachten Brauseplatz mit Kalt- und Warmdusche — je nach Belieben und der Jahreszeit

Architekten:
Hans Scharoun, Berlin,
Wilhelm Frank, Stuttgart.

Farbaufnahmen: Ernst Deyhle

216

Der Atelierraum ist nach Norden weit geöffnet — das schräge Fenster ist gleichzeitig Blumenfenster, die Tür rechts führt auf die Terrasse. Einschließlich der Schlafkammer im 20. Stock und Terrasse beträgt die Wohnfläche der Wohnung rund geschätzt 50 qm (Bild rechts)

Als besondere Attraktion für alle Besucher erweist sich die durch eine Jalousie von der Kochnische trennbare Durchreiche, zeitweilig als Bar dienend. Die Kochnische ist, ebenso wie das nebenliegende Bad, durch das Dach hell belichtet. Das Regal ist aus Eschenholz (Bild unten links)

Die verschieden bemessenen Fenster fangen das Licht von Westen, Norden und Süden ein. Die Farben des Fußbodens und der Wand- und Deckenanstriche variieren von Sandfarbe und Weiß über Rosa und Pompejanisch-Rot bis zum Ocker und gebrochenem Umbraton: eine reiche Skala . . . (Bild unten rechts)

Schlafteil mit Bettnische. Links Arbeitsplatz vor dem Fenster, gegenüberliegend eingebaute Schränke. Der Arbeitsplatz besteht aus einer Platte aus Pappelholz mit eingebauten Schubladen. Wohn- und Schlafteil sind durch einen Vorhang getrennt (Bild ganz unten links)

Mit ungestrichenen, „natürlich" behandelten Fichtenbrettern ist der Schlafplatz ausgekleidet. Aus der Wand herauszuklappen ist die schmale Ablage für Bücher, Schmuck, die Zeitung und die morgendliche Kaffeetasse. Eine zeitgemäße „Schlafhöhle" (Bild ganz unten rechts)

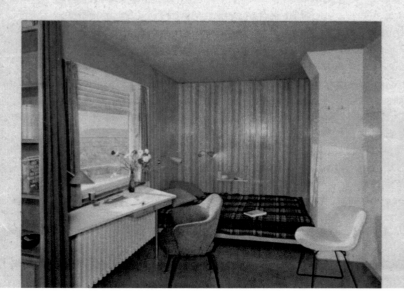

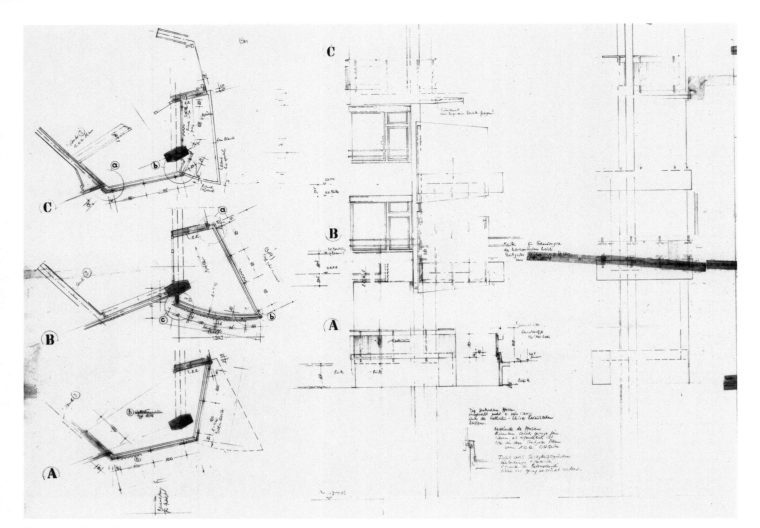

Romeo, plan of the balcony

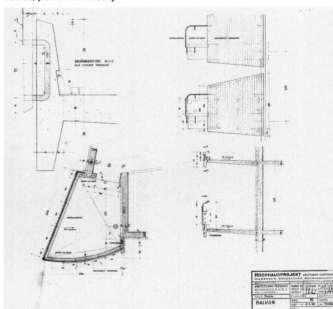

Julia, sketch of the balcony, November 7, 1955

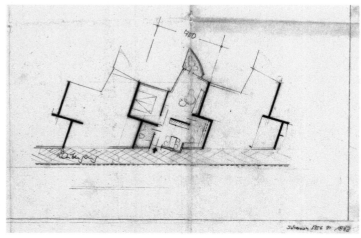

Design of a sawtooth type with quadrant-shaped balcony

of sequences and stacks lingered on as a kind of relic on the façade. Whereas the floor plans were now for single-story dwellings right across the board, the alternating rhythm of the balconies and loggias remained a virtual pointer to the duplex type. Scharoun's treatment of these dwelling-specific outside spaces attests to the disquieting productivity with which he countered those standardizing criteria that, according to the textbooks, typically define quality. Most notable among these, according to Peter Faller, are the criteria of furnishability, outdoor character, exposure to sunlight, shelter from wind, privacy, and interaction with the inside space.[30] The "gondolas" formed at the kinks in the façade were remarkably idiosyncratic figures. The element itself was identical to that of the Julia footprint, as was its location at the outermost points of the polygonal corpus. The geometry of the balconies was formulated by a dynamic, segment section of over 6 m² in area in which sinew and arc converge at an acute angle and the convex curvature is the dominant form, defining the rhythm of the whole. These balcony figures, which at their outermost refractions and folds were furnished with windbreaks made of translucent Scobalite, constitute the most unforgettable elements in this process of repetition. Rather like an ostinato—that steadily repeated, formal melody and rhythm that is so essential to Baroque music—these balconies with their distinctive form and insistent repetition were to inform all of Scharoun's future residential projects, too. The curious spikiness of the buildings—resembling mighty radiolaria planted in a cityscape—recalls Ernst Haeckel's systematization of biology and his taxonometric plates with their hexagonal orders.

The inorganic life of things, that first principle of Expressionism, informed Hans Poelzig's set for the silent horror movie, *The Golem: How He Came into the World*.[31] Rudolf Kurtz's very vivid description of that work assembles all the hallmark forms of Expressionism: "Verticals

Romeo, balcony of the duplex

span diagonally, houses meet at an angle, areas tilt to form rhomboids, the straightforward dynamism of normal architecture expressed in verticals and horizontals is transformed into a chaos of broken forms. Movements take on a life of their own, unleashing roofs all askew, planes at an angle, walls ending in acute angles and staring into space. A movement begins only to veer off its natural trajectory, after which it is picked up, perpetuated, refracted, and fragmented by another. What plays out in between—constructively, divisively, emphatically, destructively—is the magic of light, the unleashing of brightness and blackness."[32]

Scharoun's thoughts on the remodeling of the city are especially apparent in his view of Ulm Cathedral as a liberating monument to an organic city; he also shared Poelzig's fascination with the crystalline quality of the old city of Prague. That cityscape's variations in density are played out by its towers, "which in their heterogeneity are often

merely an expressive articulation of standing out from the rooftops, and while seemingly dissolving all form, in places actually lend precision to the upward thrust and dissolution."[33] The solution to the current urban-planning tasks, however, had to be sought elsewhere. "The essence and shape of the intricate medieval city can be conveyed with great immediacy. This homogeneity can no longer be developed in large conurbations. In big cities, homogeneity has to yield to complexity—the single note struck by a unified inside and outside has to yield to the whole gamut of variations and interpenetrations of an inside and outside that are not of a piece."[34]

30 Faller, *Der Wohngrundriss* 2002, p. 151.
31 *The Golem: How He Came into the World,* film, Ufa Berlin, 1920.
32 Kurtz, *Expressionismus und Film*, 1926, p. 123.
33 Scharoun, "Vortrag anlässlich der Ausstellung 'Berlin plant—erster Bericht,'" (1946) 1974, pp. 156ff.
34 Scharoun, Lecture VI/6, June 16, 1952.

Urban planning model of the Zuffenhausen-Rot development showing the high-rises and the linear building to the east of them

In his own projects in and for the modern city, Scharoun's ideas became increasingly radical to the point where the dwelling became no more than a "dot" in a very messy urban fabric.[35] As he himself acknowledged, those wishing to impose order or indeed to organize at all "prefer to take their cues from the dominant landmarks."[36] After studying images of medieval towns, Scharoun concluded the following: "Urban planning takes its cues from the dominant landmarks. The medieval city strikes a balance between the natural landmarks and the manmade landmarks."[37] The zigzagging arc of the horseshoe-shaped Julia with its access balconies and the plethora of refractions of the polygonal corpus of Romeo produced a "new style of landmark"[38] inasmuch as these "twin towers" became the most prominent landmark in the new district of Stuttgart-Zuffenhausen. Such an urbanist vision in which the "local situation of the subdivision makes it equivalent to an architectural landmark, which via 'Julia' recedes as far as Wilhelm's school,"[39] raised the question of how the similarly prominent slab building to the east of Romeo was to be treated. Scharoun wanted it to be limited to nine stories while retaining its overall length and hence its "linear character [...] Another 'landmark' would wreck the whole point of the structure in its larger context and undermine the tension between the elements."[40] On July 25, 1959, the *Stuttgarter Zeitung* blazoned its report on the opening of Julia with the headline "Die drei Riesen von Rot" ("The Three Giants of Rot"). Scharoun had spotted the fragility of the figure early on, and after voicing his concerns regarding the neighboring building to the east to Stuttgart's general director of buildings, Walther Hoss, accused him of having made a compromise to the detriment of "the whole ensemble," since "the notion of the landmark high-rise" had not been abandoned, despite the return to the "linear development."[41]

The unorthodox configuration of residential units to create such landmark buildings did not follow any straightforward, serial rules, and being polyphonic in expression was to a large extent independent of the banal development patterns taking shape around it. As Scharoun explained, adopting a fantastical, expressionistic language: "We are dealing here with point-like, structuring forces, which have an impact within a relatively indefinite space, but which need points at which to crystallize out, the which points for their part need a certain volume to sustain them. Yet the figure that best conveys the essence of this force is the star with the dotted circle. Both symbols stand for 'spiritual space' and for the space that sustains the material conditions."[42] The staggering of the building from four to seven to eleven stories built on existing dimensions, but it also triggered an acentric motion, which in the final cadence had an effect on the silhouette of the tower. Julia's tiered roofs for their part served to enhance the variety of the residential units, since they allowed the development of freely angled studio apartments and rooftop terraces. By means of the ever-changing geometrical thrust of formative elements like balconies, eaves, and rooftop studios, Scharoun created a perplexingly "Nordic" technique of repetitive motion. It was a movement without any actual beginning or end, a dynamic that sought not a radial, but rather a peripheral trajectory, and that had no real center. What Scharoun was doing was trying to work his crystallization points into the scaleless chaos of urban development. Following

35 Scharoun, "Von der Wohnung zur Gliederung der Stadt," Lecture II/12, May 30, 1950, June 5 & 8, 1950.
36 Scharoun, Lecture IA/22, n.d.
37 Ibid.
38 Scharoun, "Von der Wohnung zur Gliederung der Stadt," Lecture II/12, May 30, 1950, June 5 & 8, 1950.
39 Hans Scharoun to Prof. Walther Hoss, November 2, 1955, HSA WV 187, I, Correspondence 1955.
40 Ibid.
41 Ibid.
42 Scharoun, "Von der Wohnung zur Gliederung der Stadt," Lecture II/12, May 30, 1950, June 5 & 8, 1950.

The Stuttgart Zuffenhausen-Rot development from the west, 1959

View of Romeo and Julia from the northwest

Julia, seven-floor west wing

VIII Multiplication

Romeo, view of the east façade under construction

tency of the infinite. And in his conceptualization of Expressionism, too—which he defined through recourse to the contradiction between *élan vital* and organic representation—Worringer again referenced the Gothic or "Nordic" line, which as a dashed line did not outline anything and instead of allowing forms and background to be told apart zigzagged along between them.

By consciously harking back to the investigation of the design potential of sequences, stacking, and addition in individual residential units, Scharoun was in fact taking up one of the most important questions posed by modern mass housing—or perhaps only the most unfathomable, bearing in mind contemporary Dutch efforts to build artificial heterotopias, whose primary aim, to the exclusion of almost everything else, seems to have been the accumulation of random semantic features whose sole purpose was to break the monotony of these vast developments. What preoccupied Scharoun above all else was the transformation of the consecutive nature of the sequence and of addition into the simultaneous, simultaneity being the true principle of polyphony. Of course this was Scharoun's way of resisting the threat of repetitiveness as well as the predictable, un-

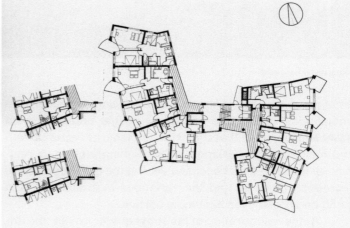

Salute regular floor plan

Heinrich Wölfflin, therefore, he deliberately dispensed with the homogeneity of form and created dissonances of the kind that Wölfflin so extolled in a model of the Neupfarrkirche in Regensburg: "The semicircular chapels projecting from the polygonal choir, their onion domes alongside the steep pavilion roof—these are contradictions to which only German aesthetics might grant legitimacy."[43] In Scharoun's case, we are dealing with a violently distorted perspective made up of projections and areas of shade and of diagonals and counterdiagonals that tend to take the place of horizontals and verticals. Sharp angles take the place of cubes and squares; acute triangles take over from curved or perpendicular lines. An analysis of the organizing lines reveals how Scharoun took advantage of what Deleuze called "lines extended beyond all measure to their meeting points, while their breaking points use accumulations."[44]

But for all the modernity exuded by the formal methods—the moving pictures, the dotted rhythms, the emphatic turnarounds, the two- or threefold parallel lines, the escalations, the ever larger intervals—they are all methods which at base rest on repetition and multiplication. Wilhelm Worringer detected a very different approach to repetition in the cryptic Gothic of early Nordic strapwork and with it the decisive difference between the endless melody of the Nordic line and the classical ornament: "Repetition in Nordic ornament [...] does not have the calm character of addition, but rather the character of multiplication, as it were,"[45] he wrote; and later in the same piece he wrote of the work of "architectural multiplication." Worringer examined this method as one of ever greater motility that eventually mutates into a state of endless motion, without allowing the sense of the organic any means of orientation. He saw in the towers of Gothic cathedrals and their accentuation of all things vertical a means of lending individual motifs the po-

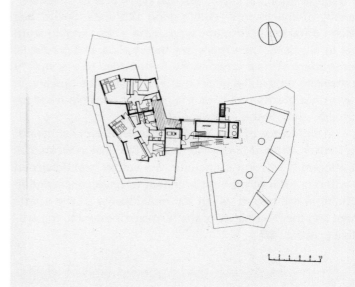

Salute, floor plan of the rooftop studio

43 Wölfflin, *Die Kunst der Renaissance,* 1931, p. 89. Wölfflin was commenting on a woodcut by Michael Ostendorfer of ca. 1521 and a wooden model of the church, neither of which was followed to the letter when the church was actually built.
44 Gilles Deleuze, *The Movement Image,* trans. Hugh Tomlinson and Barbara Habberjam, New York 1986, p. 51.
45 Worringer, "Formprobleme der Gotik," (1911) 2004, p. 201.

Salute under construction

ambiguous monotony of mass housing; and to develop the unorthodox figurations of his residential units, he once again availed himself of the extended logic of accumulation and multiplication. Variation, as something archaic—a residue, as it were—thus became a vehicle for the spontaneous recreation of form; and the variations in implementation could be spread over the whole corpus.

At the inauguration of his subsequent project, the Salute high-rise in Stuttgart-Fasanenhof, Scharoun elevated the diversity of his floor plans to a decisive principle. The act of multiplication, he explained, had given rise to a "heterogeneity of apartments—with a good 140 units 'Salute' has fifteen different apartment types with sizes ranging from one to six beds. Then there are the studios and practices. Some apartments are two-story. To be added to this variety in dwelling type is the effort made to design the building in a way that grants residents the greatest possible freedom to model their home as they wish."[46]

The history of how small apartments evolved cannot be written without some mention of the design strategies developed in relation to the city as a whole, and Scharoun is without a doubt the first architect to have succeeded in refining a method in which the individuality of the apartment and the multiplicity of the form are integral to the creative process. ●●

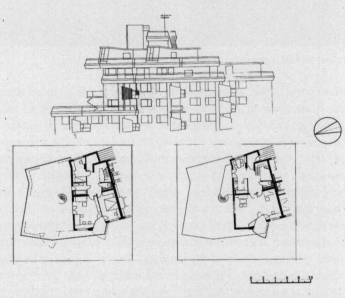

Salute, floor plan of the rooftop studio

46 Hans Scharoun, Address on Receiving an Honorary Doctorate in Rome on June 21, 1965, HSA 2907.

IX   Contemporary Pictures

by Georg Aerni

Bibliography
Image Credits
Biographies
Imprint

Writings of Hans Scharoun— Selection of the Referenced Manuscripts and Lectures

The lectures were given at the Institut für Städtebau at the Technische Universität Berlin between 1946 and 1958. Unless otherwise stated, they are now archived in the Hans-Scharoun-Archiv, which is held in the Baukunstarchiv of the Akademie der Künste, Berlin (HSA). They are not through-dated and not all of them have titles; nor do the archive holdings form a complete chronological series.

Scharoun, Hans, manuscript "Chinesischer Städtebau," lecture I/7, November 1, 1945.

Scharoun, Hans, lecture manuscript "Vorbemerkung," lecture I/1, n.d.

Scharoun, Hans, talk given at the exhibition "Berlin plant—erster Bericht, 5.9.1946," in Pfankuch, Peter (ed.), *Hans Scharoun. Bauten, Entwürfe, Texte*, Schriftenreihe der Akademie der Künste, Vol. 10. Berlin 1974, pp. 156–168.

Scharoun, Hans, lecture manuscript, lecture I/15, n.d.

Scharoun, Hans, lecture manuscript, lecture I/16, n.d.

Scharoun, Hans, lecture manuscript, lecture I/17, May 24, 1948.

Scharoun, Hans, lecture manuscript "Landesplanung," lecture I/21, n.d.

Scharoun, Hans, lecture manuscript, lecture I/26, November 26, 1948.

Scharoun, Hans, lecture manuscript, lecture IA/22, n.d.

Scharoun, Hans, manuscript "Zur Wohnzelle Friedrichshain," November 7, 1949, in Pfankuch, Peter (ed.), *Hans Scharoun. Bauten, Entwürfe, Texte*, Schriftenreihe der Akademie der Künste, Vol. 10. Berlin 1974, pp. 184–188.

Scharoun, Hans, lecture manuscript "Zur Wohnung," lecture II/4, February 20, 1950.

Scharoun, Hans, lecture manuscript, lecture II/9, February 24, 1950.

Scharoun, Hans, lecture manuscript, lecture II/7, March 3, 1950.

Scharoun, Hans, lecture manuscript, lecture II/8, May 8, 1950.

Scharoun, Hans, lecture manuscript "Normung und Typisierung im Bauwesen, besonders im sozialen Wohnungsbau," lecture II/21, May 16, 1950.

Scharoun, Hans, lecture manuscript "Von der Wohnung zur Gliederung der Stadt," lecture II/12, May 30, 1950, June 6 & June 8, 1950.

Scharoun, Hans, lecture manuscript, lecture II/13, June 12, 1950.

Scharoun, Hans and the Institut für Bauforschung, "Ergebnis der Untersuchung von Wohntypen auf ihre Eignung zur Bildung wirksamer Nachbarschaft. Zusammenfassung der Fragen," n.d., HSA 4010.

Scharoun, Hans, "Volksschule," in *Die Neue Stadt*, Sonderdruck: "Darmstädter Ausstellung im Sommer 1951" No. 5

(1951), p. 189.

Scharoun, Hans, "Die Auswirkung," lecture manuscript, lecture V/6, April 20, 1951.

Scharoun, Hans, lecture manuscript, lecture V/17A, October, 25, 1951.

Scharoun, Hans, lecture manuscript, lecture VI/6, June 16, 1952.

Scharoun, Hans, lecture manuscript, lecture VI/7, June 23, 1952.

Scharoun, Hans, lecture manuscript, lecture VI/8, June 30, 1952.

Scharoun, Hans, lecture manuscript, lecture VI/9, July 7, 1952.

Scharoun, Hans, Notizen "Das Wohnen," lecture VI/10a, n.d.

Scharoun, Hans, lecture manuscript, lecture VII/1, May 11, 1953.

Scharoun, Hans, lecture manuscript, lecture VII/2, May 18, 1953.

Scharoun, Hans, lecture manuscript, lecture VII/5, June, 15, 1953.

Scharoun, Hans, lecture manuscript, lecture IX/16, Febuary 27, 1956.

Scharoun, Hans, lecture manuscript, lecture X/18, July 15, 1957.

Scharoun, Hans, "Struktur in Raum und Zeit," in Elsässer, Martin and Werner Harting et al., *Handbuch Moderner Architektur. Eine Kunstgeschichte der Architektur unserer Zeit vom Einfamilienhaus bis zum Städtebau*, Reihe der Handbücher, edited by Reinhard Jaspert, Berlin 1957, pp. 13–21.

Scharoun, Hans, lecture manuscript, lecture X/23, June 9, 1958.

Scharoun, Hans, manuscript "Zum Begriff der Eigentumswohnung (Für Hastenteufel, Vortrag am 18.10.1960)," HSA 4843, Sheets 17–18.

Scharoun, Hans, manuscript, "Vortrag anlässlich der 31. Referendartagung 30.5.1961," HSA 2902.

Scharoun, Hans, "Das neue Wohnbewusstsein," HSA 4843, Sheets 13–16; published in Willi Oppenländer, *Bauen in die Zukunft. Lebendiges Bauen in Stuttgart*, Stuttgart 1962, pp. 7–8.

Scharoun, Hans, manuscript, "Vortrag anlässlich der Einweihung des Hochhauses Salute," Stuttgart, November 11, 1963, HSA 2970.

Writings of Hugo Häring

Unless otherwise stated, the documents are archived in the Hugo-Häring-Archiv held at the Baukunstarchiv of the Akademie der Künste, Berlin (HHA)

Häring, Hugo, "Wege zur Form," in *Die Form. Zeitschrift für gestaltende Arbeit* 1, No. 1 (1925), pp. 3–5.

Häring, Hugo, "'Bauen und Wohnen.' Bemerkungen zur Ausstellungssiedlung der Gagfa," in *Zentralblatt der Bauverwaltung* 48, No. 47 (1928), pp. 759–761.

Häring, Hugo, "Ausstellung: Die neue Küche," in *Der Baumeister* 27, Beilage, No. 2 (1929), pp. 33–36.

Häring, Hugo, "Kunst- und Strukturprobleme des Bauens," in *Zentralblatt der Bauverwaltung*, merged with the *Zeitschrift für Bauwesen* 51, No. 29 (1931), pp. 429–432.

Häring, Hugo, "Bemerkungen zur Werkbundausstellung Wien-Lainz," in *Die Form. Zeitschrift für gestaltende Arbeit* 7, No. 7 (1932), pp. 204–208.

Häring, Hugo, "Versuch einer Orientierung," talk given by the architect Hugo Häring, Berlin, at the 20th Annual Meeting of the Österreichische Werkbund in Vienna on June 7, 1932, published in *Die Form. Zeitschrift für gestaltende Arbeit* 7, No. 7 (1932), pp. 218–231.

Häring, Hugo, manuscript "strukturprobleme des bauens," talk given in Ulm and at the TU Stuttgart 1946, HHA 995.

Häring, Hugo, manuscript "grundrisse und ihre probleme," September 21, 1946, HHA 1005/2.

Häring, Hugo, manuscript "grundrisse," November 16, 1946, HHA 1005/6.

Häring, Hugo, "Neues Bauen," in *Baukunst und Werkform. Eine Folge von Beiträgen zum Bauen* 1, No. 1 (1947), pp. 30–36; reprint of "Ansprache an die architekten des 'neuen bauens' gelegentlich der zusammenkunft in aulendorf am 26. und 27. IX 1946," in idem, *neues bauen*, Schriftenreihe des Bundes deutscher Architekten Hamburg, No. 3, Hamburg 1947, pp. 21–44.

Häring, Hugo, manuscript "Disposition für ein arbeitsprogramm des fachausschusses nr. IX der forschungsgemeinschaft bauen u. wohnen," October 1947, HHA 1007.

Häring, Hugo, "Bemerkungen zum Normierungsbegehren," in *Der Bauhelfer. Zeitschrift für das gesamte Bauwesen* 3, No. 12 (1948), pp. 311–312.

Häring, Hugo, manuscript "athene apollo dionysos," June 3, 1949, HHA 1180.

Häring, Hugo, manuscript "III. Die appartement-wohnung (ausstellung 'wie wohnen' in stuttgart 1949/50)," HHA 1005.

Häring, Hugo, "Wettbewerb zur Förderung des neuzeitlichen Möbelbaus," HHA 661.

Häring, Hugo, "Geometrie und Organik. eine studie zur genesis des neuen bauens," in *Baukunst und Werkform. Monatsschrift für alle Gebiete der Gestaltung* 4, No. 9 (1951), pp. 9–18.

Häring, Hugo, "arbeit am grundriss," in *Baukunst und Werkform. Monatsschrift für alle Gebiete der Gestaltung* 5, No. 5 (1952), pp. 15–22.

Häring, Hugo, "Gespräch über organische Baukunst" [between Hugo Häring, Egon Eiermann, Alfons Leitl, and Otto Haupt], in *Baukunst und Werkform. Monatsschrift für alle Gebiete der Gestaltung* 5, No. 5 (1952), pp. 10–14.

Häring, Hugo, manuscript "vom neuen bauen," talk held at the Außeninstitut der Technischen Universität Berlin-Charlottenburg, May 27, 1952 ; HHA 885; published by the Technische Universität Berlin-Charlottenburg, Berlin 1952.

Häring, Hugo, manuscript "über das geheimnis der gestalt," talk held at the Außeninstitut der Technischen Universität Berlin-Charlottenburg, March 4, 1954, HHA 999, published by the TU Berlin, Berlin 1954.

Häring, Hugo, manuscript "Die Idee der Leistungsform," n.d., HHA 1048.

Writings of Alexander Klein

Klein, Alexander, "Versuch eines graphischen Verfahrens zur Bewertung von Kleinwohnungsgrundrissen," in *Wasmuths Monatshefte für Baukunst* 11, No. 7 (1927), pp. 296–298.

Klein, Alexander, "Untersuchungen zur rationellen Gestaltung von Kleinwohnungsgrundrissen," in *Die Baugilde* 9, No. 22 (1927), pp. 1350–1367.

Klein, Alexander, "Brauchen wir Eingangsflure in Kleinstwohnungen?" in *Bauwelt* 18, No. 21 (1927), pp. 524–525.

Klein, Alexander, "Neues Verfahren zur Untersuchung von Kleinwohnungs-Grundrissen," in *Städtebau. Monatshefte für Stadtbaukunst, Städtisches Verkehrs-, Park- und Siedlungswesen* 25, No. 11 (1928), pp. 16–21.

Klein, Alexander, "Flurlose Wohnungen," in *Wasmuths Monatshefte für Baukunst* 12, No. 10 (1928), pp. 454–460.

Klein, Alexander, "Grundrissbildung und Raumgestaltung von Kleinwohnungen und neue Auswertungsmethoden," talk held before members of the committees of the Reichsforschungsgesellschaft für Wirtschaftlichkeit im Bau- und Wohnungswesen in *Zentralblatt der Bauverwaltung* 48, No. 34 (1928), pp. 541–549, and No. 35 (1928), pp. 561–568.

Klein, Alexander, "Beiträge zur Wohnungsfrage," in Fritz Block (ed.), *Probleme des Bauens, Band I: Der Wohnbau*, Potsdam 1928, pp. 116–145.

Klein, Alexander, "Großsiedlung für 1000 Wohnungen in Bad Dürrenberg bei Leipzig," in *Die Baugilde* 12, No. 15 (1930), pp. 1458–1475.

Klein, Alexander, "Beiträge zur Wohnungsfrage als Praktische Wissenschaft," in *Zeitschriften für Bauwesen* 80, No. 10 (1930), pp. 239–252.

Klein, Alexander, "Grundrissgestaltung für Wohnung und Haus," in *Handwörterbuch des Wohnungswesens*, edited by Gerhard Albrecht for the Deutschen Vereins für Wohnungsreform e. V. Jena 1930, pp. 318–325.

Klein, Alexander, "Das Aufbauhaus," in *Die Baugilde* 13, No. 24 (1931), p. 1812.

Klein, Alexander, "Die Kleinwohnung als wirtschaftliches, wohntechnisches und raumgestalterisches Problem," in *Deutsche Bauzeitung* 65, No. 35/36 (1931), pp. 213–218.

Klein, Alexander, "Um die Frage 'Das wachsende Haus,'" in *Die Baugilde* 14, No. 6 (1932), p. 304.

Klein, Alexander, "Das Einfamilienhaus: Südtyp," in *Studien und Entwürfe mit grundsätzlichen Betrachtungen*, Serie Wohnbau und Städtebau, Vol. I, Stuttgart 1934.

Literature on Hans Scharoun

Bürkle, J. Christoph, *Hans Scharoun und die Moderne. Ideen, Projekte, Theaterbau*, Frankfurt a.M. 1986.

Blundell Jones, Peter, *Hans Scharoun. Eine Monographie*, Stuttgart, 1979.

Geist, Johann Friedrich and Klaus Kürvers, *Das Berliner Mietshaus. Band 3: 1945–1989*, Munich 1989.

Geist, Johann Friedrich and Klaus Kürvers, (eds.), *Karl Böttcher, Architekt—Bericht über meine Arbeit*, Zweites Beiheft zur Geschichte des Berliner Mietshauses, Berlin 1990.

Geist, Johann Friedrich, Klaus Kürvers, and Dieter Rausch, *Hans Scharoun. Chronik zu Leben und Werk.* Berlin 1993.

Hoh-Slodczyk, Christine, Norbert Huse, Günther Kühne, and Andreas Tönnesmann, *Hans Scharoun. Architekt in Deutschland 1893–1972*, Munich 1992.

Janofske, Eckehard, *Architektur-Räume. Idee und Gestalt bei Hans Scharoun*, Braunschweig/Wiesbaden 1984.

Kürvers, Klaus, *Entschlüsselung eines Bildes. Das Landhaus Schminke von Hans Scharoun*, Diss. Hochschule der Künste Berlin, 1996.

Kirschenmann, Jörg C. and Syring, Eberhard, *Hans Scharoun. Die Forderung des Unvollendeten*, Stuttgart 1993.

Pfankuch, Peter (ed.), *Hans Scharoun. Bauten, Entwürfe, Texte*, Schriftenreihe der Akademie der Künste, Bd. 10, Berlin 1974, Neuauflage 1993.

Thiele, Klaus-Jakob, *Über Hans Scharoun: Hinweise auf Ideen und Weg*, Berlin 1986.

Wang, Wen-chi, *Chen-kuan Lee (1914–2003) und der Chinesische Werkbund mit Hugo Häring und Hans Scharoun*, Berlin 2010.

Wendschuh, Achim (ed.), *Hans Scharoun: Zeichnungen, Aquarelle, Texte*, publication of the Abteilung Baukunst of the Akademie der Künste, Berlin, for the exhibition *Hans Scharoun—Architekt. Werkschau zum 100. Geburtstag* at the Akademie der Künste, Berlin, August 22–October 31, 1993.

General Literature

Adorno, Theodor W., *Minima Moralia. Reflexionen aus dem beschädigten Leben*, Cologne 1997.

Baillie-Scott, Mackay Hugh, *Häuser und Gärten*, Berlin 1912.

Behne, Adolf, *Der moderne Zweckbau* (1923), Bauwelt Fundamente 10, Berlin 1964.

Behne, Adolf, *Eine Stunde Architektur*, Stuttgart 1928.

Behrens, Peter and Deutscher Werkbund (eds.), *Bau und Wohnung. Die Bauten der Weißenhofsiedlung in Stuttgart, errichtet 1927 nach Vorschlägen des Deutschen Werkbundes im Auftrag der Stadt Stuttgart und im Rahmen der Werkbundausstellung "Die Wohnung,"* Stuttgart 1927.

Borsi, Franco and Giovanni Klaus Koenig, *Architettura dell'espressionismo*, Genoa 1967.

Buber, Martin, "Urdistanz und Beziehung" (Heidelberg 1951) in idem, *Werke. Band I: Schriften zur Philosophie*, Munich 1962, pp. 411–423.

Buber, Martin, *Daniel-Gespräche von der Verwirklichung*, Leipzig 1913

Buber, Martin, *Ich und Du*, Leipzig 1923.

Buber, Martin, *Pfade in Utopia. Über Gemeinschaft und deren Verwirklichung*, Heidelberg 1947.

Block, Fritz (ed.), *Probleme des Bauens*, Vol. I, Potsdam 1928.

Dorn, Gerda, Andreas Hastenteufel, and Willi Oppenländer, *Hans Scharoun. Mittelpunkt sei der Mensch*, Stuttgart 1968.

Durth, Werner, *Deutsche Architekten. Biographische Verflechtungen 1900–1970*, Braunschweig 1986.

Faller, Peter, *Der Wohngrundriss. Untersuchung im Auftrag der Wüstenrot-Stiftung*, Munich 2002.

Forty, Adrian, *Words and Buildings: A Vocabulary of Modern Architecture*, London 2000.

Frobenius, Leo, *Paideuma. Umrisse einer Kultur- und Seelenlehre*, Munich 1921.

Frobenius, Leo, *Kulturgeschichte Afrikas. Prolegomena zu einer historischen Gestaltlehre*, Zurich 1933.

Frobenius, Leo, *Auf dem Weg nach Atlantis. Bericht über den Verlauf der zweiten Reise-Periode der Deutschen Inner-Afrikanischen Forschungs-Expedition in den Jahren 1908–1910*, Berlin 1911.

Internationale Hygiene-Ausstellung Dresden 1930, official guide, Dresden 1930.

Internationale Kongresse für Neues Bauen and Städtisches Hochbauamt Frankfurt a. M. (eds.), *Die Wohnung für das Existenzminimum. 100 Grundrisse*, Frankfurt a.M. 1930.

Kurtz, Rudolf, *Expressionismus und Film. Filmwissenschaftliche Studientexte 1*, Berlin 1926.

Lübbert, Wilhelm, *2 Jahre Bauforschung. Bericht über die Tätigkeit der Reichsforschungsgesellschaft in den Jahren 1928 und 1929*, Berlin 1930.

Lübbert, Wilhelm, *Rationeller Wohnungsbau Typ/Norm*, Bonn 1926.

Muthesius, Hermann, *Wie baue ich mein Haus? Berufserfahrungen und Ratschläge eines Architekten*. 4th rev. ed., Munich 1925 (1st ed. 1915).

Ossenberg, Horst, *Was bleibt, das schaffen die Baumeister. Das Württembergische Hof- und Staats-Bauwesen vom 15. bis 20. Jahrhundert*, Norderstedt 2004.

Prigge, Walter (ed.), *Ernst Neufert. Normierte Baukultur im 20. Jahrhundert*, Frankfurt a.M./New York 1999.

Rasch, Heinz and Bodo, *Der Stuhl*, Stuttgart 1928.

Reichlin, Bruno and Adolph Stiller (eds.), *Das Haus Tugendhat. Ludwig Mies van der Rohe, Brünn 1930*, Architektur im Ringturm 5, Vienna 1999.

Reichsforschungsgesellschaft für Wirtschaftlichkeit im Bau- und Wohnungswesen e.V. (ed.), *Kleinstwohnungsgrundrisse*, Sonderheft No. 1, April 1928.

Reichsforschungsgesellschaft für Wirtschaftlichkeit im Bau- und Wohnungswesen e.V. (ed.), *Die billige, gute Wohnung: Grundrisse zum zusätzlichen Wohnungsbau-Programm des Reiches*, Berlin 1930.

Rodenstein, Marianne (ed.), *Hochhäuser in Deutschland: Zukunft oder Ruin der Städte*, Stuttgart/Berlin/Cologne 2000.

Schäfer, Carl, *Von deutscher Kunst. Gesammelte Aufsätze und nachgelassene Schriften*, Berlin 1910.

Schäfer, Carl, *Deutsche Holzbaukunst. Die Grundlagen der deutschen Holzbauweisen in ihrer konstruktiven und formalen Folge*, edited by Paul Kanold, reprint of the 1st ed. of 1937, Hildesheim 1984.

Schneck, Adolf G., *Das Polstermöbel*, Stuttgart 1933.

Sörgel, Hermann, *Wohnhäuser, Heft 1 von Handbuch der Architektur, Teil 4: Entwerfen, Anlage und Einrichtung der Gebäude, Halbbd. 2: Gebäude für die Zwecke des Wohnens, des Handels und Verkehrs*, Leipzig 1927.

Stratemann, Siegfried, *Grundriss-Lehre. Mietwohnungsbau*, Berlin 1941.

Taut, Bruno, *Die neue Wohnung. Die Frau als Schöpferin*, Leipzig 1928.

Tessenow, Heinrich, *Hausbau und dergleichen*, Berlin 1916.

Thiele, Klaus-Jakob, *Über Hans Scharoun. Hinweise auf Ideen und Weg*, Berlin 1986.

Völckers, Otto (ed.), *Das Grundrisswerk. 1400 Grundrisse ausgeführter Bauten jeder Art mit Erläuterungen, Schnitten und Schaubildern*, Stuttgart 1941.

Wölfflin, Heinrich, *Die Kunst der Renaissance. Italien und das deutsche Formgefühl*, Munich 1931.

Wolf, Gustav, *Die Grundriss-Staffel. Beitrag zu einer Grundriss-wissenschaft. Eine Sammlung von Kleinwohnungs-Grundrissen der Nachkriegszeit mit einem Vorschlag folgerichtiger Ordnung und Kurz-Bezeichnung*, Munich 1931.

Worringer, Wilhelm, "Formprobleme der Gotik" (1911) in Böhringer, Hannes and Beate Söntgen (eds.), *Wilhelm Worringer. Schriften, Band 1*, Paderborn 2004, pp. 151–300.

Bibliography

Unless otherwise stated, the originals are held at the Hans-Scharoun-Archiv (HSA) and the Hugo-Häring-Archiv (HHA) of the Akademie der Künste, Berlin

p. 148: HSA, Scharoun 3788.170.35.; HSA, Scharoun 3788.170.38; HSA, Scharoun 3788.170.42a, (top to bottom)

p. 149: HSA, Scharoun 3788.43; HSA, Scharoun 3788.41a; HSA, Scharoun 3788.46a, (left, top to bottom); Scharoun 3788.49; Scharoun 3788.47a; Scharoun 3788.44a, (right, top to bottom)

pp. 150/151: Bauaktenarchiv Berlin-Zehlendorf, Goebelstr. 1–9, Bauakte III, p. 318

p. 150: Walter Neuziel, *Messungen der Besonnung von Bauwerken. Ein neues Messverfahren und seine Anwendung auf die Bebauung*, Berlin 1942 p. 30

p. 152: *Die Baugilde*, No. 24, 1931, p. 1812

p. 153: *Deutsche Bauzeitung 65*, Nos. 35/36 (1931), p. 214

p. 154: *Deutsche Bauzeitung 65*, Nos. 35/36 (1931), p. 216

p. 155: *Deutsche Bauzeitung 65*, Nos. 35/36 (1931), p. 213(t.); TU Berlin Architekturmuseum, Inv. No. 34398 (m.); Otto Völckers, *Neuzeitliche Miethausgrundrisse, Veröffentlichung der Forschungsgemeinschaft Bauen und Wohnen*, No 1. Stuttgart 1947, p. 34 (b.)

p. 156: HSA, Scharoun 1194.170.47

p. 157: HSA, Scharoun 1194.170.46

p. 158: HSA, Scharoun WV 187, sketch 2

VII
Polygonal Apparatus

p. 160: Model photos ETH Zurich, photo: Heinrich Helfenstein

p. 161: HSA, Scharoun 1499.175.8.31(t.); HSA, Scharoun 3739. 175.47/Ewald Gnilka (b.)

p. 162: HSA, Scharoun 1299.32.1; HSA, Scharoun 1299.32.8 (l.); HHA, Häring 1198.LJ 14.6 p.164: Adolf Behne, Eine Stunde Architektur, Stuttgart 1928, p. 7 ; HHA, Häring 23/ Lehmann-Tovote (b. l.); HHA, Häring 1289. LJ 107.7 (b. r.)

p. 166: HHA, Häring 1289. LJ 107.2(l.); HHA, Häring 1289. LJ 107.22 (t .r.); HHA, Häring 1289. LJ 107.34 (b. r.)

p. 167: Internationale Kongresse für Neues Bauen and Städtisches Hochbauamt Frankfurt a.M. (eds.), *Die Wohnung für das Existenzminimum. 100 Grundrisse*, Frankfurt a. M., 1930, p.?, (l.); HSA, Scharoun 1292.107.3 (t. r); HSA, Scharoun 3715.75.3 (b. r.)

p. 168: Joedicke, Jürgen: *Weißenhofsiedlung Stuttgart*. Stuttgart 1990, p. 57

p. 169: Akademie Der Künste, Berlin, Karl-Boettcher-Archiv 38.60./ Max Krajewski (t.) and Karl-Boettcher-Archiv 38.62 (b. l.); Architekturmuseum der TU Berlin, Inv. No. 34183 (b. r.)

p. 170: HSA, Scharoun 1348.179.17 (t.); HSA, Scharoun 1348.179.15 (m.); HSA, Scharoun 1348.179.5 (b.)

p. 171: Architekturmuseum der TU Berlin, Inv. No. 34795 (t.); Architekturmuseum der TU Berlin, Inv. No. 34714 (b.)

p. 172: HSA , Scharoun 187, (top and bottom)

p. 173: HSA, Scharoun 3804.187.125/ Jakob Bohn (t.); HSA, Scharoun 1349.187.198 (m.); drawing ETH Zurich, Ulrike Tillmann (r.)

p. 174: HSA Scharoun 3818.204.33/ Dieter Storp; HSA, Scharoun WV 204, Model No. 9 ©AdK/ Merz (b. l.); HSA, Scharoun 3818.204.24a/Walter Köster (b. r.);

p. 175: HSA, Scharoun 3818.204.42a/ Cramers Kunstanstalt; HSA, Scharoun 3818.204.3a

p. 176: HSA, Scharoun 3818.204.35/ photo: Kramer (t.); HSA Scharoun 3818.204.139/Reinhard Friedrich (b.)

VIII
Multiplication

p. 178: Model photos ETH Zurich, photo: Heinrich Helfenstein

p. 179: HSA, Scharoun 1350.187.180

p. 180: HSA, Scharoun WV 187, sketch 1 (t.); HSA, Scharoun 1352.187.7

p. 182: HSA, Scharoun WV N-73, plans

p. 183: Drawings ETH, Ulrike Tillmann

pp. 183/184: *Film und Frau*, Sonderausgabe Architektur 11, No. 6 (1959), pp. 216–217;

p. 186: Balcony Romeo (t.) HSA 1356.187. 1351.187.161(m.); HSA Scharoun 1350.187.8 (b.)

p. 187: HSA, Scharoun 3804.187.185/ Wolfgang and Liselotte Fischer

p. 188: HSA, Scharoun 3804.187.68

p. 189: Landesmedienzentrum Baden-Württemberg, LMZ 812254 (t.); HSA Scharoun3804.187.151a (b.)

p. 190: HSA Scharoun 3804.187.173a/ Buderus-Werkfoto;

p. 191: HSA Scharoun 3805.187.105/ Wegert (t. l.); HSA, Scharoun 3830.217.4a (t. r.); Akademie der Künste, Berlin, Archiv Hoffmeyer-Zlotnik. 34.4

p. 192: HSA, Scharoun 3830.217.39 (t. l.); HSA, Scharoun 3830.217.36 (t. r.); HSA, Scharoun 3830.217.7a (b. l.)

VII
Contemporary Pictures

pp. 193–224: Photos: Georg Aerni

Markus Peter

is an architect and founding partner
of Meili Peter Architects with offices
in Zurich and Munich. He also teaches
as a professor of architecture and
construction at ETH Zurich.

Ulrike Tillmann

is an architect and architectural historian.
She has been working as research
assistant with Markus Peter's chair of
architecture and construction at ETH
Zurich 2006–2009 and is currently
pursuing her PhD at Humboldt
Universität Berlin.

Translations:
Bronwen Saunders

Copy editing:
Monique Zumbrunn

Proofreading:
Colette Forder

Design:
**Floyd E. Schulze /
WTHM — Büro für
Gestaltung, Berlin**

Lithography:
**Widmer & Fluri GmbH,
Zurich**

Printing and binding:
**DZA Druckerei zu Altenburg
GmbH, Thüringen**

© 2020 Park Books AG, Zürich in
cooperation with Akademie der Künste,
Berlin

**Park Books
Niederdorfstrasse 54
8001 Zurich
Switzerland
www.park-books.com**

Park Books is being supported by the
Federal Office of Culture with a general
subsidy for the years 2016–2020.

ISBN 978-3-03860-157-9